I dedicate this book to the first man I saw reading—my father.

TO BE A
BOY,
TO BE A
READER

Engaging Teen and Preteen Boys in Active Literacy

William G. Brozo
The University of Tennessee
Knoxville, Tennessee, USA

INTERNATIONAL
Reading
Association

800 Barksdale Road, PO Box 8139
Newark, Delaware 19714-8139, USA
www.reading.org

IRA BOARD OF DIRECTORS

The International Reading Association attempts, through its publications, to provide a forum for a wide spectrum of opinions on reading. This policy permits divergent viewpoints without implying the endorsement of the Association.

Director of Publications   Joan M. Irwin
Editorial Director, Books and Special Projects   Matthew W. Baker
Senior Editor, Books and Special Projects   Tori Mello Bachman
Permissions Editor   Janet S. Parrack
Production Editor   Shannon Benner
Assistant Editor   Corinne M. Mooney
Editorial Assistant   Tyanna L. Collins
Publications Manager   Beth Doughty
Production Department Manager   Iona Sauscermen
Supervisor, Electronic Publishing   Anette Schütz
Senior Electronic Publishing Specialist   Cheryl J. Strum
Electronic Publishing Specialist   R. Lynn Harrison
Proofreader   Charlene M. Nichols

Project Editor   Corinne M. Mooney

Cover   Design: Linda Steere
    Photo Credits: second from right, Image Productions; all others,
    PhotoDisc

Library of Congress Cataloging-in-Publication Data
Brozo, William G.
    To be a boy, to be a reader : engaging teen and preteen boys in active literacy / William G. Brozo.
        p.   cm.
Includes bibliographical references and index.
    ISBN 0-87207-175-8
1. Boys—Education—United States.   2. Reading—United States.   3. Boys—Books and reading.   I. Title.
    LC1396.5 .B76 2002
    428.4'071'2—dc21
                                                        2001007829

Contents

Foreword

If you have picked up this book and are reading this foreword, you probably have some inkling of the problems many boys have with reading. If you have ever struggled to get a boy interested in reading, you probably have more than an inkling. You may well be stark raving mad—pulling your hair, bulging your eyeballs, and blowing little cartoon jets of frustration out of your ears.

In any case, congratulations. If you care about boys and reading, you have come to the right place. In *To Be a Boy, To Be a Reader: Engaging Teen and Preteen Boys in Active Literacy*, Dr. William Brozo brings together research, psychology, classroom experience, obvious care for his students, and some great ideas about how to help boys become readers.

As a former boy, a former teacher, a parent, and now, a writer for kids, I found myself reading and nodding in recognition and agreement with the author again and again. Boys' literacy is a dire problem that demands urgent attention. Literacy is important to boys' developing sense of self. We need to give boys literature that speaks to their unique male imaginations. Engaging boys in reading needs to be a priority.

Presenting 10 positive male archetypes (derived from the work of psychologist Carl Jung) as a framework for books and teaching strategies, *To Be a Boy, To Be a Reader* offers us a way to speak to boys' imaginations. This is not one exclusive prescription. It's not book therapy or treatment. It's an insight into the male psyche that can help us connect boys with reading in a deep and powerful fashion. It's also got one very cool and extensive appendix of guy-friendly book titles categorized by positive male archetypes.

Brozo tells stories of his work in classrooms and lets boys, teachers, and parents tell their stories too. He shows ways he has found to attack the problem of boys' literacy. He shows himself to be a Pilgrim, a Warrior, a Prophet, and a Healer.

So enough with this foreword already. Get in there, and be a reader...to help our boys be readers.

Jon Scieszka
Author
Brooklyn, New York, USA

Jon Scieszka is a former elementary school teacher; a former boy; a parent; the author of *The True Story of the 3 Little Pigs!*, *The Stinky Cheese Man and Other Fairly Stupid Tales*, and the Time Warp Trio series; and most recently, the founder of a literacy initiative for boys called "GUYS READ" (www.guysread.com).

Acknowledgments

I am extremely grateful to all the teachers and students who welcomed me into their classrooms and the parents and sons who invited me into their lives as I researched this book. Two individuals who deserve special thanks are Patti Walter and Teri Placker. Without their collaboration, I would never have come to know Ricardo, DeWayne, James, and all the other young men and women who have strengthened my convictions about boys and reading. I am equally grateful to those who gave their voices to the Boy Talk sections in each chapter and to all the others who left their marks in the real-life stories of boys interacting with books. Each of these people breathed life into this project and made it entirely worthwhile.

To Be a Boy, To Be a Reader: Engaging Teen and Preteen Boys in Active Literacy grew out of an idea that was suggested to me several years ago by a dear friend and former colleague, Dr. Ronald Schmelzer. Soon to be "Father Ron," he has blessed this work with his incisive feedback and boundless good graces.

Of course, I owe a special thanks to the International Reading Association, particularly Joan Irwin and Matt Baker for their belief in the value of this project and Corinne Mooney for her helpful feedback and tireless fine-tuning of the manuscript.

Ultimately, though, I owe the most gratitude to my wife and fellow teacher, Carol, and our daughter, Hannah, for giving me the time, space, and inspiration to write this book. I only hope that *To Be a Boy, To Be a Reader* gives them a portion of the immense pride and joy they have given me.

Introduction

Twenty-five years ago, I began my first job teaching English at an all-black high school in rural South Carolina, USA. I came face to face with adolescent boys who, in the words of Sven Birkerts (1994), "had never bathed in the energies of a book" (p. 84). These were young men who could not read at a level necessary to understand and enjoy the stories and plays from the required anthology. William, a 6'7" 17-year-old star basketball player, was in one of my 11th-grade sections. As I handed out textbooks on the first day of class, he leaned close to my ear and whispered, "I don't know how to read." I quickly came to the realization that in order to engage William and his classmates as readers, I would need to use every bit of my creative energy. Although it ran counter to my sensibilities as an English teacher, I made a fateful decision in those first weeks to dispense with my beloved *Silas Marner* and *Julius Caesar*, and all the other vaunted poets, playwrights, and novelists of the past and experiment with young adult literature.

I was looking for something that the students would find more accessible and meaningful. I found it in Alice Childress's *A Hero Ain't Nothin' But a Sandwich* (1973). This story of an adolescent boy's maturation and alienation while growing up in Harlem transformed my class. Attendance and behavioral problems in my classroom decreased noticeably. Students were eager to read, or at least try to read. When we finished the book, they clamored for more of the same. Even William made modest progress that first year, although he dropped out the next. I would often spot his looming frame hanging out on the only street of commerce in our small, poor semicoastal town. Unfortunately, he was eventually arrested and found guilty of dealing narcotics. It was the last I ever heard of him.

Of course my own literary history is very different from that of black teens growing up in hot, dusty tobacco country, whose ancestors were slaves and sharecroppers. Nonetheless, when it comes to literacy, we all have something in common—where we begin our literate journeys may have little resemblance to where the journey takes us and, certainly, where the journey ends.

Since those days as an inchoate literacy teacher, I have spent untold hours in regular and remedial classrooms of middle and secondary school, observing and learning from other teachers, conducting demonstration lessons, and gathering research data. The overwhelming impression I have been left with is that more must be done to reach the majority of listless, detached, and struggling male readers. I have also found a clear and recurring pattern of concern among teachers: Too many preteen and teen boys do not like to read, are choosing not to read, and are suffering academically as a result.

I have written this book to share my experiences and ideas with the many teachers who are equally concerned about adolescent boys' literacy futures. The premise underpinning this book is that engaging adolescent boys in literacy should be the highest priority when developing reading curricula and seeking to foster independent reading habits. To achieve engaged reading, I propose the use of novels, informational books, and stories that are likely to appeal to boys because they are rife with positive male archetypes. To make access to this appropriate archetypal literature easier for teachers, I provide numerous titles, an extensive organized bibliography, and practical ideas for using this literature to improve boys' thinking about text and their motivation to read.

The Unique Nature of *To Be a Boy, To Be a Reader: Engaging Teen and Preteen Boys in Active Literacy*

A growing number of voices are being raised today on behalf of boys' unique psychological, physiological, and emotional needs. Books such as Michael Gurian's *The Wonder of Boys: What Parents, Mentors and Educators Can Do to Shape Boys Into Exceptional Men* (1997), Dan Kindlon and Michael Thompson's *Raising Cane: Protecting the Emotional Life of Boys* (2000), Eli Newberger's *The Men They Will Become: The Nature and Nurture of Male Character* (2000), and William Pollack's *Real Boys' Voices* (2000) have come to enjoy wide popularity, because they raise consciousness about adolescent boys' emotional development and help explain changes that occur with their burgeoning masculine identities. Although these books are helpful to parents and caregivers, they may not be as useful to middle school and secondary school teachers because they fail to address young men's academic needs systematically. Furthermore, none of these authors acknowledges the importance of literacy as boys develop a sense of self.

Books on the market that deal with both gender issues and literacy focus on either younger children's reading and ways of promoting gender equity with those children through reading curricula, such as *Reading the Difference: Gender and Reading in Elementary Classrooms* (Barrs & Pidgeon, 1994), or on adolescent girls, such as *Just Girls: Hidden Literacies and Life in Junior High*

(Finders, 1996). Kathleen Odean's *Great Books for Boys* (1998) is essentially an annotated bibliography of books for males ages 2 to 14. Although this book is a useful resource, it does not provide teaching suggestions or focus exclusively on current literature for teen and preteen boys.

To Be a Boy, To Be a Reader is the only book of its kind that provides teachers of adolescent boys with practical strategies for using literature with positive male archetypes. These archetypes will ultimately motivate adolescent boys to read, improve their reading abilities, and capture their unique male imaginations.

Why a Book Just About the Literacy Needs of Adolescent Boys?

Adolescent boys need special attention with respect to literacy. Evidence from the United States, as well as Australia, Canada, and the United Kingdom, shows that boys have the lowest scores on standardized measures of reading and verbal ability. Boys dominate the rolls of remedial reading classes and those who have difficulty learning to read. They also make up the largest group of dropouts and delinquents. These, however, are only school-related phenomena. When one considers that males (a) commit all but a small percentage of homicides, (b) are far more likely to be victims of violent crime than women, (c) take their own lives at alarming rates, and (d) make up the vast majority of drug addicts and people who are homeless (Canada, 1998; Garbarino, 1999), addressing adolescent boys' needs becomes all the more urgent.

It is well known that boys who drop out of school are likely to have weak or poorly developed literacy skills. These dropouts become vulnerable to a life of underemployment and unemployment and, far worse, are at a higher risk of becoming criminal offenders. It is also known, however, that engaged readers have a much greater chance of staying in school, expanding career and life options, and maturing into self-actualized adults.

This book, then, is devoted to describing how teachers have used literature to help teen and preteen boys find entry points into literacy. Once entry points are found, boys may develop a sense of self through active literacy and increase their chances for an expansive intellectual journey. This will ultimately lead to better lives for themselves and those around them. I have found that boys become more engaged readers and learners when motivated by exposure to literature and activities that speak to traditional male archetypes. This book presents multiple ways in which teachers, parents, and caregivers can use literature with positive male archetypes to capture adolescent boys' imaginations and improve their thinking about literature.

Organization and Content

Each chapter begins with an excerpt that relates to boys' reading and ends with two sections: "Boy Talk" and "Final Thoughts." The Boy Talk segments were written by students who were part of my reading clinic. The goal of these segments is to give voice to real-life boys who have read books. Boy Talk demonstrates the depth of understanding and levels of personal engagement that are possible when young men are given quality young adult literature to read. Final Thoughts provides a chapter conclusion.

Chapter 1 introduces the primary issues of the book and raises concerns about adolescent boys' literacy behavior. I present evidence that supports the need to help boys discover or become reacquainted with the pleasure and value of reading. I also discuss the connection between reading ability and academic success, and explore why reading sometimes disaffects male youths. Reading engagement should be the highest priority to teachers of disinterested and struggling readers, because only as boys encounter literature that speaks to their unique male imaginations are they likely to become regular and lifelong readers. I propose that creating opportunities for adolescent boys to read books with positive male archetypes is a promising way to capture boys' imaginations and help them practice active literacy.

Chapter 2 defines the archetypes and describes characteristics and examples of each. Based on Jungian theory, as well as the work of contemporary psychologists and sociologists, I explore in-depth the origins and modern applications of 10 positive male archetypes: Pilgrim, Patriarch, King, Warrior, Magician, Wildman, Healer, Prophet, Trickster, and Lover. Each description is accompanied by examples of characters from young adult literature who embody the hallmarks of the archetype. Teachers can take advantage of these positive male archetypes to further adolescent boys' literary pilgrimage.

Chapter 3 depicts numerous scenes of English, reading, science, and history teachers using innovative strategies and activities that involve young adult books rife with positive male archetypes. These teaching vignettes are organized around the 10 archetypes.

Chapter 4 presents additional ideas and practices that teachers can use to engage and keep boys reading. The approaches cut across particular archetypes and demonstrate how teachers can find appropriate books for adolescent boys and structure their classrooms to make these books accessible to young men.

Chapter 5 draws entirely from my personal experience working with two seventh-grade teachers on a teaching unit devoted to exploring masculinity with a young adult novel. The teachers and I developed, implemented, and taught the unit with a junior high school language arts class of 14 boys and 2 girls. The school is situated in an economically depressed community of primarily Hispanic Americans and African Americans. Painting scenes of classroom life, I describe how the teachers and I designed the unit, selected an appropriate young adult novel, implemented instructional strategies, and documented students' responses.

Chapter 6 describes how teachers can work with and learn from adults in the community to create conditions that give adolescent boys a chance to be readers. Every concerned adult can inspire teen and preteen boys to read, and almost anyone at home and in boys' communities can help boys continue to grow as readers and as learners. I present several vignettes of parents, relatives, friends, neighbors, and others who have had profound influences on boys' attitudes and behaviors toward literacy.

The chapters are followed by a Conclusion, which reviews the book's critical themes and briefly reflects on new pertinent evidence that supports these themes. I call on teachers to use this book as a resource to help boys find entry points into active literacy. The Appendix follows the Conclusion and presents 300 titles of current young adult literature. This literature is organized around the 10 positive male archetypes and further classified into the following categories to aid in the selection of books for teen and preteen boys: Adolescent Novels, Informational Books, and Easier Reading.

Common Questions About Working With Books With Positive Male Archetypes

What follows are some typical questions I often receive from teachers who are intrigued by the approach I advocate and interested in implementing it in their classrooms.

Question 1—Is there some way to diagnose a boy's archetypal preference, so I can introduce him to the right book?

This is probably unnecessary. My intention is not to create a prescriptive approach to active reading, but to propose that literature with positive male archetypes can make adolescent boys more engaged readers. It is only through this engagement that boys can ever be expected to become competent critical readers and thinkers. The added benefit of working with the books I recommend is that they offer a variety of masculine images.

Nevertheless, I do know a middle school teacher who has created her own inventory that consists of statements meant to represent particular archetypes. She gives it to the boys in her class and asks them to indicate which statement most closely matches behaviors and characteristics that they aspire to. With this information, she claims to be able to find reading material that matches students' preferences more efficiently than she might otherwise be able to do.

Question 2—Should adolescent boys be exposed to all archetypes?

Boys often show a strong preference for certain archetypes, such as Warrior or Pilgrim. This does not mean, however, that they should not be exposed to books with characters who possess different archetypal qualities. Remember, the primary goal in using any of the books I recommend is to capture a young man's imagination and keep him reading. One significant benefit of *just* making these books accessible to young men is that these boys may come to appreciate the many expressions of masculine identity.

Question 3—What about boys who aren't into traditional "masculine" books?

This question always fascinates me because it presumes that books for boys must automatically deal with ultramasculine themes and plots, such as the suave male who can attract many girls but discards them just as quickly, the gun-toting maverick lawman who defeats criminals coldly, or the chiseled, muscular athlete who never loses. Nothing could be further from the truth. Many of the books I recommend attest to the unique and nonstereotypical dimensions of masculinity. For example, books that have characters who embody the Lover or Prophet archetypes often present a unique and surprising face of both boyhood and manhood, because positive expressions of masculinity can come in a variety of forms and from male characters who are decidedly not "masculine." Popular media has contributed to the stereotypical construction of males as one-dimensional, incapable of self-reflection, and physically and psychologically oppressive. Exposing adolescent boys to quality literature filled with a variety of positive male archetypes can only help to provide them with realistic and in-depth images of what it means to be a man.

Question 4—Should these books be used therapeutically?

Those of us who are readers have no doubt heard other readers say, or perhaps have said ourselves, that "reading is my therapy." The use of the word *therapy* in this case is really a euphemism for an escape from the day-to-day toils that everyone experiences. In a more technical sense, therapy implies a condition or state of being that needs remedy. Boys do not need to be diagnosed with a dominant archetype, then provided with particular books as treatment.

Good books for boys should ideally capture boys' imaginations and get them hooked on reading while reaffirming their inherent goodness as males. If people expect much more from this literature, they may be setting up themselves for disappointment; however, teachers and parents have shared stories with me about how their students and sons were rescued by certain books. Some of the scenarios described in Chapter 6 leave open the possibility of using literature with positive male archetypes, if not therapeutically, at least as an important source for personal and interpersonal transformation.

Question 5—Don't most boys behave in ways that reflect a combination of archetypes?

The answer to this question is an unequivocal "Yes!" Exposure to multiple archetypes is worthwhile because it increases the chances that a young man will find something that engages him and leaves him wanting more. I present the positive male archetypes in this book in their most basic forms. Few men or boys match only one model perfectly. For example, although a young man may exhibit dominant characteristics of the Patriarch, he may also demonstrate attitudes of the Trickster, as well as other archetypes. Although positive male archetypes have been investigated scientifically and described in ways that suggest exclusivity, it would be a mistake to expect behavior from boys that is consistent with only one archetype. Exposure to a variety of archetypes helps boys affirm their true masculine selves.

Question 6—Do male characters in young adult books always embody a single archetype, or do they behave in ways that are consistent with different positive male archetypes?

Just as most boys exhibit qualities of more than one archetype, so do characters from books. Although similar to our male students and sons, they may be more representative of one archetype than another.

Question 7—I teach both adolescent boys and girls, so how can I use this approach that is just for boys?

Like most essential questions, this defies a pithy response. In answering it, I like to begin this way: As a literacy educator, former junior and senior high school teacher, spouse of an experienced teacher, and a school-based researcher, I believe I speak from experience when I assert that most teachers are desperately seeking strategies and materials to reach their male students. This desire alone can serve as the impetus for exploring the potential benefits of using books with positive male archetypes. My experiences have further shown that with some originality and risk taking, teachers of male and female adolescents can create learning environments that have special supports for boys' literacy efforts without excluding girls.

In Chapters 3, 4, and 5, I share numerous examples of middle and secondary school teachers in mixed-gender classrooms who use creative approaches to make books for boys accessible and employ teaching strategies to make these books engaging. These strategies, as will be demonstrated, may also benefit girls. Young women are just as steeped in mass media's constructions of masculinity as boys are. Books that depict males as multidimensional individuals who break masculine stereotypes do as much to erode girls' rigid conceptions of boys as they do for boys. This situation is not substantially different from one in which a teacher uses literature with diverse ethnic and cultural themes to promote pluralism and demonstrate sensitivity to students of diverse ethnic and cultural backgrounds.

Question 8—If most of the boys in my classes are already into stereotypical masculinity, why should I give them just masculine-type books to read?

The answer depends on whether these adolescent boys are already regular and engaged readers. If not, and that is what I suspect, the assumptions inherent in this question oversimplify the issue. Books with positive male archetypes may be just what these boys need to help them see that being a reader is not incompatible with their rigid self-ascriptions of masculine identity. Bo Brewster, Chris Crutcher's *Ironman* (1995), shows that he is capable of restraining his anger and outbursts, training for a triathlon, and falling in love. Boys have found that this book and others by Crutcher give them familiar glimpses of male characters while forcing them to think more expansively about what it means to be masculine. Adolescent boys who swagger with stereotypical male bravado have much to gain by exposure to books like *Ironman*, which depicts the Warrior archetype.

Question 9—Are male archetypes the only criteria for appropriate book selection for adolescent boys?

To this question, I must give a resounding "No." The top priority for all teachers and adults is to help boys find entry points into literacy; they should support any way that this can be accomplished. My ideas about archetypes are rooted in my concern that we not only engage boys as readers, but engage them with books that are identity affirming.

Question 10—Shouldn't boys read material with both good and bad male archetypes, because there are plenty of men who are bad in real life, too?

Because there are so many real-life men who behave deplorably, I stress the need for boys to be exposed to as many positive models of masculinity as possible. Keep in mind that the male archetypes described in this book are not gods. They are endowed with the same human frailties that everyone possesses. When adolescent boys read the books that I have suggested, they are reading about males who do not always make the right decisions and are not blameless; therefore, these archetypes are a good deal like the boys themselves. What separates positive male archetypes from others is that they ultimately prevail in doing what is right for the people around them. Books with positive male archetypes, then, serve as a counterbalance for both boys and girls who are daily exposed to real, deplorable male behavior and injurious popular myths regarding masculinity.

Question 11—What if I believe a book you have placed in a particular archetype category in the Appendix would be better suited to help teach a different archetype?

There is nothing scientific about the way I have categorized the young adult books in the Appendix. As previously stated, most characters and individuals exhibit traits associated with more than one archetype. A book's placement in the Appendix is based on my best judgment about the dominant archetypal qualities of the fictional or real-life characters in the book. Other people, however, may disagree with these categorizations. By its very nature, creative writing engenders different interpretations. Whether or not there is complete agreement about these categorizations is far less important than whether quality young adult literature finds its way into the hands of teen and pre-teen boys. So if the books I categorize for one particular archetype are used to teach a different archetype, I support that practice without reservation.

Conclusion

Those of us who are readers already know that the thrill of entering a book's unique world is the only reward we need to engage us in reading, although our love of books reaps other rewards as well. Active and engaged reading directly contributes to our sophisticated literacy and thinking, which has also made our professional accomplishments possible. The purpose of this book is to help boys obtain the same benefits and pleasures. Young men cannot bypass the path we have all traveled to become who we are as literate adults. *We*, however, can make the beginning of this journey possible by providing boys with appropriate and enjoyable literature and activities.

In the following chapters, the practical ideas and strategies embedded in scenes of classroom, clinic, and home-based life show how literature helped make reading an integral part of boys' lives.

CHAPTER

1

To Be a Boy, To Be a Reader

Then the whining schoolboy
With his satchel and shiny morning face
Creeping like a snail
Unwillingly to school.
—William Shakespeare, 1969, p. 257

For as long as there have been schools, there have been boys who would rather be elsewhere. It is the rare young man who faithfully attends school without grousing and with high purpose. This idea calls to mind Burris Ewell's ineloquent though pithy pronouncement in Harper Lee's *To Kill a Mockingbird* as he walks out of the Maycomb schoolhouse on the very first day, saying flatly, "I done done my time for this year" (1960, p. 27).

Teen and preteen boys who are only "doing time," who are mentally absent from school, and who are academically detached place themselves and all of society at risk. There is ample evidence to suggest that early and cumulative reading and learning failure are often precursors to unemployment (Bureau of Labor Statistics, 1999), crime (Ayers, 1999; Davis, Byrd, Arnold, Auinger, & Bocchini, 1999), drug addiction (National Institute on Drug Abuse, 1997), homelessness (National Law Center on Homelessness and Poverty, 1997), and prison (Bureau of Justice Statistics, 1991).

As adults, parents vest their futures on all children, not just their sons. And most certainly all children need adults to imbue them with hope and imagination of possibilities. This book, however, focuses on stressing the importance of engaging and keeping adolescent boys as readers to help ensure that they have successful academic futures and, consequently, richer and more meaningful lives. Mounting evidence suggests that the time has come to begin paying special attention to the literacy needs of adolescent boys. Consider these sobering facts:

11

- Boys are three to five times more likely than girls to have learning and/or reading disabilities placement in schools (National Center for Education Statistics, 2000).

- Boys in elementary school through high school score significantly lower than girls on standardized measures of reading achievement (Pottorff, Phelps-Zientarsky, & Skovera, 1996).

- Boys are 50% more likely to be retained a grade than girls (Kleinfeld, 1999).

- Fewer boys than girls study advanced algebra and geometry, and more girls than boys study chemistry (National Center for Education Statistics, 1999).

- Boys are less likely than girls to take advanced placement examinations and go to college (National Center for Education Statistics, 1998).

- The number of males earning academic degrees in traditional male professions, such as medicine and law, is decreasing, although the number of these degrees earned by females is rapidly increasing. In 1970, women earned only 8% of medical degrees and 5% of law degrees; today, those percentages are up to 39% and 43%, respectively (Sommers, 2000).

- Of the estimated 500,000 to 1 million students who annually drop out of U.S. high schools, over 55% are boys (National Center for Education Statistics, 1998).

- Five out of six children and adolescents diagnosed with attention deficit disorder (ADD) and attention-deficit hyperactivity disorder (ADHD) are boys (American Psychiatric Association, 1994).

Skillful and critical reading ability is an important tool that boys must have to become academically successful. This tool can contribute to either a virtuous cycle of successful living or a grinding cycle of difficulty and failure (Darling, 1997). Reading ability is highly related to overall academic success (Donahue, Voelkl, Campbell, & Mazzeo, 1999). In other words, good readers are better students in every subject area. It is also known that high academic achievement increases career and life options for young adults. Superior students perform better on entrance examinations, making it easier for them to access postsecondary educational opportunities and, ultimately, find better jobs. For instance, research done by Hofstetter, Sticht, and Hofstetter (1999) found that, regardless of their cultural background, people who achieve and exercise power over their lives spend more time reading than those who have less power or feel powerless. Reading, the authors assert, leads to knowledge, which is associated with power regardless of other barriers that citizens face. People who practice active literacy acquire knowledge more readily than others, and knowledge is the great equalizer in terms of access to personal and professional power.

All too common in the United States (Hedges & Nowell, 1995)—as well as in Canada (Gambell & Hunter, 1999), England (Murphy & Elwood, 1998), and Australia (Alloway & Gilbert, 1997)—are teen and preteen boys who find themselves caught in cycles of reading failure. One possible explanation as to why boys are not the readers they can and should be is that reading often conflicts with boys' sense of masculinity. Findings from recent reports (Klein, 1997) strongly suggest that the steady decline in reading achievement experienced by boys between the ages of 7 and 16 is largely a consequence of peer pressures. Adolescent boys undergo tremendous pressure not to appear nerdy or brainy, so many of them turn against reading and learning because, in the words of Browne and Fletcher (1995), it's more "cool to be a fool" (p. 74).

When boys turn away from reading, they unfortunately miss out on unforgettable, identity-affirming experiences with books. People who have had these experiences as young men share similar stories. For instance, I had this experience when I discovered a new novel at age 10 in the Montieth Branch Library in Detroit, Michigan, USA, on a rainy summer morning. Stephen Meader's *The Muddy Road to Glory* (1963) held me spellbound for days. The character of Ben Everett, a young Civil War enlistee in the Union army, embodied everything that I wanted to be. I was already a Stephen Meader junkie, snatching up any of his books I could get my hands on, although Mrs. Oshob, the librarian, did her best to keep me supplied. Meader's writing was transcendent, taking me on one gripping adventure after another. How can I ever forget sitting atop my upper bunk in the attic of my family's small, clapboard house—one house out of hundreds of blocks of blue-collar neighborhoods in a working class city—reading *Lumberjack* (1934), *Whaler 'Round the Horn* (1950), or *Boy With a Pack* (1939)? Reading these books, I felt as if I were lost in the Appalachian wilderness, sore yet strengthening day by day as I worked one end of a saw felling giant virgin red pines, or that I was the one wiping salty sea foam from my eyes as I stood at the helm of a 19th-century schooner.

Sven Birkerts (1994), a muse to anyone who has made literacy an integral part of his or her life, says of his early experiences with books,

> [R]eading was once, in childhood, a momentous discovery. The first arrival was so stunning, so pleasant, that I wanted nothing more than a guarantee of return.... Here was the finding of a lens that would give me a different orientation to what was already, though only nascently,

the project of my life. Through reading I could reposition the contents of that life along the coordinate axes of urgency and purpose. These two qualities not only determined, or informed, the actions of whatever characters I was reading about, but they exerted pressure on my own life so long as I was bathed in the energies of the book. (p. 84)

Today's adolescent boys have an equal chance of discovering or rediscovering the magic of books and the joy of flights of imagination inspired by the written word. Appealing to boys' creative imaginations by using literature that speaks to their unique male interests could help them become engaged and regular readers (Brozo & Schmelzer, 1997). Helping adolescent boys find entry points into active literacy must be a high priority for teachers, because it is from young men's early interests in books that a lifestyle of habitual reading can be nurtured (Young & Brozo, 2001).

Literature With Positive Male Archetypes: Entry Points Into Active Literacy

Teachers always are seeking new ways to reach adolescent students through innovative teaching strategies, by showing genuine displays of concern about students' day-to-day learning needs, and from learning students' future academic and personal desires. What better way to demonstrate this concern for boys than by introducing them to the right books—books that they feel comfortable reading on their own, sustain their attention, and reaffirm their burgeoning sense of male identity while offering many visions of masculinity? Young adult literature with real-life and fictional characters who represent positive male archetypes can help teen and preteen boys identify with their own masculine identities, as well as other masculine identities.

An archetype is an inherited idea or mode of thought that is derived from the experience of the race and present in the unconscious of the individual (Jung, 1955). Fairy tales contain some of the most common male archetypes of Western civilization. The hero, for instance, shows up everywhere to thwart some untoward force or rescue someone who is weak (for example, a damsel, an ailing king, and so on). Carl Jung, a Swiss psychologist, was one of the first people to scientifically investigate the uniqueness of the male psyche. In our common human memory, our collective unconscious, Jung (1968) proposed that there are archetypal or generalizable models of maleness. According to Jung, as well as other contemporary psychologists and sociologists (see also Arnold, 1995; Gilmore, 1990; Johnson, 1989; Moore & Gillette, 1992), these archetypal models are inherent within the psyche of all men. What is most fascinating about Jung's theory is that the range of positive male archetypes that exist within our culture strongly supports the idea that boys exhibit *multiple* expressions of masculine identity, which means that virtually all young men should find something familiar and reaffirming in books with positive male archetypes.

This book explores the origins and modern applications of 10 positive male archetypes derived from the work of Jung (1955) and others (see Arnold, 1995), describing each archetype and illustrating each with characters from young adult literature used by middle school and secondary school teachers to engage their male students. These archetypes are also the framework used in the Appendix for identifying and selecting appropriate books for teen and preteen boys. My intent in discussing positive male archetypes in association with young adult books is not to propose a new canon to be adhered to rigidly. As I have stated, my primary concern is to help boys find entry points into active literacy. My purpose in using the 10 positive male archetypes is to demonstrate one way (and there are potentially many others ways) in which good books for adolescent boys may be classified and how these books can be put to good use.

Developing a Love of Reading in Boys

It is one thing to say teen and preteen boys need to experience literature with positive male archetypes, but it is quite another to motivate them to enthusiastically read such literature. Teachers cannot transform boys who are unengaged readers or learners or who have poor reading skills into highly skillful and enthusiastic readers simply by handing them a young adult novel with positive male archetypes. This effect can happen for some, however. For example, many boys who did little or no free reading were instantly transformed by their infatuation with the faddish Goosebumps and Harry Potter stories. Although interest in them will inevitably wane, these books have reacquainted many nonreading boys with the joys of literacy and may compel boys to begin a lifelong search for exciting and personally meaningful literature (Weeks, 2001). In other words, Goosebumps and Harry Potter books have served as entry points into literacy for many adolescents boys. Everyone has their own entry points into literacy. What adults read may have little similarity to the texts that initially engaged them as children. However, adults' skillful reading abilities and their wide tastes and interests in literature, which they often take for granted, are traced to their initial experiences with engaged reading—or their entry points into literacy.

My experience tells me that adolescent boys who view reading as unacceptable male behavior have not fallen under the spell of a well-told story or have not found male characters in fiction, biography, or history who speak to their unique and evolving needs. Robert Chaseling, a junior high student, offers the following advice for helping boys to see reading as cool:

If you want your son to read
Get him the sort of book
Some parents don't seem to see.
It's all about image and being cool
And a lot depends on what you read at school.
Bugulugs Bum Thief
Goosebumps
Point Crime
Paul Jennings
The list goes on.
At least they are not glued
To Nintendo playing *Donkey Kong*.
So take my advice
And you'll feel quite proud
Please don't make them read aloud.
If you do
They'll quit reading like a flash
And your reading scheme
Will fall down with a crash.
So if you take my tips
And do everything right
Your son could be reading
By tonight! (Sanderson, 1995, p. 153)

Robert's lighthearted, although incisive, poem makes two critical points. First, when it comes to motivating adolescent boys to read, story content and genre are extremely important elements. Second, the very ways in which teachers offer literacy to students either draws them into reading or instills indifference.

Many teachers and administrators that I know who work with adolescents say that students' lack of motivation for learning is at the heart of many school-related problems. Regardless of the reasons, unmotivated students often find themselves in a downward spiral of declining academic achievement, diminishing self-esteem, further disinterest outside of school, and so on. Teachers know that creating positive academic experiences is critical to improving self-esteem, eliminating behavioral problems, and increasing learning involvement (Filozof et al., 1998). They also know that motivated students are more likely to learn at a deep, meaningful level and internalize their new learning whereas unmotivated students' learning is superficial, shallow, and easily forgotten (Gambrell & Codling, 1997). There is nearly universal consensus that one of the best ways to motivate student reading is through the use of interesting books (Guthrie, Alao, & Rinehart, 1997; Oldfather, 1995). This motivation translates into significant improvement in reading achievement (Taylor, Frye, & Maruyama, 1990). Unfortunately, recent U.S. surveys of the reading habits of adults (Weeks, 2001), as well as high school students, (Libsch & Breslow, 1996) reveal an overall decline in the past 20 years of the reading of books and other nonassigned material.

In the study of high school students, a stark gender gap was obvious (Libsch & Breslow, 1996). Although there has been a disturbing increase in the number of both females and males reading no books, far more females read at least one to five nonassigned books per year. Males are also reading fewer magazines and newspapers on a daily basis than females. The survey also revealed that students, particularly boys, would rather watch television or engage in other leisure activities than read. Regardless of what boys substitute for nonassigned reading, today's adolescent males are at risk of failing to develop the necessary literacy skills for future academic and workplace success (Reynolds, 1991). This is true because to a large extent, reading achievement is a function of the amount of time and energy that students invest in reading activities both in and out of school (Donahue et al., 1999).

Clearly, a highly effective way of motivating young boys to read and keep them reading is to look carefully at their interests (Baker & Wigfield, 2000). Boys have strong preferences for stories with male protagonists (Johnson & Peer, 1984; Langerman, 1990; Ollmann, 1993; Samuels, 1989). When preferences and interests are matched with books, the depth of processing and learning are enhanced (Alexander, Kulikowich, & Hetton, 1994; Glasgow, 1996; Guthrie et al., 1997); this appears to be particularly true for boys (Osmont, 1987).

Adolescent boys are also known to be especially enthusiastic for nonfiction and informational books (Herz & Gallo, 1996). For most boys, however, reading nonfiction in school consists almost exclusively of reading textbooks, which has been found to be a principal culprit in creating disaffection with reading for both boys and girls (Clary, 1991). I am always amazed at how turned-on junior and senior high students become when I pass around nonfiction and informational books. I watch adolescents shift their postures from complacency and disengagement to involvement and curiosity. These observations reinforce how rarely young adults are exposed to nonfiction books written specifically for them. There are biographies that chronicle the life stories of great men (past and present) who are emblematic of admirable male archetypes. Fact-based accounts of Galileo, Pelé, and Nelson Mandela, for example, give teen and preteen boys detailed views of heroic and creative accomplishments of men. In addition to engaging adolescents as readers, biographies help adolescents discover goodness in real-life men and introduce them to archetypes on which to base their own lives.

Juliet Turner's (1995) extensive research on motivating students within classrooms yielded specific guidelines for motivation (Turner & Paris, 1995). She discovered two critical ways for creating meaningful incentives for students to read and learn—*choices* of texts and tasks and *control* over learning. Choice is essentially self-determination or volitional engagement. Students' self-determined actions, as compared to students' actions driven by external pressure, have been found to be related to higher degrees of internal motivation, greater conceptual understanding of content, and better recall (Deci, Vallerand, Pelletier, & Ryan, 1991). In other words, students who *choose* to read have a better chance of success than students who are pressured to read. Giving students control over what they read and reading-related tasks is also essential in keeping them motivated. Control not only increases engagement in literacy and learning but allows students to reflect on their own competence (Spaulding, 1995).

Choice and control are two ingredients commonly missing in instruction provided to adolescent boys who are not reading as would be expected for their grade level and who are disinterested and reluctant readers. Typical remedial reading schemes tend to strengthen a boy's self-perception as an incompetent reader because they leave little or no room for choice and control. Although basic reading achievement may show some improvement, the boy becomes increasingly bored. An alternative approach should focus on giving reluctant or bored male readers the opportunity to choose reading materials and control the kinds of responses and extensions, such as assignments and activities, associated with those materials.

My years of work in reading clinics has verified much of the research and theoretical knowledge regarding adolescent boys and reading. Other than the obvious fact that males have always outnumbered females in clinics, I saw how boys need personally meaningful reading material to genuinely improve their literacy abilities. Otherwise, they politely go through the paces, but nothing sticks. For example, Carlos, a 14-year-old Mexican American, began making huge connections when we moved from simple skills-based activities to low-rider (a type of car) magazines and ultimately to novels such as Paulsen's (1990) *The Crossing*. With these materials, his eagerness to read, share, and respond expanded greatly. Furthermore, his response journal revealed a deep empathy and connection with Manny Bustos, the novel's main character from Ciudad Juarez, Mexico, who has many qualities of the Pilgrim archetype. As the reading clinician and Carlos worked through the book, Carlos came to see life through Manny's experiences, such as coping with the adversity of being an orphan, resolving interpersonal conflict with stronger street boys, and acting against stereotypes and racism with Sergeant Robert Locke. Before Carlos left clinic, we made sure he had an armful of other books, which he and his clinician selected together from the half-price bookstore, to take home over the summer. These included novels by Rudolfo Anaya and Gary Soto. A $10 investment is a small price to pay for a young man who now enjoys reading, knows how to make personal connections to his reading, and, because he reads regularly, has significantly improved his reading ability.

Research and anecdotal evidence support the approach we used with Carlos and continue to use with many other male students in clinic. Daly, Salters, and Burns (1998) found gender-based identification with characters from stories common among boys. A type of gender schema for boys tends to focus attention on textual personae and events that conform to their notions of appropriate male behavior. In the study by Daly et al., middle school boys, as opposed to girls, had superior recall over story content with male protagonists, particularly when the character exhibited recognizable behavior. The opposite was true when stories featured female protagonists.

Bugel and Buunk (1995) had similar results to the findings of Daly and his associates but used informational texts in their study instead of stories. Passages with traditional male topics (such as science, sports, and cars) were reported by males as being easier to read than passages with traditional female topics (such as midwifery, fashion, and so on). In addition, males had superior reading comprehension of male-oriented text versus the female-oriented text; the opposite was true for females.

In spite of fears that encouraging adolescent boys to read more of what they like—books with male characters in action and adventure plots—will strengthen gender stereotyping, concerns for listless and struggling male readers must take precedence for teachers and parents alike. Because of the diverse characterizations of masculinity found in the Jungian archetypes, books that are steeped in positive male archetypes may actually dispel stereotypical notions of what it means to be masculine.

Garnering adolescent boys' interest in reading, keeping them reading, and channeling this reading ability into academic mastery must be a priority. Books with archetypal male characters are likely to accomplish all of this. Archetypal literature that resonates in the male psyche has the power to reveal the delight and the necessity of reading to boys. It provides a reflection on their burgeoning masculinity in the form of male characters who—even though they meet physical, psychological, and emotional demands—ultimately interact caringly with others and make good choices.

Boy Talk

Gabriel, 15, Speaks of Men and Culture in Rudolfo Anaya's *My Land Sings: Stories From the Rio Grande*

A lot of people who don't know us think we're all no good. There's a piece of sidewalk on the way to school where someone wrote, "greasy spic." You can't erase it or anything. I even hear people say "wetbacks" and "beaners." They read in the newspaper and hear on television about Rodriguez or Garcia or Jimenez stealing a car or beating up his girlfriend or killing someone in a gang fight and can only think about us in that way. They don't know how rich our history and culture are. They think that because Jennifer Lopez or Ricky Martin are Hispanic Americans, everyone should like us. But people should respect us for more than that. We have worked hard to make Texas and the whole country a place that feels like home to us.

I felt proud to be Hispanic after reading *My Land Sings: Stories From the Rio Grande* (Anaya, 1999). These stories reminded me of how honest and good men of my culture are. It also reminded me that men in my culture do more than take siestas or act drunk or dumb.

In "Miller's Good Luck," Libor and Vidal are two wealthy businessmen arguing whether it was luck or hard work that made them successful. Libor thinks it's luck; Vidal thinks it's hard work. On the way to Santa Fe they meet a poor miller named Pedro Bernal. Pedro is hardworking and honest, so Libor and Vidal decide to use him in an experiment to decide who is right about how to be successful.

They give Pedro 100 pesos and tell him to do whatever he wants. Before Pedro can do anything, a hawk steals the money. They give him money again, but this time Pedro's wife accidentally trades the jar of wheat where Pedro has hidden his money. When the men come back, they think Pedro is lying about the money. Libor and Vidal go off laughing but throw Pedro a "worthless" piece of lead. This is when Pedro finally gets some good luck.

On his way home Pedro runs into a friend who is on his way to go fishing, but doesn't have a sinker. Pedro gives him the piece of lead, and his friend says he'll give him the first fish that he catches. Pedro's friend does, and Pedro's wife finds a very valuable diamond inside the fish.

Pedro gets 175,000 pesos from the jeweler for it and builds a big mill business. When Libor and Vidal return, they find that Pedro has become rich. Pedro tells them the story of his good luck, so Libor thinks he has won the argument. But then they find the first sack of money in a hawk's nest and realize Pedro was telling the truth about what happened to the money. Libor and Vidal agree that it takes some luck, but that it also takes honesty and hard work to be successful.

I think this story has a lot of meaning for my people because many of my friends say they're going to get rich by winning the lottery or some sweepstakes, or getting on some game show. They forget that, like Pedro, you have to be honest and hardworking to really be successful. My family is big and doesn't have much money, but my father works hard and is always there for us; therefore, I want to honor him by not getting involved in gangs or blowing off school. I want to be a good man like Pedro and my father. If luck comes to me it will be a surprise. I hope I take advantage of it, but I am not going to hold my breath.

The story I liked the most was "The Three Brothers" because there are three boys in my family. My two older brothers are living their lives similar to the characters of Felipé and Patricio, who wasted their lives and were always looking for someone to take advantage of. My brothers aren't that bad, but one is a dropout, working as a carpenter's helper sometimes. The other is a senior in high school, but his grades are very low, and he has no idea what he's going to do when he graduates. I want to be like Ramon's character—honest, generous, and hardworking. He eventually becomes a prosperous farmer and marries his childhood sweetheart. Ramon talks to his children about not taking the wrong path in life like his brothers did. My father has told us that many times, but I am the only one who seems to listen.

Final Thoughts

There is ample evidence that adolescent males are in an educational tailspin. As compared with girls, boys score lower on virtually all measures of verbal ability, abound in remedial classes, are delinquent and drop out of school at far greater rates, and attend and graduate from college in smaller numbers. Other data on boys' mental health and social adaptability present a grim picture of young men engaging in increasing levels of drug addiction, violence, homicide, and suicide.

Although there is no quick fix for the complex problems that face adolescent males, I reiterate throughout this book that capturing boys' imaginations through literature is a critical element of improving boys' psychological, sociological, and academic health. Reading books that appeal to and affirm young men's masculine identities in positive ways may transform a boy's sense of self and expand his academic possibilities. If middle school, junior high, and high school teachers carefully select and use good books for boys, particularly books with positive male archetypes, they may help adolescent males view reading as acceptable and worthwhile.

Literature and Positive Male Archetypes

So, you say, we have to change society first, and then boys will read good books. This is true. But if we can get just a few boys to read a few good books, we will have started the change. Cajole, coerce, do whatever needs to be done to get one book into one boy's hands, or back pocket. A book that he can make into a cave he can crawl into, roll around in, explore, for what's in there and what's in himself, you can do all by yourself, where no one can see you laughing or crying.

—Robert Lipsyte (as cited in Donelson & Nilsen, 1997, p. 259)

Teen and preteen boys may be more inclined to read "a few good books" that serve as entry points into active literacy when teachers use literature with archetypal characters. These archetypes appeal to and affirm teen and preteen boys' unique masculine identities. This literature has the chance to capture boys' imaginations, bring them into the literacy club, and ultimately bestow hope for academic possibilities and life options.

What is this literature? To be sure, it consists of books that have not been written intentionally to depict these archetypes. Writers of young adult books do not usually plan to infuse their fiction or nonfiction with archetypes that celebrate the male psyche. Glenna Davis Sloan (1991) keenly observes, however,

In literature...certain elements and structural patterns are recurrent; this is evident in works both old and new, classical and pop. These patterns or models—fundamental and ancient—recur often enough to be recognizable as aspects of all literary experience; as such, they are archetypal. (p. 48)

Because the literature I share in this book has been written either for or about boys, male archetypes are found within it; moreover, this is good literature in which boys are likely to find something identity affirming and, above all, something worth pursuing.

In this chapter, I describe characteristics of positive male archetypes. A section immediately following each description provides examples of young adult literature in which these archetypes are found. These books, and the books used by teachers in the following chapter, entice adolescent boys into the literacy club while reinforcing a positive sense of masculinity.

Finding or Rediscovering Positive Male Archetypes

Positive male archetypes starkly contrast with the mass media's spurious and injurious conceptions of masculinity. Images from popular culture assault boys very early in their lives with tales of bumbling, shallow, and even monstrous men (Kipnis, 1994). Images of men and fathers all too often depict them as incompetent, lazy, or frightening (Hewlett & West, 1998) even though studies offer counter evidence that these stereotypes are exaggerated (Parke & Brott, 1999). So, where do we find or how do we become reacquainted with positive images of masculinity in a culture that has done much to tarnish those images and saturate popular consciousness with perversions of manhood? In answering this question, I return to the ideas of the brilliant psychologist Carl Jung, whose work has been enormously influential on 20th-century thinking.

As stated earlier, Jung was one of the first to systematically investigate the uniqueness of the male psyche. According to Jung, archetypical models of maleness are inherent within the psyche of all men. For modern societies like ours, however, Jung describes a condition of "spiritual poverty" wherein we have lost the "historical symbols" of our fathers (DeLaszlo, 1959). Jung observes,

> Our intellect has achieved the most tremendous things, but in the meantime our spiritual dwelling has fallen into disrepair.... For the artificial sundering of true wisdom creates a tension in the psyche, and from there arises a loneliness and a craving like that of the morphine addict, who always hopes to find companions in his vice. (DeLaszlo, 1959, p. 300)

According to Jung, in order for a male to become a true man, he must rediscover his spiritual, inner self. This journey of rediscovery can be difficult, fraught with pitfalls and challenges. In the words of Jung, though, it "proves to be the indispensable condition for climbing any higher" (DeLaszlo, 1959, p. 302). Jung continues, "The prudent man avoids the danger...but also throws away the good which a bold but imprudent venture might bring"

(DeLaszlo, 1959, p. 303). It seems that boys must be willing to endure hardships associated with a kind of "right inner passage" to become fine young men and honorable adults. Positive male archetypes are an adolescent boy's guides along the often dark and jagged way of this interior journey.

In support of Jung's theory on male archetypes, contemporary psychologists and sociologists (Arnold, 1995; Johnson, 1989; Moore & Gillette, 1992) have discovered that the qualities that most societies consider masculine are remarkably consistent. Cultures as diverse as those of North American Natives, the island people of Truk in the South Pacific, the Mehinaku Indians of South America, the Samburu of Africa, the Samina of New Guinea, and many others share an understanding of what it means to be a mature man. One example of a consistent model of masculinity is the "big man" of New Guinea, the "muy hombre" of Spain, and the "worthy man" of Samburu who are all protectors, providers, and procreators. All show courage in the face of danger, are thoughtful risk takers when necessary, protect their families and communities, and exhibit extraordinary endurance to achieve laudable goals. They embrace these roles to nurture their families and build their communities (Gilmore, 1990). These different cultures share not only similar broad understandings of masculinity but also many specific male archetypes, such as Healer, Trickster, Prophet, and Warrior (Moore & Gillette, 1992).

The journey to manhood in almost all of these cultures involves, by design, inward and outward struggles that assure a new generation of men of goodness and strong spiritual connections. After exhaustive study of worldwide cultures, David Gilmore (1990) concludes that manhood is a test in most societies. In these societies, manhood ideologies "force men to shape up on penalty of being robbed of their identity" (p. 221). He further offers "when men are conditioned to fight, manhood is important; when men are conditioned to flight, the opposite is true" (p. 221). Gilmore does not necessarily refer to male fighting from an antisocial standpoint, but, rather, states the importance of men remaining strong for their families and communities. Male flight, on the other hand, is prevalent in societies such as the United States, where there is remarkably high tolerance for divorce and paternal absenteeism. Male flight from communal responsibility is further conditioned in cultures, again similar to the United States, that accept definitions of men as loners and rugged individuals.

Our own culture, says Patrick Arnold (1995), is also responsible for "indoctrinated hostility to spirituality" (p. 12). Far from enthroning men, as many have argued, periods in the history of Western civilization such as the Enlightenment and the Industrial Revolution have disconnected men from their homes, their religions, and their inner selves. In Arnold's words,

It is no exaggeration to say that modernity has created generations of Numb Men who cannot *feel* their own experiences, much less articulate them. Capitalism...has fabricated the Incredible Shrinking Man, a merely utilitarian robot programmed...to create capital. (p. 14)

Leaving children a legacy of economic prosperity is not enough. Children also must be shown how to lead lives of mission, purpose, and ideals. For boys, this means helping them persevere and thrive academically and imparting a positive sense of their uniqueness as males. The templates for this uniqueness are found in masculine archetypes of humanity's collective past.

Ten Positive Male Archetypes

An archetype, as previously stated, is an inherited idea or mode of thought that is derived from the experience of the race and present in the unconscious of the individual (Jung, 1955). Jung theorized that each man possesses a masculine soul, the *animus*. He found evidence for archetypes of the animus in the nearly identical motifs and tales of manhood that appear in widely separate cultures. Tribal stories, songs, poems, and fairy tales of different cultures—originating in antiquity before modern communications made worldwide connections possible—speak of manhood not as an entity, but as both an inner and outer test of courage. According to Jung, deep knowledge residing in the collective unconscious makes up the archetypal core of man. Exhumation of the animus is one result of archetypal study.

I present the 10 positive male archetypes to help teachers guide adolescent boys through the archetypal world of the male psyche. These images of masculinity, derived from the work of Jung (1955) and Arnold (1995), may be thought of as signposts along a boy's psychic journey to claim or reclaim an honorable masculine identity. The archetypes include Pilgrim, Patriarch, King, Warrior, Magician, Wildman, Healer, Prophet, Trickster, and Lover. These archetypes are the focus of the literature and teaching strategies presented here and in Chapter 3. Using archetypes to interpret literature is a highly common practice in literary criticism (Cowden, Viders, & Lafever, 2000; Cutler, 2000; Schaum, 2000).

Pilgrim

The Pilgrim archetype is one of male wanderlust. He is a searcher and wanderer, filled with hope, faith, and the need to improve life. Deliberate pilgrimages are a featured practice of major ancient religions. A male's pilgrimage is a quest for spiritual freedom, which he reaches by seeking a special holy place. A Pilgrim endures great hardship across many miles, enacting this sacred ritual. In the process of pilgrimage, a man must give up the comforts of familiarity, because only through detachment from that which impedes his progress can he find his way to higher forms of selfhood. The Pilgrim's spirit is characterized by Jung as the "highest freedom, a soaring over the depth, deliverance from the prison of...timorous souls who do not want to become anything different" (DeLaszlo, 1959, p. 303).

It is critical to a boy's consciousness to become reacquainted with his inner Pilgrim; if not, he may grow up to be like so many adult men in lockstep that leads to mental stagnation, emotional numbness, and spiritual starvation. Adults do boys few favors by turning a blind eye to undisciplined and habitual video watching. Recent reports suggest that the average 5 to 7 hours per day that children spend in front of television and computer screens, regardless of content, results in less intellectually stimulated and more emotionally disconnected adolescents and adults (Greenspan & Lewis, 2000). Boys who are mired in this video malaise take fewer and increasingly limited flights of imagination and ignore their inner Pilgrim. Young boys need and crave, especially in their souls, meaningful and vibrant interaction with others who can keep them in touch with the wanderer within.

Wandering is meaningful for adolescent boys when it is borne of intense needs or desires for life-altering experiences. In this way, Pilgrims search for great solutions to seemingly insoluble problems. Solutions may come at a significant price; however, this is part of the test of Pilgrims' commitment. As Jung suggested, these inner journeys are not for the cautious because they require bold action and risk taking.

Adolescence is itself a metaphor for a pilgrimage. Boys travel unfamiliar physical, emotional, and sociological terrain in this phase of their lives. Adult role models must help teen and preteen boys clarify the goals of their pilgrimages and support their pilgrimages to higher levels of selfhood.

A Pilgrim in Young Adult Literature. Adolescent boys will find an ideal Pilgrim in the character of Lincoln Mendoza in Gary Soto's *Pacific Crossing* (1992). Growing up in the Mission District, the barrio of San Francisco, California, USA, Lincoln's interest in martial arts does not go unnoticed by his high school principal, who selects him to be an exchange student in Japan. During his 6 weeks there with a host family, Lincoln learns more about himself as a stranger in a foreign country than he has in his own country. He also realizes that he must accept his own identity as a Mexican American. His journey to the East brings some life-changing adventures, the most notable of which involves Lincoln and Mitsuo, his Japanese brother. They must find a way to save Mr. Ono, who has been bitten by an extremely poisonous spider while the three of them are visiting a temple at the top of a mountain. Lincoln also experiences pain and failure at the hands of superior *kempo* (a type of martial arts) opponents. In the end, however, he realizes that the mastery of *kempo* is a lifelong process, and that the practice of it has more to do with self-control and pride than defeating any combatant. Similar to all Pilgrims, Lincoln must search his inner and outer selves for his essence—and he does so with dignity.

Patriarch

Patriarch, as well as King, is one of the most important archetypes of respon-sibility. The Patriarch represents the masculine form of care, nobility, and self-sacrifice. His energy provides a family with "emotional stability, sturdiness, firm correction, world-wisdom, constructive criticism, moral principles, and a sense of fun" (Arnold, 1995, p. 38). Like all other positive male archetypes, the role of the Patriarch has been tarnished by images from pop culture, but the archetype continues to burn within each boy. It remains there to be dis-covered or rekindled.

There would appear to be a need in our society for the reemergence of Patriarchal fathering and mentoring for young boys (Blankenhorn, 1995). Margaret Mead's (1969) scientific studies on fathering reveal phylogeneti-cally (from an evolution perspective) that male care for offspring has been ten-uous. Males have learned, however, to overcome their primal inclination to leave after impregnation and "commit themselves to their families and soci-eties as nurturers and care-givers in a uniquely masculine fashion" (Arnold, 1995, p. 37). Patriarchal care is characterized by its firmness, consistency, de-pendability, and fairness. For thousands of years, Patriarchs—in their social roles as fathers, tribal leaders, and judges—have been responsible for creating orderly and lawful societies and institutions for the personal and aesthetic wel-fare of the community.

Feminists and other modern critics of patriarchy are not unfounded in their claims of its historical and current abuses. Rigid, violent, and misogy-nistic forms of male dominion have prevailed throughout the ages. I must agree with Arnold, however, who argues "it is unfair, unscholarly, and unwise only to characterize a system by its abuses. One rarely hears an...account of patriarchy that also takes into account its vast contributions to human history" (1995, p. 37).

Sylvia Hewlett and Cornel West's *The War Against Parents: What We Can Do for America's Beleaguered Moms and Dads* (1998) asserts that one of the caustic messages of the 1990s is mass media's negative stereotyping of moms and dads. In a case of pop culture irony, say Hewlett and West, the television wasteland of the 1950s, which unrealistically portrayed U.S. parents and families, at least paid tribute to mothers and fathers by reaffirming the importance of parenthood. In subsequent decades, progressive sensibilities were offended by the patriarchal nature of stereotypical television families. Hewlett and West argue, however, that in dismissing the fantasy elements of television parenthood, parents have been dismissed altogether. Open season on parents is evident everywhere in the mass media, from talk shows and contemporary movies to popular songs, books, and magazines. This parent bashing sends a clear message that fathers no longer deserve respect that once came with being a dad. Fathers are increasingly portrayed as klutzy and bumbling fools, or vicious perverts, whereas children are cast as "saviors"—coolheaded sons and daughters who are far more stable and resourceful than their neurotic parents. Hewlett and West summarize this trend as follows:

> Over a forty-year period, the entertainment industry has moved from celebrating to denigrating the parental role and function; where once parents were portrayed as loving and wise, they are now portrayed as neglectful and abusive.... More and more parents feel demoralized and devalued. They listen to Beavis tell Butthead "Your mother is a slut" and remember a time when television, movies, and popular music routinely paid homage to moms and dads and reinforced the values they taught. Now they feel locked in a daily battle to protect their children from the negative messages spewed forth by these same sources. (p. 133)

As honorable masculinity declines in our society, the first qualities to fall away are, historically, the last to develop—namely, patriarchal responsibility and nurturance. Modern cultures eschew initiation rites of adult males, leaving boys with fewer reference points for responsible masculine behavior. Instead of expecting male irresponsibility to reverse itself by bashing or dismissing men, as is common, people should excite the consciousness of boys and restore a sense of masculine pride and responsibility.

In addition to being responsible for others, the Patriarch is generous and gracious. Arnold describes the Patriarch as "the archetype in the masculine psyche that offers to father those who are not so fortunate, who are orphaned or lost or helpless or who need guidance and wise direction" (1995, p. 89). Exploration of this archetype teaches young men to understand what it means to be a father. Adolescent boys can also find expression for this fatherhood in ways that serve others just as powerfully as these boys will come to serve their own children. The ideals of the Patriarch, for example, can inspire boys to provide community service, such as helping homeless people, reading to patients in children's hospitals, and participating in beautifying and cleanup efforts. Helping boys access this archetype makes *all* of society a better place.

A Patriarch in Young Adult Literature. George from Chris Lynch's *Shadow Boxer* (1995) possesses many of the qualities that adolescent boys admire in the Patriarch. George becomes the man of the house after his father dies of boxing-related injuries. He must teach his younger brother, Monty, important lessons about boxing and life that George first learned from their father. George's dad taught him how to take care of himself and how to fight but also taught him "how not to be a fighter, how to walk away" (p. 7). This is the most important lesson that George helps Monty learn because Monty sees boxing as his legacy. In order to protect Monty and help him realize that too many physical blows brought on their father's demise, George gives his younger brother just enough space but remains at hand to catch him when he inevitably falls. George is not superhuman, but like any Patriarch he does his best to support his mother and provide fatherly counsel and love to his brother.

King

The King embodies male greatness. He is trustworthy and wise, and he engenders excellence in others as well. Filled with spiritual generosity, dignity, and composure, the King accompanies people into places they do not wish to go, but must. Every male who wants to be a leader should explore this archetype to better understand magnanimity, difficult decision making, and equanimity.

At first glance, it would appear that most boys and men today would have difficulty identifying with the concept of King. As a boy, I was immersed in the adventures of courtly intrigue with Danish Prince Valiant, who appeared in the Sunday paper; the legendary tales of ruthlessness at the behest of Henry the VIII; or Daniel Dravot's cunning and illegitimate rule of Kafristan in Kipling's "The Man Who Would Be King" (1999). These images formed my model of kingly behavior. Most males develop notions of kingship from the popular conception of an all-powerful monarch, luxuriating in pampered, carefree living and exercising his prerogative at will. With this model in mind, it is little wonder that boys become overwhelmed by this grandeur; furthermore, U.S. boys are steeped in democratic ideals of representative government and self-rule, not in those of a monarchy. I distinctly remember my fifth-grade teacher, Sister Rose Thomas, vilifying King George III for his efforts to crush the insurrection of democracy-minded New England colonists.

There is little room in the political and social milieu of the United States for this kind of King. Yet, as Arnold points out, "regardless of these conflicting attitudes, any man who finds himself in a position of power over others...needs to develop this archetype successfully if he is to govern well and keep from becoming a Tyrant" (1995, p. 112).

Given the exceptional goodness of the King archetype, nothing could be more honorable than to encourage adolescent boys to imitate it, regardless of their personality. The qualities of King described in Psalms in reference to King Solomon—who, in spite of his riches, comforts, and power, saw as his duty to tend to the needs of his lowliest subjects—are clearly worth emulating by all of us:

> He gives justice to poor people,
> And saves the children of poverty.
> He frees the lowly and helpless who call on him,
> He takes pity on the poor and the weak.
> The souls of powerless he saves...
> The lives are precious in his eyes (72 Ps. 4:12–14, New American Bible)

Modern-day figures whom boys can readily recognize and admire for their similarities to the King archetype might include the school principal who sets high standards of conduct and scholarship, personally knows his students, and works tirelessly on the students' behalf to help them achieve their potential; the boss who wins the trust of employees, cares about employees' well-being, encourages both the janitor and the highest executive to speak freely about their concerns, and brings about equitable pay for office staff; and the military officer who openly discusses problems raised by his troops and works diligently to provide affordable and comfortable accommodations for military personnel and their families. And consider former U.S. President Jimmy Carter who, with his bare hands, helps build low-cost housing for the poor and less privileged—now that is Kingly behavior.

A King in Young Adult Literature. There was a great man who was a leader of the United Kingdom during its most troubling years in the 20th century. Instead of having a crown and a scepter he wore a top hat and smoked a long cigar. The man is Winston Churchill, the prime minister who found special inspiration from the King archetype. John Severance affectionately tells Churchill's story in the fascinating biography *Winston Churchill: Soldier, Statesman, Artist* (1996). This is a classic story of a man who develops his King archetype to rescue his besieged nation. Recall that when Churchill became prime minister of England, the country had recently entered into the war against

Hitler and the Nazis. British forces had been routed in Belgium and needed a miracle to escape complete annihilation from the Germans. Soon after, the bombing of Britain commenced. Every night brought new destruction to London, Liverpool, Manchester, and Birmingham. Presiding through it all with a stiff upper lip and a gallant stride was Churchill. Wearing the cloak of governance with total devotion, he rallied his people to never lose hope or give in to Nazism, and to fight back. Churchill is similar to legendary Kings who brought life-sustaining energy to despairing subjects even though their kingdoms were at their lowest. When Churchill saw devastating bombardments eroding his kingdom, he brought new life to his people and inspired a new spirit of determination, which ultimately lead to victory over Germany.

Severance offers little-known insights about Churchill. Beginning with Churchill's election to Parliament in 1900 and ending with his resignation as prime minister, readers come to know him first and foremost for his public service, which stretched over half a century. Readers also learn just how human Churchill was through his proclivity for alcohol, tobacco, and other vices. Although he sometimes domineered and bullied others, the King within Churchill shone more brightly throughout his life, inspiring a generation of British citizens, as well as their World War II allies, to give of themselves for the common good. Churchill's often quoted words of praise for the resilient British citizens during the height of the Battle of Britain sum up his kingly essence—Never have so few given so much, for so many (Severance, 1996). This delightful and engrossing book demonstrates that there are modern-day Kings who, although they may be born without royal lineage, are capable of leading others to a better future.

Warrior

Lurking in the souls of all males is the Warrior. He is brave, edifying, and honorable. In defining the Warrior archetype, it is important to avoid using female passivity as the subordinate concept. The definition of the Warrior should contrast with male greed, selfishness, and lack of humanitarian spirit.

Violent males are not Warriors, although this image has been appropriated by U.S. movies as the most salient and the most profitable; furthermore, emotionally wounded boys find the Warrior archetype so compelling that they may join gangs to gain a sense of misguided self-respect. This cheapened form of the Warrior is built on violent, self-righteous retaliation and the duty to protect neighborhood turf. These modern perversions make it difficult for both males and females to embrace this archetype's glorification. The Warrior's true masculinity is based on self-control and moral courage, and has nothing to do with a lack of behavioral volition or the sway of impulse and rage (Jordan, 1995). The Warrior's sacred obligation, which is recognized in almost every culture, is to never act violently out of blind anger or revenge, but to deliberately and strategically plan and take full responsibility for actions. As in the past, today's Warriors should be initiated and educated in ethical codes of "personal honor, noble restraint, magnanimity to defeated rivals, and individual humility for one's deeds" (Arnold, 1995, p. 104).

Although most modern-day males rarely need their inner Warriors for physical combat, they still need the Warrior's strength for everyday psychological and psychic battles. Warriors find expression in steadfastly training the mind and body, girding themselves for the onslaught of naysayers and detractors, and courageously defending an honorable cause.

Understanding the origin of the Warrior archetype helps illuminate its importance. The paradigm was an outgrowth of the Paleolithic hunter, around whom mythology, rituals, ethics, and art were developed as an homage to this central role in early human societies. "Lauded by poems, songs, and stories, celebrated and sanctified by rituals, and blessed by the gods, the Warrior has come to epitomize the noblest qualities of masculinity: bravery, self-sacrifice, stamina, and skill" (Arnold, 1995, p. 101).

No archetype symbolizes the opposition to evil more powerfully than the Warrior. Today this opposition involves battling disease, attacking drug use, and waging war on poverty and ignorance. Teachers, parents, and others need to help teen and preteen boys discover their inner Warriors as a source of fortification for a variety of meaningful causes. As R.W. Connell (1989) discovered, however, this is not an easily obtained goal. In his study of the interplay between masculinity and school, the construction of masculinity for teens from homes with either unemployment or absentee fathers involved a process of "getting into trouble" or blindly fighting school authority. Following these teens into adulthood, Connell documented their confusion and frustration in developing a patriarchal masculinity based on the mixed messages they received from home and school. This resulted more often than not in the recapitulation of the cool guys, nerds, and wimps models of masculinity from their working-class communities. Those trying to help boys access the Warrior persona will confront similar blocked paths; indeed, it is the inner Warrior that emboldens people to accept the challenge in the first place.

A Warrior in Young Adult Literature. The best real-life Warrior is a man who goes to great lengths to avoid aggressive action, but when he must act, does so with confidence, resolve, and honorable intent. Such is the Warrior power of Nelson Mandela, who is engagingly described in *Nelson Mandela: Voice of*

Freedom (Hughes, 2000). Born in a thatched hut in a peasant village in South Africa, Mandela was raised by his uncle and attended a local missionary school. When he was a young man, he ran away to Johannesburg to work in the mines. Eventually, he was admitted to law school and began to recognize the need to fight the racism of his homeland. Mandela became the leader of the African National Congress in the 1960s, which was committed to dismantling apartheid and restoring social justice for people of every race. The South African government (comprised of only white people) arrested and imprisoned Mandela for his radical views on racial equality, and he spent over 27 years in jail. Due in large part to his efforts to raise international consciousness about the atrocities of apartheid, the stress of embargoes and other policies of economic isolation finally pressured the South African government to release Mandela and modify its constitution to give blacks full participation in the political process. Within 4 years of his release, Mandela was elected president of the Republic of South Africa. Similar to all honorable Warriors, Mandela withstood both extreme physical and psychological hardships because of his devotion to the welfare of others. He was gracious in victory, imposing strict policies that criminalized reprisals against whites and forging stronger interracial relationships to ensure prosperous coexistence in South Africa.

Teen and preteen boys cannot help but become absorbed in Hughes's moving account of a man whose conviction brought a nation and the world closer to the ideal of social justice and human rights for all. Mandela illustrates how boys can potently channel the Warrior archetype into socially constructive and peaceable causes.

Magician

The Magician evokes amazement through his intuition and cleverness. According to Sallie Nichols (1980), the paradigm of the Magician and his wand is extremely ancient. Ancient wisdom has it that the Magician is the first major psychological archetype out of 22 symbols and situations of people's collective unconscious (Pearson & Seivert, 1995). Pop culture has, unfortunately, reduced this archetype to sleight of hand hucksters for sideshow amusement or high-priced, glossy deception for television. These superficial renderings have little connection with the deeper level of the Magician archetype. Within men's core, the Magician engages psychic resources. According to Arnold (1995),

> Many modern men are appallingly unaware of the tremendous psychic potential that lies within them unused; educated in a left-brain/material-

istic worldview, they insist that things are just what they appear, that what you see is what you get, and any other viewpoint is just superstition and religious hocus-pocus. (p. 107)

Adolescent boys should be guided in the ways of prayer and meditation to nurture their intuition and conjure their inner Merlin. We think of intuition as a female trait; indeed, a common synonym is "female logic." Yet primal societies gave elevated status to men who, inspired by hunches or feelings in their bones, could locate the best sources of game, water, or shelter. Pearson and Seivert (1995) report that men who develop their inner Magician follow business hunches that pay off, perceive subtle changes in the emotional moods and needs of loved ones, and notice how coincidences lead to special opportunities in their personal lives. For some the Magician archetype connects them to the universal mysterious and pervasive force that guides all creation. This is the force that strengthens people to reconcile with their enemies, restores people's pride after defeat, and helps people recognize blind luck or good fortune as the handiwork of the Magician.

To access the Magician archetype, boys need to become acquainted with their intuitive selves. Teachers may help boys become comfortable with this archetype by finding both ancient and contemporary examples of males who have used their intuitive powers to improve their lives and the lives of those around them.

A Magician in Young Adult Literature. Imagine being able to throw a baseball on a straight course from beyond the outfield directly into the catcher's perfectly positioned mitt to tag out a runner from third base. That's what Billy Baggs, the main character in Will Weaver's *Striking Out* (1993), can do. His magic on the field extends to the plate as well:

> Billy drove forward low and hard with his rear leg. His eyes followed the ball all the way to his bat. The ball floated in as large as a softball. For an instant he saw it bulge and flatten against the thick part of the bat—then it was gone with a hard, stinging *crack!*... King watched Billy's ball rise straight out over second base toward center field. The center fielder took one step back, then stopped. Hands hanging straight down at his sides, his mouth open, he turned to watch the ball soar overhead.... The ball shrank away white against the gray-and-white clouds and disappeared far over the center-field fence. (p. 67)

Billy's magic, however, must be worked on his father, who cannot forgive him for what happened to Robert, Billy's deceased older brother. The story takes place on a Minnesota farm, where Robert dies after allowing Billy to drive the tractor. Something goes horribly wrong, and as the machine jerks forward, Robert falls off and is crushed by its massive tires. Billy cannot escape the sullenness and wrath of his father, which includes his disdain for Billy's membership on the Flint Sparks baseball squad. Billy recognizes, though, that his baseball prowess is not the only gift he possesses; he can also help his parents and himself come to terms with the loss of Robert. Billy Baggs is endowed with many of the Magician's admirable characteristics, which allows teen and preteen boys to identify with and revere him in *Striking Out*.

Wildman

The Wildman archetype is characterized by lustiness, unpredictability, and independence. He is the ancient male paradigm of one who yearns for freedom. He is the original man frolicking in the lush, beast-filled expanses of Eden. Arnold (1995) describes the Wildman as follows:

> He is a figure representing man's primordial connections with nature; in the myths, he dwells in the wilderness in swamps, caves, or lonely desert tracts. Totally liberated from the trappings of modern civilization...he represents male earthiness, that grubby and gritty manly energy radically free from the effete effects of deodorized and cosmetic modern male narcissism.... That's the Wildman—that dangerous and attractive fellow beckoning us out of our ruts and into the wilderness. (p. 35)

For many, the word *wildman* evokes a host of negative images, such as tattered and unshorn street dwellers or undisciplined or lunatic social rebels. People lock their car doors when they see the wildman hitching a ride with a makeshift duffel at his side. On city streets and in subways, people walk briskly past the wildman shuffling toward them with matted down hair and an outstretched palm. How unfortunate that boys have so few opportunities to encounter the authentic Wildman, who resides deep beneath modern consciousness (Anderson, 1990).

If we could go back far enough in time, we would discover that all men were Wildmen. Primal man was as wild as the beasts he hunted. Enslaved by and in awe of natural forces, primal man explained the mysteries of birth and death through myth and paid homage to large unexplained forces in an attempt to contextualize his existence. With the invention of agriculture, however, humanity changed forever. Men, no longer at the mercy of indifferent natural processes, learned to exploit nature for their own purposes. This process has yet to cease; consequently, boys and men living in modern civilizations have become disconnected from the former natural order of things. Most are now estranged from their inner Wildman.

The Wildman remains alive within the male psyche, though. Introducing an adolescent boy to his inner Wildman can be a daunting experience. When I reflect on this process of reunification, I envision the flash of recognition not unlike the kind that sweeps over the spouse of *The Man With the Twisted Lip* (Doyle, 1930). In this Sherlock Holmes tale, a gentleman dons the disguise of a hairy, deformed beggar in an attempt to repay a debt from a poor investment. He panhandles by day and changes into proper clothes each evening, returning to his wife and children as if nothing were untoward. Through a coincidence, however, after his wife spies him in the window of a notorious opium den—his safe haven for changing out of his disguise—he goes missing and is feared murdered. Holmes, of course, gets to the bottom of the mystery by deducing that the beggar and the gentleman are the same man. In a public unmasking before his wife, the man with the twisted lip is forced to remove his disguise. The reader sees the line between man and Wildman disappear. This dualism is also evident in Robert Louis Stevenson's *Dr. Jekyll and Mr. Hyde* (1994) and other stories from the late 19th century.

Teachers and parents should be cautious, though, when choosing books that present the Wildman archetype. The authors of the narratives from the late 1800s were influenced by the burgeoning fields of psychology and psychoanalysis and the work of Freud and Jung, and their tales invariably reveal the dark side of the Wildman archetype—the destructive, wanton nature of wildness. Even real-life Wildman Chris McCandless, from Jon Krakauer's *Into the Wild* (1996), leaves boys with little to emulate. Although McCandless embodies many positive qualities of the Wildman, such as eschewing materialism and seeking a state of oneness with nature, his ill-fated adventure is nothing more than escapism, or a complete turning away from family and friends, into what one might characterize as a pathological drive to be apart from everything and everyone.

The Wildman archetype helps boys both escape the demands of modern life and exploit the archetypal inclination to improve their families, communities, and society. The Wildman emboldens young men to challenge the status quo, and question their own and others' complacency, conformity, and popular ideologies. The voice of the wilderness is, today, the voice within that tells boys to reject false promises and replace them with genuine behavior. This voice also helps adolescent boys see through fads and strive for solid and permanent values instead.

A Wildman in Young Adult Literature. Wildmen look for adventure, although sometimes get more than they bargained for. Such is the case with Gabe Rogers and Raymond Providence in Will Hobbs's gripping action tale

Far North (1996). This is the kind of thrill-a-minute book that I consider traditional boy material. Similar to most of Hobbs's young adult novels, in *Far North*, there is more than meets the eye. Beneath the account of Gabe and Raymond's physical struggle to survive in Canada's Northwest Territories against seemingly impossible odds is a story of inner survival. The 15-year-olds are roommates from a boarding school on the shores of Great Slave Lake in the city of Yellowknife. Gabe's father is a professional driller from Texas, working at a remote site near the Arctic Ocean. Raymond's heritage is one of Athabaskan Indian descent. Gabe, because he is looking for adventure, and Raymond, because he has dropped out of school, find themselves on the same plane bound for Raymond's village on the Nahanni River. When the plane is lost over the mammoth Virginia Falls, the boys must dig deeply into the survival power of their inner Wildmen. Initially, tempers are high and feelings run bad because Gabe sees Raymond as a quitter for escaping the academic and social demands of the boarding school. Eventually, however, they discover that only through working together will they find their way to safety.

This gripping adventure is likely to engross boys after reading only the first page. Reading this book will help them learn of the Wildman's power to reconnect males with nature. The book also celebrates the virtues of the Wildman by demonstrating how boys' infatuation with rock music, MTV, and other teenage fads loses importance when compared with the solid values of friendship and cooperation. Raymond's survival lessons ultimately give him the resolve to return to school and take up the challenges of survival in a new academic and social culture.

Healer

The Healer archetype is mystical, spiritual, and capable of bringing wholeness to people and societies that are incomplete and suffering. Rituals of healing are deep in the histories of mankind. Well before the arrival of Jesus, for instance, baptisms by water were common throughout the Hebrew culture because they were viewed as a ritual to cleanse impurities and heal the wounds of sinfulness. Jessie Weston (1997), the renowned authority of medieval legends, shows how the processes of birth and rebirth and sickness and healing were integral to ancient fertility rites. In the Fisher King myth, for example, the ruler of a land that has become barren must endure sickness and disease before life-giving waters return to heal him and restore the fertility of his land.

Healers are powerful archetypes in many worldwide cultures. They cure physical, emotional, and spiritual illnesses of their tribes or societies. Ancient healers regarded most afflictions as spiritual in nature. The work of the healer, therefore, was to cure disease and injuries by invoking good spirits who were more powerful than the evil demons who plagued the sufferers.

Remnants of the Healer archetype continue to reside in the male psyche. Unfortunately, it has become extremely difficult for boys and men to access the healing side of masculinity because of a pop culture that depicts men as violent and destructive. To become Healers, boys must first learn to heal themselves. This self-healing is distinctly masculine. John Grim (1984) describes the process of a healer or shaman receiving his healing powers through a harrowing spiritual journey, whereby the young and vulnerable healer must endure and conquer physical and emotional trials that require him to marshal a great force of positive spirits. This rite of passage is viewed by cultural peers as a miracle not only for the individual, but for everyone, because the shaman can then devote his healing powers to lifetime service of the wounded and sick tribespeople.

Self-healing must be dealt with carefully for boys living in today's instant-cure world. As Arnold points out, "The healing process takes place in a much more mysterious, complex, and individual fashion than the spiritual salesmen would have us believe, in league with forces and on a timetable not amenable to our conscious direction" (1995, p. 136). Teen and preteen boys need models of the Healer archetype who fit into their complex and high-tech worlds. Teachers should work to guide boys through the inward journey of self-healing while encouraging boys' outward acts of public service for those who are hurting.

A Healer in Young Adult Literature. Healers have special gifts that they use to heal wounds, make people whole, and bring people together. This power is illustrated by 13-year-old Weyr in Harald Bakken's *The Fields and the Hills: The Journey, Once Begun* (1992). The book depicts a fantasy world in which nations and races create elaborate psychological and institutional barriers to pluralism and cultural harmony.

Weyr's powers include the ability to see and hear things that others cannot. These abilities are the source of his healing power. The Tam and Agari tribes avoid each other at all costs, sharing a mutual hate and fear of each other. Adults in each tribe tell stories to their children about how members of the other tribe are monsters, kidnappers, and even witches. When Weyr, a member of the Tam, uses his special abilities to save the life of an Agari, the Agari tribespeople show genuine gratitude and thanks. The Tam realize that these characteristics are very similar to their own. As he spends more and more time traveling with the Agari, Weyr discovers the true nature of their cultural uniqueness but also how similar their hopes, fears, and pleasures are to those of the Tam. The Agari come to see Weyr's special abilities as helpful, not sinister, and their overall attitude toward this trait changes, because they no longer view this as a source of Tamish witchcraft. Other stereotypes eventually fall by the wayside as the Agari learn the full depth of Weyr's goodness.

Bakken portrays Weyr as a boy with classic powers of the Healer. While on his journey with the Agari through their lands, Weyr makes a spiritual excursion to find a new source of confidence and self-knowledge. He then uses this new understanding of himself and his extrasensory gifts to heal wounds of fear, hatred, and division between people. Weyr possesses qualities that adolescent boys can recognize in their own lives, making *The Fields and the Hills* a highly useful source for helping boys access their inner Healer.

Prophet

When people think of a modern-day Prophet, they might think about a self-ascribed, television clairvoyant who predicts love, fame, and fortune for gullible callers. Other people may envision a wizened man who can predict the future, utter divinely inspired revelations, and effectively speak for a cause or concern. The Prophet archetype embodies all these qualities and more. He causes controversy and piques consciousness. He is "a spiritual figure of great antagonism who insists on battling falsehoods and telling the truth to society without regard to his own safety, success, or welfare" (Arnold, 1995, p. 33). This archetype has no room for pretense or false commitment. A spiritual friend of mine described the Prophet archetype to me in a homespun way that makes clear this last point. He said, "The Prophet is like the ham in a ham and egg breakfast. Whereas the chicken makes a partial contribution to the meal, the pig makes a full commitment by giving his life. This is the Prophet" (R. Schmelzer, personal communication, December 29, 2000).

The Prophet's power to see and tell the truth makes him a most admirable paragon in the male psyche. He stands up to lies, is blunt, and possesses an intuitive lie detector. With these characteristics, why would anyone not want all adolescent boys to be guided by the power of this positive archetype? Like all of the archetypes I have described, the true Prophet is a very masculine figure. Endowed with a kind of spiritual virility, the Prophet stands up to assaults from people and society in denial about conscience. Arnold (1995) says,

> Indicting, judging, accusing, attacking, exhorting, and exciting, his words sometimes wound and always irritate, and inevitably provoke and scandalize.... To the complacent, he hurls warning; to the desperate, hope. He tells us what we do not want to hear when we do not

want to hear it. That is why society is always so intent on finding ways to eliminate him from its earshot. (p. 148)

It is rare to see someone in society speak as truthfully and lovingly as a Prophet does. Teachers should strive to find books that embolden male youth with this insight and the power of truth. Boys who have access to this archetype are capable of living and leading others to honorable and honest lifestyles. Providing boys with models of real-life men who love the truth, as well as examples of male literary characters who embody Prophet-like qualities, can help boys more readily access this powerful archetype for lifelong inspiration.

A Prophet in Young Adult Literature. *Prophet* is a heavy moniker. As evidence, consider its sparing ascription over the course of recorded history and particularly in modern time. To have Prophet-like qualities, however, does not automatically entail highly superhuman powers of prediction and uncanny insight. Perhaps the most ideal Prophets are those individuals who are not yet fully aware of their own gifts, but who pursue truth, justice, and goodness with innocence and humility. A unique fictional character in young adult literature who seems to embody the aforementioned qualities is Jeffrey Lionel Magee, better known as Maniac Magee. Jerry Spinelli's (1990) moving tale of the same name follows the exploits of a young man who wanders into a segregated Pennsylvania town and shakes the citizens out of their complacency forever.

Whether intentional or not, Spinelli imbued Maniac with characteristics reminiscent of biblical prophets. Maniac seems to appear in the small town of Two Mills almost out of thin air. Spinelli (1990) opens his book by describing Maniac in this way: "They say Maniac Magee was born in a dump. They say his stomach was a cereal box and his heart a sofa spring" (p. 1). Similar to John the Baptist, Maniac soon has the townspeople exchanging stories about his unusual feats, such as how fast and how far he can run, how in baseball he hits a "frogball" for an inside-the-park home run, and how many touchdowns he scores. His real accomplishment, however, comes in the form of challenging long-standing views regarding racial integration. The East End and West End of Two Mills are separated by an invisible line that segregates whites and blacks. Again, similar to the powerful biblical prophets, Maniac disrupts the status quo by being the first to cross that line, leading the community to a new level of consciousness.

With true Prophet-like strength, Maniac's color blindness and innocent courage show people a truth they had yet to glimpse. Boys have found and will continue to find *Maniac Magee* a story that piques their unique male imaginations. Using athletic prowess as the hook, Spinelli carves a figure of an adolescent boy who can also impress with his gifts of truthfulness and righteousness. Maniac Magee is an ideal model of the Prophet archetype for male youth.

Trickster

The Trickster archetype is irreverent, funny, and satirical. This archetype is the impish side of the masculine spirit, poking fun of pomposity, ostentation, and self-righteousness. His ancient role was to mock arrogance to make way for new, honest leadership. Shakespeare's jesters and sprites, such as Feste in *Twelfth Night* (1998) or Ariel in *The Tempest* (1994), express the aura of this archetype very well when they take advantage of interludes in the play's action to speak directly to the audience about the folly and overwrought emotions of the main characters, engendering satiric laughter.

This archetype lives on in the male psyche. The Trickster is the source of unconscious antics, as well as the spice and flavor in routine lives. The male Trickster is the office prankster who lightens moods; the teacher who is always ready to inject levity into the discussion of an otherwise turgid topic; or the buddy who teases in ways that remind his friends that life is not so bad, and that it does not hurt to laugh at themselves. The Trickster is the comedian, the political satirist, and the musical parodist who reminds people of their frailty and humanness in delightful ways.

The Trickster is a worthwhile role model for young men because he instills humility. For example, if a boy becomes conceited because of his athleticism during a baseball game, the Trickster finds a way to have him fall over his own feet on his way from third base to home and tagged out. When a young man starts taking his sex appeal too seriously, his inner prankster makes certain that a piece of spinach is stuck in his front teeth when he tries to make a date in the lunchroom. Both boys and men are all equally susceptible to the antics of the Trickster, but they are also capable of exploiting its puckishness to bring themselves down to earth after their own arrogance balloons and induce a smile in the most churlish of peers.

A Trickster in Young Adult Literature. Most teen and preteen boys are familiar with the stories *Willy Wonka and the Chocolate Factory* (Dahl, 1998) and *James and the Giant Peach* (Dahl, 2000). If so, they know the biting satire of the author, Roald Dahl. Dahl has also written an immensely entertaining autobiography titled *Boy: Tales of Childhood* (1988), which colorfully recreates his days growing up in England and Wales. What becomes clear in this enchanting tale is that the tricksters, pranksters, and practical jokers who abound in Dahl's creative works have their origins in the real-life misadventures of Dahl himself.

Like all effective Tricksters, Dahl zeroes in on those around him who behave pompously, contemptuously, or wickedly and makes them the objects of his acerbic wit or victims of his practical jokes. In the chapter titled "The Great Mouse Adventure of 1924," Dahl puts a dead mouse in the gobstopper jar at Mrs. Pratchett's candy shop to get back at her for her ill-humored manner toward him and other neighborhood kids. In another instance, the young Dahl finds a way to retaliate against his sister's smug fiancé by filling his pipe with goat dung.

Bringing truly nasty adults down a few pegs is a motif that runs throughout Dahl's fiction, as well as in these exciting sketches of his own life. Nowhere in his book is this more apparent than in his struggles with the blind and often brutal authority so wantonly displayed by headmasters at the various boarding schools Dahl attended. According to Dahl, the headmaster at Llandoff Cathedral School was particularly odious. Anytime Dahl attempted to expose the dark side of boarding school life there, he would get whipped on the back or ankles with a cane. Undeterred by these harsh punishments, Dahl, drawing on the full power of his inner Trickster, continued to find ways to defy school authority by employing a clever array of practical jokes on both teachers and bullies.

Dahl's uncommon adventures are not meant to give legitimacy to irreverence or disobedience. Instead, they demonstrate how wit and trickery can be used to expose phoniness, hypocrisy, and arrogance. These are the Trickster's gifts, which Dahl possessed in abundance. Boys are sure to find his autobiography of childhood through adolescence funny and sometimes painful, but always interesting.

Lover

The Lover archetype is giving, caring, and intimate. Without love, human beings cannot go on. The Lover is the primal energy, passion, and appetite for all human hungers, such as for food, well-being, reproduction, creativity, and meaning (Moore & Gillette, 1992). Mostly, the Lover is the symbol of man's connectedness to all other people.

The word *lover* has been appropriated by popular culture to simply mean a sexual partner. This cavalier definition is detached from all deeper and aesthetic meanings, making it difficult to talk to young boys about the authentic and intimate nature of the Lover archetype. Love as a narcissistic urge to satisfy one's own primal hunger is an abomination of true love as embodied in the inner Lover of all males. Young men need to find expressions of love beyond the heat of romantic passion. There is love in generosity to friends or strangers, in the compassion of forgiveness, and in other acts of selflessness. It motivates us to form alliances, to place a common shoulder to the wheel, and to recognize that in helping others we are also helping ourselves. Jesse Goodman (1992), in reference to the importance of "connectionism" between people, says,

> Each individual's self-actualization can be fully realized only within a just and caring society. Individual goals must be balanced by deep and sincere attitudes of altruism, compassion, cooperation, and civic responsibility and the social structures that support them. Freedom within this context suggests nonexploitative psychological, social, and economic relations and the belief that our individual identities cannot be seen as separate from the organic, interdependent system of humankind.... (p. 9)

The Lover, then, has the capacity for deep empathy. He is profoundly sensitive to the pain and joy of his family and friends and to those in the community in need of assistance and caring. To talk about love in such terms may make this archetype difficult for most adolescent boys to access because these qualities are stereotypically feminine. So it remains highly challenging for many teen and preteen boys, whose notions of masculinity are steeped in popular culture, to connect with this sensitive form of masculinity. This does not mean, however, that boys are incapable of establishing or reestablishing contact with their inner Lover.

When young and mature men appropriately access the Lover archetype, they feel alive, enthusiastic, compassionate, empathic, energized, connected, and romantic about their lives, work, goals, and achievements (Moore & Gillette, 1992). This is because the Lover is humane and gives positive, meaningful purpose to the other masculine archetypes. All males, then, need to strengthen the Lover archetype throughout their lives to stay connected to those around them and to avoid slipping into isolation and loneliness. To radiate love, adolescent boys must love themselves and return the love of others. Teachers must find books that help boys learn to love in an honorable and uniquely masculine way.

A Lover in Young Adult Literature. Boys need palpable, contemporary depictions of men who love honorably, so that they can find connections between their own efforts to act lovingly. A contemporary model is the Lover of peace, former U.S. President Jimmy Carter. In *Talking Peace: A Vision for the*

Next Generation (1993), Carter speaks directly to adolescents about the many experiences he has had, as Presidential statesman and human rights advocate, striving to bring about world peace. Carter summarizes his commitment to "waging peace" with these words:

> The existence of war is incompatible with our basic needs as human beings.... It is one thing to say that we each have the right not to be killed. It is another to say that we each have the right to live comfortably, with adequate food, health care, shelter, education, and opportunities for employment. It is even more powerful to say that we each have the right to worship as we choose, to say what we choose, and to be governed by leaders as we choose. And perhaps the most powerful statement of all is to say that we each hold these rights equally—that no one person is more entitled to any of these rights than the next, regardless of his or her sex, race, or station in life. (pp. 21, 27)

Carter avoids self-indulgence by speaking directly to young people about how they too can make a commitment to peace. He punctuates his narrative with the voices of students, friends, and activists who have also channeled their talents into improving understanding between people. Carter emphasizes how peace can be waged in neighborhoods, living rooms, ball fields, and classrooms. Offering specific guidelines about how to actively improve the lives of others, he makes such suggestions as becoming a Big Brother to an underprivileged child, donating time to homeless shelters or soup kitchens, and turning empty lots into city gardens. This is a valuable book for teen and preteen boys who are searching for honorable expressions of their inner Lover.

Boy Talk

Jermaine, 12, Makes a Statement About Men and Slavery Based on Reading Ann Cameron's Adaptation of *The Kidnapped Prince: The Life of Olaudah Equiano*

My granddad says all of us have slaves in our past. Our people come from Mississippi. They moved to Texas to work on the farms, but mostly Mexicans do the field work now. I listen to Granddad and the other old men on Greenwood Avenue talk about when Corpus had separate schools and parks for black people, and separate places for them to sit in movies and restaurants. We were called "Negroes" then. I would have hated living at that time, but being a slave is the worst thing that could happen to a person.

I had never heard of Olaudah Equiano before I read *The Kidnapped Prince: The Life of Olaudah Equiano* (Equiano & Cameron, 2000). As I read, I found out that there are not many books by slaves because they weren't allowed to read or write. *This* book was written because Olaudah was a prince before he was kidnapped and forced to become a slave. This is like taking some rich guy's kid, making him work for free all day in the heat, giving him hardly anything to eat, and making him walk every-where. The worst was when Olaudah was put on a ship and sent to the West Indies. Slaves were jammed into the bottom of the ship. There was no room to move, there were no lights, and it was dirty. The slaves also got seasick. If you made it out okay, you had to work in the sugar cane fields.

I'm proud to be an African American. Being a slave meant you were nothing. The people who forced Olaudah to become a slave didn't have any respect for him and whether he was a prince. They just thought, "You're black and you're strong, so you work for us or else." When he finally got out of slavery, he wrote this book, and a lot of people bought it. This was back in the 1700s. Somehow Olaudah kept his pride. My granddad says people can take a lot of things from you, but they can't take away your pride.

Final Thoughts

Exposing teen and preteen boys to books that embody the 10 positive male archetypes described in this chapter may not automatically transform them into active readers, although it is this kind of literature that has the potential to present boys with a reason to read. Archetypal literature that resonates in the male psyche has the power to reveal the delight and necessity of reading. This kind of literature provides a reflection on boys' burgeoning masculinity by depicting male characters who struggle with similar life choices. Teen and preteen boys concern themselves daily with questions about what it means to be a man. The images of masculinity that they receive from popular media and their immediate surroundings may have little resemblance to authentic and archetypal masculinity. In his book *Reaching Up for Manhood: Transforming the Lives of Boys in America*, Geoffrey Canada (1998) says,

> Our beliefs about maleness, the mythology that surrounds being male, has led many boys to ruin. The image of male as strong is mixed with the

image of male as violent. Male as virile gets confused with male as promiscuous. Male as adventurous equals male as reckless. Male as intelligent often gets mixed with male as arrogant, racist, and sexist.... We must all spend more time trying to understand what happens to boys—and how we can help shape them into better men. (p. xiii)

Teachers who use books with positive male archetypes may improve their chances of reaching boys, of helping boys find entry points into active literacy, and of getting boys to think critically about text and about what it means to be a man. Chapter 3 describes numerous ways in which teachers have used archetypal literature with these expectations in mind.

Teaching Positive Male Archetypes With Literature

Properly, we should read for power. Man reading should be man intensely alive. The book should be a ball of light in one's hands.

—Ezra Pound, 1968, p. 7

This chapter provides descriptions of teachers using good books as vehicles for exploring the 10 positive male archetypes with their students. I chose to include these particular descriptions because of the teachers' creativity in structuring innovative, meaningful, and engaging learning experiences around excellent young adult literature.

Teaching the Pilgrim Archetype With Literature

Philena is a ninth-grade language arts teacher. She has 14 boys and 3 girls in her last-period basic English class. The gender makeup in this class is not dissimilar to her other classes for freshmen who have the lowest scores on the state reading achievement test. Philena works closely with the teacher of U.S. history who has the same students, so as to help these struggling readers and learners use literacy skills to improve their understanding of subject-area content.

During the study of the Great Depression, or more specifically of the Dust Bowl, Philena's language arts class read *Children of the Dust Bowl: The True Story of the School at Weedpatch Camp* (Stanley, 1992) to complement their learning of the topic in history class. This masterly crafted book traces the history of southwestern farmers who were forced to leave their dust-ravaged farms in the 1930s in search of better land and a better life. Punctuated by archival photographs, this book tells the story of men striving to achieve lives of dignity for themselves and their families in the midst of economic despair. In an effort to sensitize her students to the power of the Pilgrim archetype in the lives of the men and boys described in *Children of the Dust Bowl*, Philena employed some highly effective strategies.

Strategies Using the Pilgrim Archetype

Philena asked students to compare how men in *Children of the Dust Bowl* embody the Pilgrim archetype versus the way that the men in other books embody the Pilgrim archetype. Students identified traits and motivations of the Pilgrim in Inman, the main character in *Cold Mountain* (Frazier, 1997), which Philena had read aloud to the class earlier that year. Inman deserts the Confederate army and makes a long and treacherous pilgrimage to his home and his wife on Cold Mountain, escaping a war for which he no longer has any heart. Inman shares several similar traits with Elmer Thomas, a character from *Children of the Dust Bowl*, who is from Muskogee, Oklahoma, USA. In the manner of all good Pilgrims, Elmer seeks a better life for his family in a land of bounty (California) after escaping the ravages of drought. Students recorded their findings on a compare-contrast chart.

The class also engaged in a *storypath* activity (McGuire, 1997), in which students take on the identities of people from the era or place that they are studying, which in this case was the Dust Bowl in Oklahoma and California. First, students individually created their own storypath character by providing pertinent personal information, as in the following example:

1. Name: Amos Brown

2. Age: 45

3. Date of birth: 1895

4. Birthplace: Ada, Oklahoma

5. Distinguishing features: A long scar on my arm from getting it caught in a combine

6. Occupation: A farmer in Oklahoma but now trying to find work in California

7. Family: My wife, Erma; three daughters, Julie, Barbara, and Thelma; and two sons, Amos, Jr. and Billy

8. Personality characteristics: Stubborn and don't want to take anything for free; I want to work and need to find a steady job

9. Leisure activities: Whittling, playing horseshoes, and singing

10. Interesting anecdote: Joined the army when I was 22 and was sent to Belgium to fight the Germans; guess I can say I've been to Europe

Once students created characters for themselves, Philena organized them into logical family, work, and community groups and subgroups (such as farm owners, laborers, children, and so on). Next, Philena had her students create a large, colorful mural that was taped to one of the classroom walls. The students' mural contained drawings of fertile farmland, tents and shanties, jalopies, mountains, big farmhouses, and a police station. The mural allowed students to translate images of community that they gathered from both the history textbook and *Children of the Dust Bowl* into an identifiable context for storypath activities.

The real heart and soul of storypath teaching occurs once the characters and the setting have been established, and once the episodes are introduced. Episodes are issues and concerns that the teacher may inject into the storypath community; they are historically valid and relevant to the characters' lives. Teachers should design episodes to generate focused discussion and problem solving among students as they role-play their characters. Philena introduced the following episode to her class, asking them to call a community meeting to discuss it:

> The men earn 25 cents per hour doing farm work but can't support their families on that wage. In order to pay for just the absolute basics, such as food and clothing, they need at least 35 cents per hour. If they demand a higher wage from the farm owners they'll be fired. What should they do?

The students role-played a camp discussion from the perspectives of their characters to brainstorm possible solutions. One student, Wally, said, "We need to fight the farm owners to make them give us more money." To this remark, "Amos" responded,

> We can't forget that everything we do must be for our families. We have to make sure our kids have food to eat. Twenty-five cents isn't much, but at least we can buy food with it. If we go to jail or get kicked out of California, who will look after our families?

Teaching the Patriarch Archetype With Literature

It is not uncommon in high schools to find just about anyone teaching reading. Thankfully, this arrangement does not always have unfortunate consequences. Emory, the basketball coach and reading teacher in a midsize, racially mixed high school, has been able to help young people, especially males, approach reading with new enthusiasm. He does this in two critical ways:

(1) by saturating his students with reading material and (2) by emphasizing the importance of boys as readers.

One book he reads with his students is Walter Dean Myers's *Hoops* (1999). He knew that this book would be a hit from the moment he discovered it. After all, nearly all his male basketball players find themselves in his reading class. Many of the female "roundballers" are also in one of Emory's classes. First and foremost for Emory is finding reading material that his students will want to read and are likely to have success with given his supportive instruction. One of Emory's biggest goals is to supply his students with a steady diet of literature that provides them with adolescent and adult models worthy of emulation.

Lonnie, the central character in *Hoops*, is an outstanding basketball player who is befriended by Cal Abbot, a former professional player who is now a high school coach. When readers meet Cal, he has fallen from glory because of his involvement in a point-shaving scandal. As a coach, he dedicates himself to helping other promising young athletes avoid his mistakes. The story climaxes when Lonnie discovers that bookies have been pressuring Cal to bench Lonnie to ensure that his team will lose the tournament championship. As seconds dissolve at the end of the crucial game, both the reader and Lonnie wonder whether Cal has, once again, succumbed to the allure of easy money. In a display of patriarchal self-sacrifice, however, Cal repudiates his dishonorable past and sends Lonnie in to help win the game.

Many of Emory's black and Hispanic American basketball players do not live with their biological parents. Their families and community offer limited examples of men who honor their paternal responsibilities; therefore, Emory designed class strategies meant to emphasize the positive qualities of Cal Abbot, the principal adult male in *Hoops*. Some of Emory's class activities are described in the following section.

Strategies Using the Patriarch Archetype

As they read the book, students kept a list of the ways in which Cal acts with Lonnie that are similar to how they would have wanted Lonnie's real father to act. (Lonnie was raised by his mother.) At the book's conclusion, students referred to this list to write letters to Cal, praising him for mentoring Lonnie. One student's letter read,

> Dear Mr. Abbot:
>
> Thanks for helping Lonnie reach his dream of being a basketball champion. He couldn't have done it without you. You told him to stay away from drugs and alcohol. And you coached him on what it is really like to

be a big-time player. At the end you showed Lonnie that you don't have to cheat to win.

Your friend,
Elton

Students also rewrote parts of the story into short scenes and in small groups presented them in a Readers Theatre format. Two students reenacted the last couple of minutes of the championship game. Another group acted out the scene when Cal talks to Lonnie about how professional basketball is high-pressure and how it requires more than just skill. A third group presented the conversation between Lonnie and his girlfriend, Mary Ann, as they talk about making it out of the projects.

Another activity the students participated in involved identifying men on television who had similar archetypal qualities to Cal Abbot and explaining *why*. Among the television men who the students said "were not super-human" but trying to be good mentors to their sons and daughters were Heathcliff Huxtable (*The Cosby Show*) and Robert Peterson (*The Parent 'Hood*). The students said that these men demonstrated the capability of honoring patriarchal responsibility.

Teaching the King Archetype With Literature

In an alternative high school in South Texas, USA, Ruben works with adolescent boys and girls who have been marked for failure. Most of these teens are already well acquainted with the criminal justice system. Virtually all of them have family histories that would make most people shudder. Yet Ruben believes that none of these students are lost causes and that literacy is the key to turning their lives around.

The school operates as a kind of academic boot camp with tight controls over students' freedoms outside the classroom. Inside the classroom, however, because the usual system has not worked for these students, each teacher is encouraged to employ innovative strategies and approaches, especially if they are successful in reaching these adolescents.

From experience, Ruben knows that his students' literacy skills and self-esteem are dismal. In an attempt to deal with these concerns simultaneously, he uses books and literature therapeutically. He has found that reading material with cultural appeal tends to be more successful in sustaining his students' attention. Ruben looks for fiction or nonfiction books that present Hispanic Americans as people worthy of emulation. One such book is titled *Cesar Chavez* (Franchere, 1970). Written on a fifth-grade level, this simply told biography of an important leader in the Hispanic American community stirs his students' curiosity. The book also sparks controversy among his students because many of them have a heritage of migrants including fathers and grandfathers or older brothers and uncles who spent many hot days toiling in the citrus fields of South Texas. Here are some strategies with which Ruben found success when he taught *Cesar Chavez*.

Strategies Using the King Archetype

Ruben and his class brainstormed the qualities of a leader. Ruben wrote these on a large poster in a column labeled "A Leader." Then, as they read, students added the qualities of leadership that Chavez exhibited in an second column labeled "Cesar Chavez." In a third column labeled "How I Lead" were examples that the students gave of when and how they have demonstrated leadership, and to what extent it resembled the ways of Cesar Chavez.

Every entry on the chart spawned lively discussion in Ruben's classroom. For example, Omar told the class that he led his gang in a war with a rival gang to settle a dispute over drug turf. After the students both ridiculed and praised this example, Ruben redirected the discussion by asking everyone whether that type of behavior would have been endorsed by someone like Chavez. Questions included the following:

Did Cesar use guns and weapons to lead our people?

Did he teach his fellow migrant workers to fight with their fists or their minds?

Even though he didn't carry a gun or teach violence, did Cesar have the support of his people, our people?

With these and other similar questions, Ruben's class was able to look more critically at which of Chavez's qualities brought about nonviolent leadership.

Another strategy Ruben employed was the display of additional books that depicted characters from fiction or real-life who embody attributes of the King. These books typically vary in level of difficulty from easy (plenty of pictures and photographs) to more challenging (novels and historical biographies). Students were required to make oral presentations comparing and contrasting Cesar Chavez with a leader from the book they read. After reading *A Picture Book of Jackie Robinson* (Adler, 1994), Philipé shared how both Chavez and Robinson

were told by Anglos they couldn't have what they had. And they both fought hard for their people and for respect. Robinson was black and

Chavez was Mexican but the people looked up to them. After Robinson, black people could play baseball with white people. After Chavez, Mexicans had more rights.

Lupé, one of the more accomplished readers in Ruben's class, took on a much longer biography, *The Tall Mexican: The Life of Hank Aguirre All-Star Pitcher, Businessman, Humanitarian* (Copley, 2000). Lupé shared the following:

> Like Cesar Chavez, Hank Aguirre grew up in poverty. He had to make thousands of tortillas every day for his father's little restaurant. This must have given him a strong arm because he became a great pitcher. Aguirre was like Chavez because, even though he got famous, he never forgot about his people.
>
> This guy, Robert Copley, who wrote the book was a good friend of Aguirre, and he told a lot of really neat things about him. When Aguirre quit playing baseball, he wanted to help our people, so he set up a business called Mexican Industries. It made a lot of money, and he gave jobs to Latinos, blacks, and people of other minorities.

Teaching the Warrior Archetype With Literature

As a high school history teacher, Angie notices how the boys in her classes tend to show more enthusiasm for topics involving war. "Weaponry, bombs, blood and guts—all that stuff really turns them on," she comments. "It's as though nothing else happened in the history of civilization." These adolescent interests are likely fueled by the way popular culture portrays war and warriors; that is, war is often glorified, and the leaders are invincible. To help her students, particularly the boys, appreciate the multifarious nature of the Warrior archetype, Angie makes sure that they read about and explore what she calls the "nonwar Warrior." A book she finds particularly suitable is Laura Jeffrey's *Simon Wiesenthal: Tracking Down Nazi Criminals* (1997). Following is a description of some different strategies she employed with this biography, as well as other books.

Strategies Using the Warrior Archetype

One of Angie's strategies was to begin each semester in both her world and U.S. history classes by teaching lessons about the Warrior archetype. She found that this allowed her to use literature throughout the study of various leaders and their conquests. Angie also read *Simon Wiesenthal* aloud to her students. She engaged her classes in discussion about the characteristics of a warrior and encouraged them to identify past and present people who might fit this characterization. John said warriors have to be super tough and named Jackie Chan, Rachel said Angelina Jolie was a warrior, and Damien said Shaquille O'Neal was the best warrior he could think of.

Picking up on Damien's example, Angie asked the class to consider the qualities that make Shaq O'Neal a warrior even though his battleground is not filled with tanks and guns. This led to recognition that words like *fight*, *battle*, and, most importantly, *Warrior* have figurative as well as literal meanings. Angie said that a popular movement in the 1960s called "the War on Poverty" could be thought of as a war and suggested that the people who fought it could be thought of as Warriors. Her dialogue with the class follows.

Angie:	If we think about the figurative meaning of the word *Warrior*, how does that change our sense of who qualifies?
Derrick:	With what you have said, all kinds of people can be Warriors. Like, people who fight for something that's not a fight like in the parking lot, you know, like a doctor who fights for a way to cure someone.
Carrie:	How about people who try to save animals and nature and stuff?
Angie:	I think those examples fit our definition, don't the rest of you? What do you think, Michael?
Michael:	Blacks didn't have any rights until someone fought for them.
Angie:	So the people who fought for civil rights for blacks could be considered Warriors, couldn't they?

This kind of class discussion made it possible for students to expand their understandings of the Warrior archetype and its diverse forms.

When Angie finished *Simon Wiesenthal* with the students, which took no more than 3 weeks of reading 15 minutes per day, she asked students to research the life of a nonwar warrior of their choosing. She reminded them of the example Wiesenthal set as a warrior who struggled for justice for himself and others who were victims of Nazi war crimes. Angie also reminded her students that he fought these battles with only courage and moral conviction. She provided students with regular library time to gather print and electronic sources for their research papers.

Angie had her students present their research papers in first person, as though the student was the historical figure. As part of the presentation, she required students to provide a brief biography with pertinent information, such as birth date and place and family members; include at least one interesting anecdote; describe important professional accomplishments; and explain what makes them a nonwar warrior. Students also had to be prepared to answer questions, use simple gestures and props, and behave in a manner consistent with what they had learned about their nonwar warriors. They could use their scripts but were not allowed to read directly from them.

David's portrayal of Morris Dees, the cofounder of the Southern Poverty Law Center, was exemplary. Standing before his classmates in a blue, button-down shirt with the sleeves rolled up to his elbows and a stylish tie, he intoned with just a hint of a southern U.S. accent:

> Hello, students. My name is Morris Dees of the Southern Poverty Law Center. I was born in 1936 in a small Alabama town called Shorter. My father was a cotton farmer, and in high school I was named the Star Farmer of Alabama by the Alabama Future Farmers of America. When I graduated from the University of Alabama School of Law in 1960, I started a mail-order publishing business and opened a law office. My publishing business was very successful. I sold it in 1969. In the mid-60s, I began taking cases that were unpopular with whites in Alabama. In 1968 I filed suit to integrate the all-white Montgomery YMCA. In 1971 we set up the Southern Poverty Law Center. We don't work for a profit because we want to make sure the poor and minorities get justice.
>
> People always ask me why I gave up a business that was making a lot of money to run a nonprofit center. It came to me one night in a Cincinnati airport. I grew up in the South and every day saw how prejudiced whites were against blacks. I agreed with the Civil Rights movement but was not involved. Then, while I was sitting around in the airport because we were snowed in, I decided to do something to help my black friends. I decided to sell my publishing business and become a civil rights lawyer.
>
> I am a fighter. I don't use my fists and I don't carry a gun, but I work as hard as I can to help poor people and minorities get the justice they deserve. I also fight against racism, neo–Nazism, and all hate groups.

Teaching the Magician Archetype With Literature

"I want my students to enjoy the magic of science," says Terrell, "and one of the best ways to do that is to present the people who made and continue to make amazing scientific discoveries as Magicians." Only a few hundred years ago, the conjurer, alchemist, magician, and scientist were regarded by people as the same. Today, new scientific and technological breakthroughs and discoveries occur with such frequency that everyone, particularly young people, has become immune to the enchantment of science. Terrell's efforts to imbue his students with a sense of enchantment with science involves revealing the human stories behind the science. What everyday forces influence individuals who made and make important scientific discoveries?

When his ninth-grade class was immersed in the study of Newtonian laws of motion, Terrell read *Rocket Boys: A Memoir* (Hickam, 2000) aloud to his students. Homer Hickam used his magic, inspired by the inchoate U.S. space program, to construct his own rockets from the most improbable of launch pads—a 1950s West Virginia mining town. His rocket wizardry led to a gold medal at the National Science Fair in 1960, which is a feat unimaginable by a rural miner's son. This feat is all the more wondrous because of Homer's perseverance in the face of his parents' tense and contentious marriage, as well as his father's dim view of Homer's "impractical" dreams.

This book engaged Terrell's students not only because of its science content, but also because of its poignant and inspirational coming-of-age tale, which depicts relevant adolescent themes. Here are some strategies Terrell used to help his ninth graders make connections between the text and their own inner Magicians.

Strategies Using the Magician Archetype

Terrell asked students to keep a learning log throughout the reading of *Rocket Boys* in which they made daily entries in response to various prompts that Terrell provided. Terrell constructed these prompts around the categories of content-based writing inspired by the SPAWN technique (Martin, Martin, & O'Brien, 1984). The SPAWN acronym stands for *special power, problem solving, alternative viewpoints, what if,* and *next. Special power* allows students to change an event from history or a story, then explain the consequences of this change; *problem solving* poses a problem from the story that students must solve in advance of learning about the actual solutions; *alternative viewpoints* asks students to consider a story's topic, event, or scene from a fresh or unique perspective; *what if* lets students think up new consequences for alternative scenarios that they have been given by the teacher; and *next* urges students to predict what will happen next in a story based on what they have learned or read to that point. For example, one day Terrell's students entered class and were asked to get their logs (which Terrell kept on a classroom shelf) and write a response to the following:

> You have the power to change one aspect of your life to make it more similar to Homer Hickam's life. Write what you would change about your life, why you would change this aspect, and what you think would happen as a result of this change.

Based on this prompt, Eddie's entry read,

> If I could change something about me it would be so I would stick to
> something. I always start something then I give up. I would change this
> because I like how Homer never gives up making his rockets work. If I
> stick with science, you never know, maybe I would find a cure for AIDS
> or figure out how to end polution [*sic*].

Because *Rocket Boys* is a story about how Homer uses the magic of science to live out his dreams, Terrell created an assignment called "Using the
Magic of Science to Solve Problems" to ask his students how they might do
the same thing. After forming groups of three or four students, he gave them
the following task:

1. Identify a problem in the world that your group would like to solve.
   No problem is too big, so think big.
2. Formulate hunches about how you might solve the problem. Use your
   imaginations, and don't let negative thinking block your group's brainstorming. If you can dream it, it may be possible.
3. Research whether your hunches have been tried and, if so, how successful they have been. Identify possible solutions that your group
   thought of that have not been tried.
4. Describe what kind of time and resources it would take to implement
   your possible solutions.

One group decided to take on the challenge of finding a cure for cancer. The scope of this problem was just what Terrell was hoping his students
would define for themselves with this assignment. In their hunch-forming
stage, someone mentioned that he thought he heard that sharks are one of
the only creatures that do not get cancer. The idea of investigating sharks for
a cancer-fighting hormone or enzyme became a possible solution.

From there, the group members went about gathering information on research that might have been done with sharks. Using the Internet as their
principal resource, they found articles and references to research done on
sharks' livers by Eugenie Clark in the 1970s, although they did not find more
current research than that. The group thought more research should be done
because Clark's findings were inconclusive. They prepared a list of resources
that they would need to study possible cancer-fighting properties of sharks'
livers, including such things as a marine lab, various kinds of sharks, shark bi-
ologists, medical and genetics researchers, cancer researchers, and test animals
such as rats and primates.

When the groups completed their work, they made a formal presentation to the class. The group members had created a PowerPoint presentation that identified the problem of cancer and its worldwide significance, explained hunches about possible cures, described the results of their research into sharks' livers, and detailed resources they would need for further study of sharks.

In another activity designed to reinforce the connection between science and magic, Terrell invited a local magician to perform for the class. The magician was asked to perform his usual tricks, but be prepared to slow down a couple of them, so the class could see how they were done. Terrell's students were required to think of scientific principles that could explain theses tricks.

Teaching the Wildman Archetype With Literature

To many, the name Farley Mowat is instantly familiar. His book *Never Cry Wolf* (1983), which was later made into a successful feature film, has become a favorite of teachers and students alike. Its pro-environment theme on the role that modern people should play in preserving and protecting wild animals makes the book an ideal companion in the study of the natural world. Like all worthy naturalists, Mowat's approach to understanding the environment is to enter into it humbly and as a kindred spirit with all creatures. He embodies the contemporary Wildman.

Similar to Mowat, Toby spends most of his time in the wilderness. During the rest of the year, however, he is a 10th-grade environmental science teacher. Leanne, his wife, is just as drawn to nature as her husband. Their schedules and the fact that Leanne teaches 10th-grade English in the same high school make this shared avocation possible. Each year they braid as much of their curriculum as feasible, so as to reinforce the expanded language and thinking skills, and content knowledge of the students they share.

One such shared effort focused on modern Wildman Farley Mowat. During a 3-week unit, Leanne's English class read and engaged in activities related to *Never Cry Wolf* while Toby's environmental science class explored Mowat's autobiography, *Born Naked* (1995). *Never Cry Wolf* is an account of Mowat's struggle to survive in the Arctic Circle while studying wolves for the Canadian Wildlife Service. Alone in the tundra to investigate caribou slaughter by wolves, Mowat soon discovers that, far from bloodthirsty hordes, wolves are caring and resourceful providers whose survival is threatened by bounty hunters and government exterminators. *Born Naked* is a story of Mowat's rural Canadian childhood. Readers learn how his wilderness experiences and his relationship with his writer-librarian father shaped his love for books, animals, and nature.

To engage their students in meaningful reading and to help them better understand the importance of a modern Wildman in improving interspecies harmony, Toby and Leanne employed the following strategies and activities.

Strategies Using the Wildman Archetype

To reinforce text connections and create multiple opportunities for practicing writing, Toby and Leanne had their students compose dialogues between Mowat, the young naturalist from *Never Cry Wolf*, and either Mowat the child or another person from Mowat's memoir. Trent wrote an e-mail conversation between Mowat (on the Arctic prairie) and his father, Angus, (in Saskatoon, Alberta, Canada). It read,

> To: Angusm@toon.com
> From: Farleym@nature.com
> Subject: advice about voles
>
> Dear Dad,
>
> As you can imagine, it's cold, windy, and gray here most of the time. But the weather wouldn't be so bad if my little shelter wasn't full of voles! The little buggers are everywhere. They're eating everything, too. With your years of experience in the country, what do you suggest I do?
>
> I've got to go now, one of the adult wolves I've been watching has just come out of its den. Thanks for any advice you can give me.
>
> Love,
> Farley

> To: Farleym@nature.com
> From: Angusm@toon.com
> Re: advice about voles
>
> Dear Farley,
>
> I've had mice in my tent, but I have never had a problem like yours before. I have one possible solution. It's a bit crazy but here goes: Try eating them. If you cook them well, they'll probably taste okay. Several of them would make one meal, so you'll be able to get rid of a lot of them in a short time. Good luck.
>
> Your loving father,
> Angus

To: Angusm@toon.com

From: Farleym@nature.com

Re: advice about voles

Dad,

Your suggestion was brilliant! I'm catching and eating voles every day. I roast two or three on a stick at a time, and that makes one good meal for me. They're good with salt and pepper. Thanks for your great idea.

Your adoring son,
Farley

Toby and Leanne also took their students on a field trip to the nearby Smoky Mountains to learn more about the elk repopulation project. They also wanted to bring students into contact with park rangers, conservationists, and scientists. Leanne and Toby structured the field trip so their students could gather research; afterward, the students were required to write reports on topics related to environmental conservation and job opportunities in that field.

Leanne and Toby asked the students to generate questions in advance for the rangers, conservationists, and scientists. These questions could be related to the elk repopulation project, as well as general occupational and environmental issues on which the experts were likely to have specialized information and informed opinions. Leanne and Toby compiled the students' questions to eliminate redundancy and organize them into logical clusters. This approach makes efficient use of everyone's time and avoids random topic-hopping.

During their trip and after their return, students also were required to answer questions about the elk repopulation project from Mowat's point of view. For example, Leanne and John asked the following:

How would he feel about this project?

What problems would he expect with such a project, and are they similar to those of the actual project?

What role would Mowat want in the project?

Students kept all their notes and written responses in a science log, which they took on the field trip. The logs are spiral-bound notebooks with personalized covers; they were stored in Toby's classroom. Students responded to writing prompts every day either before or after a lesson. They dated these responses and made sure to write the prompt as well.

The final activity that Toby and Leanne created was based on their ability to combine their classes for occasional group activities. One of these activities was a mock trial based on the following premise: Wildmen like Mowat have an important role to play in modern society. Leanne's class was required to defend this position; Toby's class had to disprove it. Students developed arguments, identified lead counsels and legal teams, obtained witnesses, and role-played a jury that rendered a verdict.

Attorneys for the opposition argued that Wildmen like Mowat are out of touch with what most people want. Wildmen are free to do whatever they wish, these lawyers argued, but they do not have the right to pretend that they are better than everyone else, and they do not know what is best for others. To bolster their case, the lawyers questioned a student who role-played a scientist, who reported that many of the claims of environmental degradation are exaggerated.

In defense of Wildmen like Mowat, defense attorneys argued that important discoveries in nature, such as certain medicines, would be missed without them. They also argued that new ideas emerge by questioning the way things have always been done. To support these assertions, the lawyers introduced a witness (a student dressed in outdoor attire) who offered impassioned oratory on behalf of the animals and the trees. The witness made it clear that humans are connected to all living things and reminded everyone that field scientists who braved the bleak wilderness of the southern icecap discovered the gaping hole in the ozone layer. That discovery by Wildmen has led to serious international attention to ways of preventing further deterioration of the ozone layer.

Teaching the Healer Archetype With Literature

Peg made a very deliberate decision to introduce her 11th graders to Robert Lipsyte's *The Chemo Kid* (1992). After fighting a successful battle against leukemia, Peg found that Fred Bauer's own fictional struggle to overcome cancer resonated with hers. Peg's English literature class is structured around American themes such as multiculturalism, human rights, and biodiversity. One of her favorite themes is American archetypes. While recuperating from a bone marrow transplant, she read many books about healing. With this reading came the realization that the Healer archetype—one not previously explored in her curriculum—had been expressed in a variety of forms in U.S. literature (for instance, in Walt Whitman's Civil War memoranda and in William Gibson's play *The Miracle Worker* [1984]). Peg's search for a young adult book that possessed the Healer archetype led to the discovery of *The*

Chemo Kid, a contemporary tale of healing at the hands of a young man, who happens to be in the same grade as her own students. To her delight, it proved to be a real hit with the students.

Although this intriguing novel is inherently appealing to adolescents, Peg made the power of the Healer archetype the focus of the students' examination of *The Chemo Kid*. Following is a sampling of Peg's strategies.

Strategies Using the Healer Archetype

To introduce the archetype, Peg had her students fill out and discuss an "opinionnaire." An opinionnaire is comprised of declarative statements centered on a critical concept, such as friendship, technology, or in this case, healing. Peg's students responded to each statement using a format ranging from "strongly agree" to "strongly disagree." A "maybe" or "not sure" option was not included because Peg had found that many students chose it as an easy way out. White and Johnson (2001) discovered that opinionnaires are highly beneficial in furthering the goals of readiness for learning. When their readiness potential is fully exploited, opinionnaires can activate and build relevant prior knowledge for specific topics, build interest in and motivation to learn more about a particular topic, and help students set meaningful purposes for reading and learning. See Figure 1 for the opinionnaire that Peg used to introduce the Healer archetype.

When students finished responding to these statements, Peg asked them to form small groups to discuss answers. This brought out many different ideas, experiences, and opinions that reinforced, extended, and challenged the students' responses. Peg followed group discussions with a class discussion, listening to input from each group and facilitating student-to-student dialogue.

The students' principal assignment was the completion of the Healing Project, which required students to support the healing of someone in their lives (family member, friend, or a person in the community). Peg defined this healing in its broadest sense—making people and their living conditions better. The assignment required that students maintain a journal with regular entries describing how they supported healing, as well as the results of their efforts. The goal of this project is to help demonstrate the potential healing powers that reside in each person.

One student, Gilbert, took advantage of a program at a neighborhood community center for senior citizens where his mother worked. The center enlisted volunteers to visit and interact with severely mobility-impaired or bedridden individuals. Gilbert's mother introduced him to Alfonso, an 85-year-old man with severe arthritis, and the two hit it off immediately. Gilbert's

FIGURE 1
Healer Archetype Opinionnaire

Directions: After each statement, write SA (strongly agree), A (agree), D (disagree), or SD (strongly disagree). Be prepared to explain your answer.

1. Only doctors can heal the sick.

2. There are people who are not doctors who have special healing powers.

3. It is important to know how to heal yourself.

4. I can help a friend heal by just being supportive.

5. Healing can apply to more than sickness of the human body, such as the degraded environment, poverty, homelessness, and broken families and friendships.

6. When I have a physical or emotional need to heal myself, I can do it.

7. To heal is to make people and living conditions better.

8. Our society is sick and in need of serious healing.

9. Each of us should take care of our own healing.

10. If I had a serious disease like cancer, I could only be healed with medical treatment.

11. I spend time being supportive to friends and others who are trying to heal.

12. If I knew how, I would get involved in projects that support healthier living conditions for others.

Healing Project journal entry reflects his surprise at finding his conversations with Alfonso so enjoyable.

> October 23, 4:30—Healing Project Journal
>
> I had my first meeting with the guy at my mom's work. His name is Alfonso and he can barely walk because of arthritis in his leg joints. I

talked with him for almost an hour. I discovered he used to play baseball on a black team in Florida. He told me about meeting Joe DiMaggio and Ted Williams when they played exhibition games with big league teams during the winter. He seemed happy to talk about those days, and I liked just listening to him.

Talking baseball was a good icebreaker, but by his third visit, Gilbert found Alfonso speaking more openly about things that bothered him. He complained about his legs; his children, who he said did not stay in touch; and being a poor man who was dependent on Social Security. Alfonso's reality challenged Gilbert to develop more resourceful ways of healing. Gilbert's entry describing his fifth visit reflects his efforts to be helpful and create a positive atmosphere for Alfonso.

November 4, 4:30—Healing Project Journal

Alfonso's got a lot of problems that I'm not able to help him with. He seems to be in pain nearly all the time. He doesn't have much money. And just listening to him doesn't make him feel any better as far as I can tell. I got him to agree to sit in the cafeteria area and play checkers. It's open and bright in there with lots of windows. He doesn't go there too much because it's a long way from his apartment, and he doesn't have a meal plan because he says he can't afford it. Playing checkers seemed to take his mind off other things. He even beat me a couple of times. That made him feel pretty good.

Although the journal was a requirement, Peg encouraged students to document their Healing Project through other means, such as photographs, audio, or video, to enhance their oral reports on their experiences. Gilbert used several pictures—some of him and Alfonso playing checkers and some of Alfonso by himself—when he presented his report.

Peg also wanted to draw attention to the traits *The Chemo Kid* character, Fred, exhibits that are consistent with the Healer archetype, so she and the students created a large chart on poster board and attached it to the wall. She split the chart into two large columns. The class used the left side of the chart to list different ways in which someone might demonstrate healing. In the right column, the class chronicled the progression of Fred's behavior through the novel, noting instances in which his healing powers were applied. See Figure 2 for an example.

FIGURE 2
Sample of a Healing Comparison Chart

The Healer	The Chemo Kid
Uses his gifts to make people who are in pain feel better.	Uses humor to improve his own and other people's recuperation process after receiving chemotherapy.
Helps restore all life to good health.	
Is equally concerned with society's physical, emotional, and spiritual health.	Becomes committed to eliminating environmental pollution by a local plant that's dumping chemical waste in the community's reservoir.

Teaching the Prophet Archetype With Literature

Seaward's self-contained classroom for students who have difficulty learning to read is one that other junior high teachers in his building visit often. He is the kind of teacher who decided early in his career to design curricula that was truly special for his learners. Instead of taking the view that his students' academic challenges required him to narrow teaching and learning possibilities, Seaward has embraced the charge from his principal to "Do whatever you can to help these kids make progress." *Innovation* and *meaningful learning* are the watchwords that guide his practice, and using language in all its forms is emphasized.

Seaward spent his teenage years in Detroit, Michigan, USA, assisting his parents in the fight for civil rights and workers' rights. His proudest memory is of meeting Dr. Martin Luther King Jr. at a union rally when he was 8 years old. During Black History Month in February, Seaward engaged his class of nine black boys and four black girls in a variety of activities designed to inform and uplift them. The unit emphasizes Dr. King and his legacy. Seaward described King to his students as the "brown prophet." Seaward filled the classroom with books about King and read several of them aloud to his class. *Martin Luther King: The Peaceful Warrior* (Clayton & Hodges, 1996) is his favorite, and he designed several language and learning activities around it. What follows are other activities that Seaward used with his students during the study of Dr. King.

Strategies Using the Prophet Archetype

In order to help his students recognize the power of Martin Luther King's gifts of prophecy, Seaward had his class brainstorm the Prophet's characteristics. While students offered input, he drew a word map on the board (see Figure 3).

Another activity Seaward used was the creation of an informational chart. As Seaward read aloud, he discussed critical events in King's life and time, as well as King's ideas and tactics for bringing about racial equality. Seaward asked students to identify prophetic statements made by King, then to consider whether they had been foretold accurately and what had come to pass. Seaward compiled this information in a chart. Figure 4 shows a sample of some of the students' entries.

Throughout the month, students scanned the newspaper for articles that dealt with human rights and racial and ethnic prejudice. They then pasted any appropriate articles to a large piece of poster board. On an index card, they wrote a caption or summary of the article identifying any issues of human rights or prejudice that they discovered in the article. Students also wrote what they thought King would think or say about it. (Seaward supplied the newspapers and all other material for this project.) He and his aide worked closely with students in identifying appropriate articles, reading the articles, forming article summaries and captions, and if necessary, writing the summaries and captions.

Student posters were placed on the walls throughout the classroom. Each student was responsible for making a brief oral presentation about his or her

---

FIGURE 3
Word Map of the Prophet's Characteristics

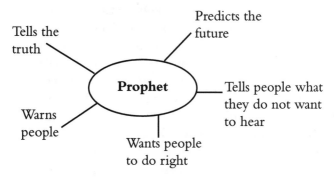

FIGURE 4
Sample of the Informational Chart Entries by Seaward's Students

King's Prophecies	Accurately Foretold	Current Situation
Blacks and whites will eat in the same restaurants.	Yes	
Blacks will get same pay as whites.	No	This is still not the same.
Black and white children will play together.	Only in some neighborhoods	Many blacks and whites still live in different neighborhoods.

poster. Tremayne's poster had an article about the mistreatment of ethnic Albanians by Bosnian Serbs in the former Yugoslavia. His caption read, "These people are kicked out of their houses because they are different." When making his oral presentation, Tremayne commented, "Martin Luther King Jr. would be very sad about this, but he wouldn't stand around and do nothin'...he'd do whatever he could to help those people. He wouldn't use no gun."

Teaching the Trickster Archetype With Literature

It would seem that some people are born Tricksters. I briefly described Roald Dahl's autobiography in Chapter 2, noting that, similar to many of his fictional characters, he was a habitual prankster. Hideki, a world history teacher, was playing practical jokes as far back as he can remember. When I spoke with him, he recalled with some amusement, if not pride, his best prank. Once, to get back at his Aunt Miko for chastising him for his bad table manners, Hideki mixed pieces of his mother's false fingernails with shaved coconut and sprinkled them on Aunt Miko's Jell-O. When she realized what she had eaten, she coughed and spit her dessert on the dining room table before running from the room.

Hideki's pranks continue. His students enter class every day alert for some new trick or gimmick. To begin a unit on medieval Europe, for example, he walked into class in a monk's robe and sandals, with what appeared to be a newly shaved head. He was actually wearing an actor's wig, but the effect induced considerable laughter and speculation among class members. He passed around a marvelous book that day, which captured his students' imaginations. The book was John Morressy's (1999) *Juggler*.

"The clown, jester, or trickster is a common figure from medieval times," Hideki explained. "His jokes and antics were entertainment, a way of making a living. But remember that more truth is said in jest. In other words, the trickster could use humor to disguise serious truths about royalty, society, religion, or particular individuals who thought too much of themselves." Beran the juggler must use all his willpower to survive the sacking of his village and the murder of his master, and overcome the Devil's contract on his soul. The teaching and learning strategies that Hideki employed in conjunction with *Juggler* are described in the following section.

Strategies Using the Trickster Archetype

The class designed and published a medieval newspaper titled *Ye Trickster Broadsheet*. The newspaper had columns lampooning politicians and celebrities of today using pseudonyms of "olde," such as King George (U.S. President George W. Bush) and Lady Madonna (Madonna). Other sections included jokes, classified ads, cartoons, and "The Trickster Calendar," which gave information and dates of upcoming performances by clowns, jesters, and jugglers. One classified ad read, "Wanted! Someone who can perform tricks, juggle, and entertain with the tongue. Must be capable of telling the truth in ways that amuse. Apply in person at Sir Phillip Funnybone's castle in North London." Another installment of the *Broadsheet* titled "The Merry Prankster Speaks," written by one of Hideki's own class clowns, took aim at ostentation and arrogance by suggesting how certain innocent pranks might be employed to remind the guilty of their hubris.

Students also compared modern-day tricksters with those from medieval times. Hideki showed a video of political satirist Mark Russell and played the zany compositions of Harry Shearer. These men combine music and biting wit to poke fun at and raise consciousness about U.S. politics, as well as a host of social issues. Hideki also read excerpts from books (Radin, 1969; Willeford, 1969) that included descriptions of medieval tricksters. The students created a Venn diagram (see Figure 5 for example) to compare and contrast modern and medieval tricksters.

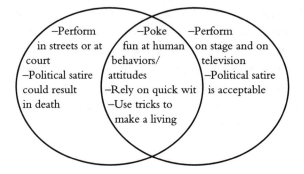

Teaching the Lover Archetype With Literature

Love is the most prevalent literary theme. For Tanya, finding embodiments of the Lover archetype was not difficult, although selecting just the right book for her class of 12th-grade basic English students, most of whom were male athletes, posed a special challenge. She wanted a book that could hold the students' interest and offer a clear and forceful message of love, compassion, and doing the right thing. When Tanya discovered *Jack and Rochelle: A Holocaust Story of Love and Resistance* (Sutin, Sutin, & Sutin, 1996), she knew she had found the perfect book.

Jack and Rochelle Sutin are Polish Jews who escaped from Nazi labor camps. They tell their terrorizing story of how they reunited and managed to elude and strike back at their would-be captors until they were finally liberated by the Russian Army in 1945. Above all, theirs is a story of love in the midst of intolerable conditions, both during and after the war, and while raising their family. The authors weave the theme of love of oneself and others into a gripping narrative of escape and survival. These exciting details engaged Tonya's reluctant readers, and Tanya, with her innovative teaching, made their experience with *Jack and Rochelle* more understandable and memorable. Examples of this innovative teaching follow.

Strategies Using the Lover Archetype

Throughout the reading, Tonya explored what it means to love. In a class discussion to begin the book, many of her students, particularly the boys, had a difficult time speaking seriously about love or even using the word *love*. When the conversation stalled, Tonya asked students to record personal statements in which they use the word *love*. After the students wrote these in their journals, Tonya asked students to volunteer statements that she could write on the board, such as the following:

Greg: I love Tennessee football.

Tiffany: I love my Mom.

Josh: I love Faith Hill.

Vanessa: I love nature.

Brandon: I love Burger King Whoppers.

Dwight: Christ said to love your neighbor.

Tonya then asked the class to work with a partner and decide whether the word *love* was being used in the same way for each statement. Soon the class was abuzz with conversation. Students began to think seriously about the true nature of love and what it means to love something or someone. When Tonya brought the class back into discussion, the students told her of their revelations:

Josh: When I said I love Faith Hill, I didn't mean I actually love her. It's just that I love her music, you know, her voice and all. That's not the same as loving someone like my mom or grandma.

Greg: I think it's how strong you feel about something and what you're willing to do for it. I love Tennessee football, plain and simple. I'd love to play for that team someday, and I'm working hard now, so maybe that will happen. I love my mom, too. I work hard to make sure she's okay. I don't see any problem with that.

Tiffany: It's like nothing else or nobody else matters when you love something or someone. You'd do anything for that person.

Dwight: Christ's love ain't nothing like loving a hamburger. Those are two completely different things. It's silly to compare them.

Tonya followed this discussion by soliciting ways in which people can behave in truly loving ways. As a result of the previous discussion and brainstorming activities, her students were able to provide more relevant responses. The list of behaviors the class generated included the following:

- Helping someone whose car has broken down
- Giving a homeless person clothes and food
- Helping the environment, so people can have clean air and water
- Forgiving someone and not holding a grudge
- Working with neighbors to solve a problem

To help her students appreciate the various expressions of genuine male love, Tonya used *Jack and Rochelle* in way that made it possible for her male students to find connections between the text and their own lives. One activity Tonya had students engage in at several junctures in the book was reader-response writing (Brozo & Simpson, 1999; Petrosky, 1982). Students were given questions such as

- At this point in the story, what aspect of Jack's love for Rochelle did you find most interesting or moving?
- What are your feelings and attitudes toward this?
- What experiences have you had that may help others understand why you feel this way?

Students worked with a feedback buddy during the drafting process. Tonya usually allowed up to three drafts before students were required to submit a paper for a grade. She also encouraged volunteers to share their compositions with the class to reinforce the need for people to connect with an audience when they write. Greg read the final draft of his reader-response essay to the class.

> At this point in the story, Jack and Rochelle are hiding in a swamp. The German soldiers are trying to find them. If they do, they will be killed. Even so, Jack is always showing concern for Rochelle and thinking about what he can do to make sure she survives even if he doesn't (even small things like telling her every day how much he loves her and saying things to keep her spirits up).
>
> This makes me feel good and bad at the same time. It makes me feel good because I think it's neat how much Jack loves Rochelle, so much that he would give his life for her. It makes me feel sad too because my mom and dad divorced when I was little, and I've never seen them in

love or treat each other like people who love each other, like Jack and Rochelle. When you grow up like I did, never really seeing my father and mother together, you think it's the way most married people live. Most of my friends' parents are divorced too. But this true book says married people can love each other all the time and treat each other good.

I hope I can be like Jack when I get married. And I hope I can find someone who's strong like Rochelle.

Tonya also reaffirmed the multiple ways in which mature males can demonstrate genuine love by inviting men from the community to speak to the students. These were men whom Tonya regarded as excellent models of the Lover archetype. She began searching for these particular guests by referring to the list of loving behaviors that she and her class had created just before they had started reading *Jack and Rochelle*. She then made her own list of people and various occupations that might fit these behaviors. Ultimately, four male guests were able to speak with the students to recount their unique experiences and answer the students' questions.

Tonya required the students to plan for the guest speakers by creating questions relevant to the speaker's occupation and background. A group of students was also responsible for filming the guests; Tonya granted them appropriate planning time.

The first speaker, Bernie, survived the Holocaust. He began by sharing his experiences in a concentration camp. The spellbound students, having just completed *Jack and Rochelle*, were brimming with questions. Bernie's most significant answer, however, was his revelation that he no longer harbored any ill will toward the people who mistreated him. This illustrated genuine love.

Wallace, a director of a homeless shelter, described who homeless people are, giving these "throwaway" people an identity, a personality, and a history. He went on to talk about how he became interested in helping homeless people, starting with volunteer work at his church's inner-city missionary project and continuing with his current full-time job of maintaining the church's shelter. Wallace told the class that he earned a college degree in hotel and restaurant management, but he decided to follow his calling and put his training to use in the shelter instead of starting a business.

Rodney is a nurse in a Doctors Without Borders program. His sobering stories of disease and starvation, as a result of poverty, famine, and war throughout the world, kept Tonya's students attentive, although uneasy. Rodney explained how a doctor, with whom he assisted in the university hospital, recruited him into the local program. In response to a question from one student about why someone would intentionally put himself or herself in the middle of mass suffering, Rodney replied by saying,

> There's a sense of duty about it. I'm a nurse, so I'm trained to help people who are sick and dying, but it's more than that. There's a story that's always stuck in my mind involving two guys who are talking. One asks the other, "Why did God make so much suffering in the world?" The other answers, "So you'll help ease it."

Rodney's anecdote helped the students understand his compassionate love.

Bryan's experiences as a volunteer firefighter have involved middle-of-the-night calls, smoke inhalation, irritated eyes, and the occasional surprise. Saving lives and limiting overall property damage are the two priorities of firefighters. Bryan made it clear to the class that as a volunteer he also had a regular job. He decided to volunteer because he wanted to guarantee that his family and those of his neighbors were protected in a fire emergency.

Tonya was pleased with each of her guests' unique expressions of forgiveness, generosity, and caring—all forms of genuine love. After their presentations, the men were asked to remain for a small in-class reception with food and refreshments, allowing the students one-on-one interaction.

Boy Talk

Richard, 14, Relives an Experience From Will Hobbs's *Bearstone*

I didn't go to school until I was 8; my parents were into this thing about traveling the country like their Indian ancestors. My parents really were wild Indians. They rode Harleys first, then bought an old school bus when I was born. They didn't have me until they already had gray hair.

I guess I'm proud to be an Indian, but I don't think about it much. I look just like everyone else. Most people think I'm Mexican or something. My hair is black and straight, and my skin is a pretty brown color. Dad says we're part of the Tarahncua, the first people to live in this part of Texas. I still feel different sometimes, not because I'm an Indian, but because my parents are so weird. None of my friends understand me when I tell them I don't really have a place I can call home. I was born in Oklahoma, and I've lived in 14 different states. Before moving here, we were in Florida. Mom thinks we're going to stay here because our native roots are here. I hope so.

I kind of know what Cloyd was going through in *Bearstone* (Hobbs, 1989). He's the same age as me, and he's an Indian, but in a lot of ways we're very different. He didn't have his parents around, and he pretty much stayed in one place out in Utah. My mom says I stayed in Utah for a while, but I was just a baby, so I don't know where it was.

What's really weird is I had an experience a lot like Cloyd's, or I guess I should call him Lone Bear; at least, that's what he calls himself. The part I'm talking about is when Walter, the white guy who owns the ranch, finds out that Lone Bear can't read. I knew just what Lone Bear must have been feeling; that is, you wish you never had to look at another book again in your life or write another word. For me it happened when I went to my first school. It was in Arkansas, and I was in first grade. I don't like to tell this story too much because it reminds me of how much I hate my parents for doing this to me. Anyway, I was a lot bigger than the other kids. Most of them were only 6. The teacher passed out our reading books and called on kids to read. Thank God not everyone knew how to read, but some of the girls did, and they were pretty good too. When the teacher called on me, I got real scared and thought I might get sick or something. I finally said that I couldn't read without my glasses and had left them at home. She was nice and didn't force me to try. At recess she asked me if I knew how to read, and I had to tell her that I didn't. I felt terrible because, even though I should have been in the third grade, I still didn't know how to read.

That first-grade teacher was never mean about it and always tried to help me, so I learned fast. I decided I would never be embarrassed in class again, so I worked real hard to catch up with the students who were my age. Since I've been in Texas, I've been able to be in the same grade as the other kids my age. I know that reading a lot has really helped me. I like to read after school and at home even though none of the guys I know do.

Lone Bear was lucky to have someone like Walter who didn't make fun of him because he couldn't read. I was lucky to have a nice teacher. Boys need adults who won't make them feel bad if they have trouble in school; they might just give up. I'm not saying I'd rather read than play football, ride my skateboard, or hang out with friends. But I like to read enough that if I have something really great, like *Bearstone*, I'll read it just to find out what happens in the end.

Final Thoughts

The teaching vignettes provided in this chapter demonstrate that books for teens and preteens that depict positive male archetypes can be used in many innovative ways to foster language development, critical thinking, and an expanded consciousness of what it means to be a boy and a man. The young adult novels, biographies, and informational books in this chapter may serve as entry points into active literacy for adolescent boys, especially those who have become reluctant readers. When teachers help boys find these entry points by using books that celebrate the goodness of the male psyche, they prepare boys for literary journeys toward honorable masculinity.

Creating Successful Book Experiences for Boys

> I would let [a boy] at first read any English book which happens to engage his attention; because you have done a great deal when you have brought a boy to have entertainment from a book. He'll get better books afterwards.
>
> —Samuel Johnson (as cited in Boswell, 1979, p. 121)

Achieving a language curriculum with positive male archetypes is similar to using literature for the purpose of developing other themes and literacy skills. The critical difference, of course, is the choice of reading material used by teachers to expand students' literacy abilities. This is no small matter, however. Evidence abounds that language teachers are more likely to select and use narrative fiction that may be less appealing to boys. Anne Simpson (1996) argues that many language teachers "reward particular kinds of literacy practices which girls take to like ducks to water" (p. 275).

The previous chapter described numerous teaching strategies centered on books that are likely to appeal to boys—books with positive male archetypes. This chapter will provide additional ideas, strategies, and suggestions to help teachers make book choices that are better for boys. This chapter is also devoted to establishing guidelines to help teachers identify, select, and develop teaching strategies around books with positive male archetypes. I have peppered these guidelines with descriptions of instructional strategies designed and implemented by teachers to help their male students become active readers. Drawing from my firsthand observations, I share these scenes of innovative and successful teaching for the benefit of other teachers attempting to create similar learning conditions in their own classrooms.

Curricular Guidelines for Teaching With Archetypal Literature

Discover Boys' Outside-of-School Interests

Plucker and Omdal (1997) point to a number of causes for student antipathy toward learning, such as lack of intellectual challenge or lack of understanding about how to apply their learning. They champion classrooms that promote active learning, employ a student-centered curriculum, and, above all, capitalize on student interests. Teachers will never make significant progress eradicating boys' difficulty with reading and learning unless they dedicate themselves to discovering boys' interests and acquainting boys with quality books related to those interests.

I admonish my student interns that it does not make sense to ask children new to our clinic questions like "What do you like to read?" More often than not, these children, who have had a history of reading failure, will have very little to say to such a question. Why? The majority of them would not be coming to the reading clinic if they enjoyed reading. Students who think reading is pleasurable are already good readers and readily talk about favorite books, authors, and topics. Conversely, struggling readers are short on specifics regarding these preferences; therefore, the direct approach to discovering what a struggling reader likes to read may do little more than reconfirm the student's status as a weak reader or a nonreader. An oblique approach to finding appropriate books for struggling readers is better. Teachers, then, should first discover what adolescent boys' interests are outside of school in order to ultimately introduce them—particularly struggling and reluctant readers—to enticing literature. The following sections include strategies for learning students' outside-of-school interests, such as My Bag, companion introductions, interest journals, and interest inventories.

Another "My Bag" Success Story. The Texas Coastal Bend is not known for its beaches the way California, Hawaii, or Florida is. To a hardcore group of young sailboarding junkies, however, the wind-tossed waters off Padre and Mustang Islands offer an undiscovered paradise. Delfino's interest in windsurfing came to my attention when he shared his *My Bag* with me on the night when his clinic teacher was absent. At the time, I was director of the reading clinic at Texas A&M University in Corpus Christi, Texas, USA, which provided diagnostic and tutorial services to children and adolescents from the local community.

I've been using the My Bag strategy for many years as a way of getting to know students. It allows them to showcase their strengths, loves, hobbies, and dreams. The strategy involves placing items in a bag or some other comparable container (Delfino used his backpack). The decision-making process used to select items for the bag forces students to think critically about themselves and about how certain items symbolize different aspects of their life.

I began working with Delfino that evening by sharing items from the My Bag that I keep in my office and update regularly. My approach is to take items from the bag and use them as prompts for other students to ask questions. I do this instead of a show-and-tell, to build questioning strategies and encourage students to show genuine interest in their classmates. Delfino asked me several questions when I showed my guitar pick, such as how long I had been playing, what kind of music I played and liked, and if I played in a band. He was especially curious about a photo of me running on the beach. After brief conversation that revealed how I try to stay fit by jogging and my fondness for jogging along the Mustang Island shore, Delfino said he knew that beach like the back of his hand. To prove it, he rummaged through his backpack and pulled out a photograph of teenage boys in wetsuits, standing next to their sailboards. Behind them was Bob Hall Pier, a landmark of that beach. Delfino was one of the boys in the picture. What happened with Delfino over the course of the semester only reinforces the power of the My Bag strategy to reveal personal information so critical in matching boys' interests with good books.

Once I found out how enthusiastic Delfino was about windsurfing, I knew the book he would have to read, *Lockie Leonard, Human Torpedo* (Winton, 1991). The remainder of items from Delfino's My Bag did not include a single book or magazine. In spite of his intense attraction to his hobby, he was not reading about it. I probed Delfino for details about his school life, as I do most young adults who come to clinic, only to discover that he could not remember a single teacher ever recommending a book for him to read besides his required reading. This is not an isolated story. I have evaluated numerous reading programs around the United States and have found (particularly at the secondary level where the problem is most acute) that it is rare for students to (a) use school libraries except for required projects, (b) be exposed to alternative text sources beyond the core textbook, and (c) be encouraged to simply read a book for pleasure.

When Delfino returned the following week, I had already decided that I would continue working with him. The anticipation of reading *Lockie Leonard* together, as a way of garnering Delfino's interest in reading, building his comprehension skills, and deconstructing aspects of teenage masculinity, was too much to pass up. I started by asking Delfino to keep a journal to track his responses to our discussions, as well as his personal reactions, questions, and connections, resulting in a kind of "my life-his life" analysis. Before we even began reading, we both responded to the following journal prompt: When do we feel happiest and most in control? I no sooner got these words out of my mouth before Delfino started writing. He wrote the following in a stream-of-consciousness format:

> That's easy...for me there's nothing like boarding.... I don't like school that much and I don't like all this football and basketball jock stuff...but I love being on my board...there's nothing like it...you should try it Dr. Brozo...it's like nothing else matters when you're out there.... You know you can get up to 30 or 40 miles an hour...man that's fast and you feel it in every part of you.... But sometimes when the water and wind are just right, you could be floating on a magic carpet...that's the name of my board and rig, you know, Magic Carpet.

I handed Delfino his copy of *Lockie*, which had Lockie on the cover "hanging ten." A smile came over Delfino's face, acknowledging an instant connection with the book's theme. We read the inside cover together:

> The sun was almost down as he caught his last wave, leaning and cutting across its orange glistening surface as it rolled toward the beach like the twist in a great monster's tail. It hissed behind him. His hand trailed in the smooth, faceless wall; he tossed his head back and hooted as the whole pitching funnel of his insides shot him down the line. He wasn't thinking of anything. He didn't need to. (Winton, 1991)

I then asked Delfino to compare what he had written with this description of Lockie's boarding experiences. He immediately drew a comparison between himself and Lockie by pointing out how he had written "nothing else matters when you're out there," whereas Lockie "wasn't thinking of anything. He didn't need to." "Only those of us who get out on the water on boards understand what we're talking about," Delfino said. Before we had read the first page, he was bonding with his water buddy, Lockie Leonard. Winton's books have had an equally powerful effect on many boys. (Winton has reprised his character in at least one other novel, *Lockie Leonard, Scumbuster* [1999].) Teachers who have made Lockie Leonard books available to their students have reported on the life-changing impact the books have had on them (Sanderson, 1995).

As we progressed through the book, I asked Delfino to point out passages that resonated for him. For example, in the first chapter he read to me:

> No joke. Lockie Leonard could surf. He was lousy at football. He could be counted on to entirely screw up a cricket match, and he wasn't even

any good at Monopoly, but he could sure ride a board. Genuine surf rat.... (p. 12)

Delfino drew my attention to his journal entry again, pointing out how both he and Lockie felt disinterested in popular sports but knew they could handle their boards.

We spent a considerable amount of time each week critiquing other male images in the book. These males included Lockie's father, Sarge, and a variety of "bogans," which is Australian slang for teenage tough guys. We generated a variety of responses with these male characters: we listed their behaviors and qualities; we identified people we personally knew, and people we knew from history and popular culture who were similar; and we discussed whether their male behavioral traits were worthy of emulation. Delfino characterized Lockie as wanting to be wild and free, much like himself, and not too complicated. I helped Delfino see that there was more to Lockie than this. For instance, Lockie demonstrates honorable qualities when he refuses to fight with the bogans, escorts his girlfriend away from trouble on the beach, and exercises self-control in the face of his girlfriend's sexual overtures.

When I think back to Delfino and our time with *Lockie Leonard*, I cannot help but reflect on the importance of connecting boys to books related to their interests. The French philosopher Rousseau says in *Emile, or on Education*,

> Reading is the curse of childhood.... A child has no great wish to perfect himself in the use of an instrument of torture, but make it a means to his pleasure, and soon you will not be able to keep him from it.... Present interest, that is the motive power, the only motive power that takes us far and safely. (1979, p. 213)

Delfino, the adolescent boy who had equated reading to torture, became reacquainted with books after being introduced to the kindred spirit Lockie Leonard. Delfino also discovered honesty, humility, and innocence in this fictional Wildman—admirable qualities that he thought worthy of imitation.

Delfino's final journal entry epitomizes the power of books with characters and themes that interest the male reader. Delfino constantly mentioned how he was more eager to read *Lockie* each week than any other book he had ever encountered. This permeates his final response to the book:

> I still don't like to read much...but after Lockie Leonard, I like it more than I used to. This was the best book I ever read in my life. It was so cool to read about someone that was a lot like me. Lockie never made a big deal about how much he loved surfing and how good he was at

it, but kids gave him a hard time anyway. Only my friends know I wind-surf. Even my p.e. [physical education] coach thinks I'm no good at any sport...he hasn't seen me on the bay. I wish teachers would let students read stuff they're interested in. If when I was a kid teachers let me read books about surfing and stuff I think I would be a better reader now. I'm going to look for other books about surfing and also tell our librarian to get books on surfing. The next book I'm going to read is the other Lockie Leonard book.

I have shared my experiences with Delfino to demonstrate how I selected *Lockie Leonard, Human Torpedo* through the My Bag strategy. Delfino's mother had already told me that he disliked reading, had low grades in English and most of his other classes, and did not read for pleasure. To have asked Delfino what he likes to read would have yielded nothing. Because of the My Bag strategy, I discovered Delfino's windsurfing hobby. Only teachers who are concerned about boys' lives outside of the classroom have a chance of successfully engaging them with literature, because the literature these teachers choose will directly relate to the boys' life worlds, or lives.

Grouping for Reading Interests Using My Bag. Jared, an English teacher, supplements the My Bag requirement to ensure that he has a permanent record of his ninth graders' out-of-class interests. In addition to assembling bags to share in small groups, students must also make a written list of the items in their bags, with brief notations on each item's importance. After the bags are shared, Jared still has a list of the students' items on file. This allows him to share books related to students' interests, or group students with common interests to explore books related to certain class topics.

Jared's heightened concern for the males compelled him to find books with positive male themes and archetypes related to the students' interests (as revealed in their bags). For example, Jared formed groups around such interests as low riders (a type of car), football, music, and African American pride. Each group read books that portrayed real-life or fictional male characters who were somehow connected with these interests.

One group of three black students had shared My Bag items related to their families and culture. Jared introduced this group to the comic and deeply moving novel *The Watsons Go to Birmingham—1963* by Christopher Paul Curtis (1995). Students in this group enjoyed the weird and hilarious world of Kenny Watson and his family. Living in Flint, Michigan, USA, in 1963, Mr. Watson decides it is time to visit Grandma in Birmingham, Alabama, USA. The story of their drive through the heart of the South, at a time when blacks were segregated, and their eventual rendezvous with one of the darkest and most turbulent moments in U.S. history made for a riveting literacy experience for Jared's students. Mr. Watson's strength and unflagging commitment to his family left a lasting impression on the three black teens. As stated throughout this book, images of men like Mr. Watson are becoming too scarce in the lives of many minority boys. Young adult books that display images of positive masculinity for minority boys and provide these boys with concrete, attainable models of honorable male behavior is a combination too powerful for teachers to ignore.

Companion Introductions. In addition to the My Bag strategies, there are numerous ways to discover boys' hobbies, loves, and dreams. The *companion introduction* is another successful approach to learning about students' out-of-school lives. For the past few years, Patty Walters's seventh and eighth graders have established a buddy relationship with one of my undergraduate secondary reading classes. (Please refer to Chapter 5 for details on a special teaching unit conducted with one of Patty's classes.) This buddy relationship entailed at least two visits per semester to either Patty's school or my university classroom where the middle school and college students participated in joint learning activities. First, students from our classes paired up. To get to know each other and to share what each learned with the class, partners talked about their lives (family members, pets, role models, personal and career goals, proudest accomplishments, and what they do for fun and like most about school).

The unique aspect of this process came when personal introductions were made before the entire class. Students introduced their partners by role-playing one another. When it was my group's turn, I sat silently while Noe stood behind me and stated,

> Hello, I'm Dr. Bill Brozo. I'm married. My wife's name is Carol, and my daughter's name is Hannah. Hannah is 10 years old. I have a cat named Oscar, a dog named Teddy, and a parakeet named Rosie. I like to read, jog, travel, play music, and Roller Blade with my daughter. I've been to Europe and South America. The person I admire most is Jimmy Carter. My goal is to write classical music. My proudest accomplishment was publishing a book. The part of my job that I like the most is helping students become good teachers.

When Noe finished, we changed places, and I introduced him:

> Hi, I'm Noe Soliz. I'm 13 years old and in the eighth grade at West Oso Junior High School. I have three sisters and one brother. I have a small dog named Pepe. I love basketball and play guard for the Bears. The person I look up to is Michael Jordan. My goal is to make the high

school basketball team and maybe go to college and play. My proudest accomplishment was scoring 18 points in one game. I like p.e. the best because I can give my brain a rest.

My students and I always have a great deal of fun with these introductions, as well as other activities with Patty's students. Teachers can also conduct these companion introductions to equal effect within their own classrooms and just with their own students. An astute teacher gleans valuable information about students' interests from the introductions. Consider what the class learned about Noe. Knowledge of his fervent attraction to basketball alone offers a link to good reading material to match his interests. Appropriate for Noe would be Bruce Brooks's *The Moves Make the Man* (1996), Mark Stewart's *Hakeem Olajuwon (Grolier All-Pro Biographies)* (1996), Brad Townsend's *Shaquille O'Neal: Center of Attention* (1994), and Eloise Greenfield's *For the Love of the Game: Michael Jordan and Me* (1997). These books would likely motivate Noe because of their basketball content; they also present fictional and real-life sports figures who embody honorable masculinity. In an era when athletes repeatedly exhibit poor sportsmanship, adopt supercilious attitudes, or openly dismiss their responsibilities as role models, Michael Jordan, Hakeem Olajuwon, and Shaquille O'Neal have conducted themselves with dignity both on and off the court. Displays of these basketball stars' generosity are apparent in their foundations that help disadvantaged children stay in school, scholarships that enable disadvantaged children go to college, and general relief for children and families in poverty, refugees, and victims of famine. These books demonstrate to boys like Noe that they can aspire to play basketball like the greats but should also learn the value of dedication and masculine largess.

Interest Journals. Another way to gain insight into the life worlds of teen and preteen boys is through the use of *interest journals* (Bromley & Powell, 1999). First, a word of caution about journal writing in general: In spite of compelling testimonials that journaling helps develop students' writing abilities (Atwell, 1987; Bromley, 1993; Popp, 1997), using this strategy requires special attention to the unique nature of male propensities. Boys often find journal assignments requiring them to express feelings and emotions much more difficult than their female peers do. If teachers insist on this kind of emotive response only, writing may become a turnoff for boys in the same way that reading has become a turnoff when they are exposed to a steady diet of books unrelated to their interests (Ivey, 1998). Alternative response modes are likely to yield a desired level of language production and keep boys interested in writing. It is critical to remember that any book that provides pleasure and engages boys in reading is good because novice readers learn through reading; thus, the same holds true for writing. Boys should be allowed latitude in journaling. If they desire to focus on a story's action rather than their feelings toward the story's characters, teachers should accept it. This does not excuse boys from delving into their feelings to understand characters' motivations for certain behavior, but it emphasizes that language production is the most important goal of journaling. Journaling based on students' interests is an inherent motivator just as reading books and other material related to students' interests is.

Simply defined, interest journals are a form of journaling in which students write about topics that interest them. Teachers who use interest journals often structure the activity in a way that allows peers or themselves to interactively respond to students' journals and entries. This approach makes journaling ideally suited to discovering boys' likes and dislikes. Tonja has been successfully using interest journals with her sixth graders for several years. She tells me there is no better way to get to know her students at the beginning of the year (while also supporting the writing habit) than with this form of journaling. One of her testimonials stands out.

Bo, a diffident, thin, and small boy, entered Tonja's classroom just after the Christmas holidays. His military father had recently been assigned to the local naval airbase, moving from Saudia Arabia to the Texas Gulf Coast. Bo's belongings had not yet arrived at their new residence, so he was unable to share a My Bag with the class. Instead, Tonja got him started with an interest journal. Within a couple of weeks, Bo's journal entries revealed his fascination with airplanes (not surprising because his father is a navy pilot), computer games, and baseball. Another clue to Bo's out-of-school interests was provided in the following entry:

> If I didn't have to go to school, I would play golf every day. Maybe in 2 or 3 years I could play like Tiger Woods. He's the greatest golfer in the world. So far, my dad has taken me golfing about five times but not in Corpus Christi yet. When he gets the time, he said he would take me. I also like Tiger Woods because I found out his mother is from Thailand, and guess what? My mom is too!

Armed with this knowledge, Tonja was able to supply Bo with books from the school library and her own collection, including Bill Gutman's *Tiger Woods: Golf's Shining Young Star* (1998), Laura Driscoll's *Slugger Season: McGwire and Sosa* (1998), and David Adler's *A Picture Book of Jackie Robinson* (1994) and *Lou Gehrig: The Luckiest Man* (1997). Not only are these books directly related to Bo's interests in baseball and golf, but they also depict admirable men who are worthy of imitation.

Interest Inventories. *Interest inventories* are simple to construct and easy to fill in, making them useful tools for discovering students' interests outside of school. Generally speaking, the easier the response mode, the more likely it is that students will make the effort to complete the inventory. Figures 6 and 7 present two different types of interest inventories developed by secondary reading teachers. The first sample inventory (see Figure 6) asks students to circle a number between 1 and 4. These numbers correspond to the students' feelings toward a given activity. Notice that there is also space at the end of the activities list for students to add their favorite activities. The second sample inventory (see Figure 7) requires students to complete sentences regarding their activities and preferences outside of school.

FIGURE 6
Sample Interest Inventory

Directions: Circle the number that matches your feelings about the following activities.

Activity	Excellent	Good	Okay	Not Interested
1. Playing sports	4	3	2	1
2. Watching TV	4	3	2	1
3. Hunting/fishing	4	3	2	1
4. Playing computer games	4	3	2	1
5. Dancing	4	3	2	1
6. Surfing the Internet	4	3	2	1

Please add your favorite activities in the space below.

_____

_____

_____

FIGURE 7
Sample Interest Inventory—Complete Each Sentence

Directions: Please complete each sentence to let me know what you like to do outside of school.

1. After school I like to_____.

2. My favorite thing to do on weekends is _____

_____.

3. _____is my favorite sports team because _____

_____.

4. I really think the music of _____is cool because

_____.

5. _____is a movie I would see

over and over again because _____

_____.

Teachers like Hector, who teaches high school reading, survey their students' general interests with similar inventories at the beginning of the school year and once or twice during the term. These inventories give up-to-date information on each student's likes and dislikes. Preferences evolve in the ever-changing life of most adolescents, so that what may have been a student's strong interest in September may be a lower priority by April, or earlier.

Antonio, one of Hector's 10th-grade reading students, could not spend enough time talking about bodybuilding during the fall. Hector learned of Antonio's obsession with weight lifting after reviewing his first interest inventory. So when Hector gave a book talk on Chris Crutcher's *Ironman* (1995), you would have had to nail Antonio's feet to the floor to keep him from racing up to select that book for independent reading. By January, though, bodybuilding had been supplanted by wrestling as Antonio's new obsession. He had had such an enjoyable experience reading *Ironman* that he begged Hector to give him a good novel about wrestling. Hector was eager to oblige and plucked two books from his shelf for Antonio. One of the books, Matt Hunter's *Wrestling Madness: A Ringside Look at Wrestling Superstars* (1999), showcases the pantheon of popular television wrestlers (with whom Antonio was familiar) with colorful photos.

Hector's selection of narratives about wrestling, even though they would seem to celebrate traditional or even stereotypical masculine behavior, may leave some people uncomfortable. Roger Simon (1987) reminds us that we should respect boys' reading preferences to avoid demeaning their lives; furthermore, when helping boys find entry points into literacy, people should always bear in mind that they had modest beginnings on their own literacy paths. For example, some of the most renowned women, from novelists to Supreme Court justices, found entry points into literacy with such "artless" texts as those from The Bobbsey Twins and Nancy Drew series (Cooper-Mullin & Coye, 1998). The point is this: Only after years of traditional print explorations do people come to pride themselves on their sophisticated and flexible reading abilities. Teachers should, therefore, resist the tendency to withhold what young men desire to read, because boys already filled with disaffection toward books cannot bypass the journey that others have also taken to arrive at a point of active literacy and expanded consciousness (Young & Brozo, 2001). Ultimately, no one knows where a young man's first exciting print experiences will lead him.

The other book that Hector gave Antonio was John Irving's *The Imaginary Girlfriend: A Memoir* (1997). This book tells of Irving's own story of college wrestling. Devoid of the smoke and mirrors, loud threats, and bizarre outfits and makeup seen in televised wrestling, Irving recounts his wrestling experiences in pure and vivid images. He captures the atmosphere of the wrestling room and reveals through anecdotes that he and his buddies were not a bunch of "dumb jocks"; intercollegiate wrestlers expend a great deal of physical and emotional energy to be successful. Irving shows the reader how common sports themes such as fair play, graciousness in victory, and cooperation really do apply to life. This is a splendid book for adolescent athletes to enjoy and appreciate for its portrayal of honorable masculinity.

Hector allowed Antonio to do his 6-weeks' project on the similarities and differences between professional and amateur wrestling. On a large poster board, Antonio created two columns. Each column listed information about the two forms of wrestling in parallel fashion. For example, a statement under the Professional Wrestling column read, "Every wrestler can fight any other wrestler." Directly across from this statement, in the Amateur-College Wrestling column, Antonio wrote, "Wrestlers are in weight classes and only wrestle guys in the same class." Antonio's major breakthrough, however, was his acknowledgment of the disingenuous nature of professional wrestling. One of his entries read, "Pro wrestlers never act afraid and only talk about beating the other guy," whereas the other column read, "College wrestlers never brag in public and often get really nervous and sometimes even sick in the locker room before a match." On another line Antonio included the following statements for each column: "Pro wrestlers know how each match is going to go and who will win. College wrestlers have to be ready for any move from the other guy, and nobody knows who's going to win the match."

How many teen and preteen boys are passing through life without knowing that outstanding fiction and nonfiction books that speak to their interests are readily available? Antonio is one of the lucky ones. Hector made it possible for a male teen to be introduced to exciting books directly related to his interests. As a result, Antonio read three books, which is more than what he might otherwise have done. The benefit of reading is well documented in the professional literature; however, the boost to his self-esteem and reaffirmation of a positive male identity that Antonio gained from reading is of incalculable value. The lesson here is that it is essential for teachers to discover male adolescents' interests and involve themselves in an ongoing search for quality literature that will capture boys' interests.

Introduce Books Through Book Talks

Using the titles listed in the Appendix, teachers should have little difficulty finding books with positive male archetypes within the aforementioned genres. For example, Chuck, a middle school reading teacher in a small town, allowed his class to form small groups around a novel of their choosing. He keeps an extensive collection of trade books in his classroom and reads most of them himself. Chuck purchases many of his books at garage sales or discount bookstores for a fraction of their original cost. When students forget to return these books or lose them, Chuck merely requires a donated replacement of another suitable book.

Chuck introduces novels and other books to his students through *book talks*. A book talk is a short, exciting glimpse of a book that is, in essence, a way of selling students on a book through a personal introduction. Think of a film trailer as an analogy: The film's most exciting or intriguing moments are packed into a highly condensed advertisement designed to lure audiences to see it. Likewise, a book talk that includes an enthusiastic delivery, expressive reading of excerpts, and a cliff-hanging conclusion is especially useful for enticing reluctant readers.

Another powerful aspect of book talks is that they allow teachers to demonstrate their concern for their students' literacy by reading books written especially for the students. This is no small matter, given evidence that the most common reason students give for selecting a particular book is that someone made a recommendation; that someone is often the teacher (Kragler & Nolley, 1996).

Four boys, two who were football players, formed a group around a book titled *The Heartbeat of Halftime* (Wunderli, 1996), which Chuck had used for a book talk. The book is based on Wunderli's own experiences coaching his son's peewee league team to a championship even though it was the underdog. The story revolves around Wing, a 13-year-old player on the Mighty Titans, whose football team has the longest losing streak in the conference. Determined to end the humiliation, Wing rallies his teammates to many longshot victories as they complete their last season together before high school. In the midst of championship fever, Wing's father, who has been his mentor and private coach, becomes seriously ill, forcing Wing to decide what is most important to him. Wing's fight for a dad he truly loves and victory on the field casts him as an ideal Warrior.

As a former student of mine, Chuck had become sensitized to the important role he plays for his teen and preteen students. He knows how rare it is for his students to interact with adult men who are also avid readers, so he takes great care to be a role model of active literacy. With this in mind, he took full advantage of the opportunity to acquaint his boys with the honorable displays of masculinity in *The Heartbeat of Halftime*. Chuck and the group evaluated Wing's and other male characters' behavior against a standard of honesty and bravery. They also discussed what it means to "fight for a valorous cause." As described in Chapters 2 and 3, Warriors do not need to fight with their hands. Warriors can fight with their minds and hearts to improve themselves and the lives of those around them. Wing demonstrates this power when he fights against great physical and emotional odds.

Create a Guys' Rack

A remarkable man himself—born into poverty, he later became a paraplegic from a diving accident and is now wheelchair bound—Kenny is a constant reminder to his seventh-grade students, most of whom qualify for free or reduced-price lunches, that by dint of sheer effort, personal goals can be accomplished. Kenny is also a former student of mine. He invited me to his classroom to see the progress he had been making with his male students by using some simple but powerful strategies that made it "safe" for boys to choose to be readers.

I watched as Kenny maneuvered freely and competently throughout the room while guiding and cajoling his students to a higher level thinking with *Sniper* (Taylor, 1989). He handed me a copy so I could follow along with the class. As students were reading and discussing the action, I noticed the initials G.R. printed on my book's spine. When we finished that day's chapter, students dispersed throughout the room to work on projects, discuss compositions with the teacher, or find a comfortable spot for reading. I wandered to the long bookshelf at the side of the room and began perusing titles when I found what the initials on my book stood for. Three full shelves of paperback novels, nonfiction, informational books, and magazines were in a section labeled "Guys' Rack." I saw a couple of boys walk directly to these shelves, select a book, and flop down on a beanbag to read. I also saw at least one girl do the same thing.

I later pressed Kenny for information about these books. He told me that when he began teaching 3 years earlier, his male students were rarely self-selecting books because of fear of ridicule. If a boy chose something that other boys deemed a "girl's book," the book would likely be returned to the shelf, becoming a "pariah" among the males. Fear of ridicule was a powerful incentive for the boys to find "boys' books." Kenny said he wanted his male students to be able to select books without fear, so he decided to label certain books as just for boys. These became the books that formed the Guys' Rack. Boys in his classes now have no doubt which books are likely to be more interesting to them; however, neither males nor females are discouraged from choosing reading material from anywhere on the bookshelves. Kenny's female students do not feel disenfranchised by his system because they know they are free to read a Guys' Rack book as well.

To confirm Kenny's description of his male students' new attitudes about self-selecting books, I talked with 12-year-old Evan after watching him choose a magazine from the Guys' Rack. I sidled next to Evan at a reading table in the back of the classroom and asked what he was reading. It was a computer game magazine. He told me about his interest in computers and his ambition to become a designer of computer games. In response to my questions about choosing reading matter from the boys' section, Evan said,

"The stuff I like to read is already in one place on the bookshelf...that makes it easy for me to find things to read. I don't look anywhere else because I know the interesting stuff for me is right there."

"What was it like before the 'Guys' Rack'?" I asked.

"It took, like, a long time to find things to read...at least for me."

I probed further, "Did you ever pick a book that your classmates thought was not something a guy like you should be reading?"

"Yeah, they give you a hard time and everything.... When the books were all mixed up, you know, the boys' and girls' books all together, you didn't know if you had a good book until you read some of it."

"Can you remember any particular book when that happened?" I asked.

"I really like baseball, and I found this book about baseball. When I started reading it, I found out it was about girls' baseball. [The book Evan was referring to is *A Whole New Ball Game: The Story of the All-American Girls Professional Baseball League* by Sue Macy (1995).] I didn't know. The cover said something like 'a new ball game' or 'a whole new game' or something like that, and it wasn't until Lucy, who sits next to me, told me it was about baseball for girls that I figured it out. But then she told some of my friends, and they were passing notes and laughing and stuff. I ended up not reading it."

It is important to keep in mind that even if Evan's decision not to read a book because of peer pressure seems to be an unworthy excuse, the net result was one more boy choosing not to read. I have elaborated on this point in preceding chapters, but because time spent reading is linked to reading competence, boys like Evan are likely to fall behind academically (Anderson, Wilson, & Fielding, 1988; Mullis, Campbell, & Farstrup, 1993). The reverse, however, has been shown to be true; that is, people who have a hard time reading can become much more competent simply through voluntary reading in areas of personal interest (Fink, 1995/1996).

Kenny's goal, then, was to create a classroom environment that would nurture interest reading and that would not hinder personal book selection. The Guys' Rack has made it possible for Evan and other male students to quickly find reading matter of high interest and to enjoy books without fear of ridicule. At the same time, the girls in Kenny's classroom feel entirely free to find something to read from the boys' shelves; thus, this important tool for male students does not alienate female students.

Know and Locate Books for Boys

Know Books for Boys. As established earlier and throughout this book, boys need help finding books that are both pleasing and identity affirming. Ray Nicolle (1989) chided his fellow school librarians for their lack of attention to preteen boys' reading needs. He asserted that there was virtually nothing for boys to read once they entered what he termed the "five-year void," which is the period between the ages 7 to 12. Without apology, Nicolle stated that boys will not read "watered down, insipid, cloyingly sweet" (p. 130) books but prefer books with genuine action, adventure, and villains. Placing suitable books in teen and preteen boys' hands is also one of the goals of education officials in the United Kingdom. Trends similar to those we are witnessing in the United States show British boys reading far fewer books than girls and scoring significantly lower on measures of reading comprehension (Benton, 1995). The concern among U.K. officials is that "teachers have not been choosing the kind of literature that would most interest their male pupils" (Hoffman, 1999, p. 12). Teachers have been urged to include in their language schemes "stirring tales which appeal to young boys," so as to avoid the "serious danger of developing the idea that reading is...not a manly undertaking" (p. 12).

I am pleased to report that the volume and variety of excellent books for teen and preteen boys has grown considerably over the past 2 decades. It is now easy for teachers to find books from a range of genres to match the unique needs of their male readers. Results of surveys and research studies that focused on adolescents' reading interests (Diaz-Rubin, 1996; Langerman, 1990; Ollmann, 1993; Simpson, 1996; Wicks, 1995; Worthy, Moorman, & Turner, 1999) point unwaveringly to the following genres favored by males who participated in the studies:

- Humor
- Horror
- Adventure and/or thriller
- Informational and/or picture
- Science fiction
- Crime and detective
- Monster and/or ghost
- Sports
- War
- Biography
- Fantasy
- Historical

Form Alliances With Librarians. I often speak to teachers about how to make reading and writing more lively and meaningful for their teen and preteen students. All teachers, regardless of subject matter expertise, need to be enthusiastic models of active literacy behavior to show their students the benefits and pleasures of literacy.

Recently, I was speaking to a group of high school teachers on the importance of paying special attention to adolescent boys' reading habits. I displayed and described various trade books that had been found to be particularly appealing to boys (see Baines, 1994; Brozo & Schmelzer, 1997). I shared some of the following books:

- Stephen Biesty's *Cross-Sections: Man-Of-War* (1993)
- George Sullivan's *Sluggers: Twenty-Seven of Baseball's Greatest* (1991)
- Isaac Asimov's *Isaac Asimov's Great Space Mysteries* (1994)
- James Robertson's *Civil War: America Becomes One Nation* (1992)
- Ron Schultz's *Looking Inside the Brain* (1992)
- Rupert Matthews's *Explorer* (1999)
- Bill Littlefield's *Champions: Stories of Ten Remarkable Athletes* (1993)
- Ted Wood's *A Boy Becomes a Man at Wounded Knee* (1995)

We were situated in the school's library. As I passed around and commented on each book, I noticed that someone had gotten up and was moving among the bookshelves, although I did not give it a second thought at the time. When I concluded sharing these books, a male teacher sitting in the back of the group confronted me: "That's all well and good what you're saying about encouraging boys to read, but we don't have those kinds of books in our school." Before I could reply, the person who had been roaming among the library shelves shouted, "Yes we do," and held up every one of the titles I had just mentioned. The person, of course, was the school librarian.

I tell this story to make the case that a teacher's best friends in the struggle against adolescent boys' aliteracy are librarians. Even in school libraries that have what some might consider paltry holdings, there are always books capable of speaking to boys' inner struggles, hopes, and lifelong goals. Not long ago, I toured the junior high school library of a small school district in South Texas and discovered a cache of those wonderful Stephen Meader books (see Chapter 1). These timeless books of adventure are sure to keep most young men riveted page after page. Because of her meager budget, the librarian had devised an ingenious way of giving these books new life. With the help of students, the librarian re-covered the lifeless aqua, brown, and red bindings from the 1960s with enticing laminated collages that suggested the books' themes.

Students found that these fresh covers helped do away with the stigma of reading old, boring books.

Because of their vast knowledge of young adult literature, librarians can also save valuable time by finding and grouping material specifically for male readers. Teachers can work with librarians to create special "just for boys" sections in the library, giving male students a place to search for reading material that matches their interests. These books can also be checked out of the library and kept in the classroom, where teachers can provide book talks and make the books available for sustained and self-selected reading. Teachers may also simply ask librarians to order books that appeal to boys by either requesting these books directly or sensitizing the librarian to the need for such books. In my experience as an evaluator of reading programs, most librarians speak regrettably about how unusual it is to receive order requests from teachers despite regular solicitations for such requests. Consequently, any teachers willing to take advantage of this opportunity to shape the character of the library's holdings will likely have many of their reading material requests met. Teachers choosing to act on any of these ideas will form a critical alliance with librarians in the struggle to engage all boys in active literacy.

Use Book Guides to Find Boys' Books. One of the first questions I get when talking with teachers about using quality books with honorable male characters is "Where do I find books like those?" The answer is, from anyone or any source that has this information. Good librarians are perhaps the best guides to finding these books because of their abilities to point teachers in the right directions, find the material quickly, and most importantly, make themselves immediately accessible to others. This book is also a guide to books with positive male archetypes appropriate for teen and preteen boys: The Appendix is a lengthy list of these books and will help teachers, parents, and other concerned adults identify and procure reading material that will motivate males to read.

Numerous other resources are available to help teachers find books that will appeal to teen and preteen boys. A list of what I consider to be the best of these guides appears in Figure 8. Although these guides are not specifically for boys, with the exception of Odean's, they index, categorize, and annotate a range of books. The astute teacher, however, will find countless titles within these guides to motivate their male students to read.

Invite Men Who Read to the Classroom

How else will boys become familiar with what male readers look like than to observe men reading? As noted, most teen and preteen boys rarely see

FIGURE 8
A Select List of Book Guides

Adamson, L.G. (1998). *American historical fiction: An annotated guide to novels for adults and young adults.* New York: Oryx Press.

Barr, C., Thomas, R.L., & McDaniel, D. (1998). *From biography to history: Best books for children's entertainment and education.* New York: R.R. Bowker.

Benedict, S., & Carlisle, L. (1992). *Beyond words: Picture books for older readers and writers.* Portsmouth, NH: Heinemann.

Berman, M. (1995). *What else should I read: Guiding kids to good books.* Englewood, CO: Libraries, Unlimited.

CheckerBee Publishing. (1999). *Science fiction: A reader's checklist and reference guide.* Middletown, CT: Author.

CheckerBee Publishing. (1999). *Young adult: A reader's checklist and reference guide.* Middletown, CT: Author.

Christenbury, L. (1997). *Books for you: An annotated booklist for senior high students.* Urbana, IL: National Council of Teachers of English.

Coffey, R. (1997). *America as story: Historical fiction for middle and secondary schools* (2nd ed.). Chicago: American Library Association.

Donelson, K., & Nilsen, A.P. (1996). *Literature for today's young adult* (5th ed.). Reading, MA: Addison-Wesley.

Gath, T. (1996). *Science books and films: Best books for children 1992–1995.* New York: American Association for the Advancement of Science.

Hartman, D.K. (1994). *Historical figures in fiction.* New York: Oryx Press.

Kennemer, P.K. (1992). *Using literature to teach middle grades about war.* New York: Oryx Press.

Kies, C. (1992). *Presenting young adult horror fiction.* London: Twayne Publishers.

Kilpatrick, W., Wolfe, G., & Wolfe, S.M. (1994). *Books that build character: A guide to teaching your child moral values through stories.* New York: Touchstone.

Matulka, D.I. (1997). *Picture this: Picture books for young adults.* Westport, CT: Greenwood Press.

Nakamura, J. (1999). *High-interest books for teens: A guide to book reviews and biographical sources* (3rd ed.). Farmington Hills, MI: Gale Group.

Odean, K. (1998). *Great books for boys.* New York: Ballantine.

Orion Society. (1995). *Bringing the world alive: A bibliography of nature stories for children.* (1995). New York: Author.

Rodriguez, M., Rasbury, A., & Taylor, C. (1999). *Sacred fire: The QBR 100 essential black books.* Chichester, UK: John Wiley & Sons.

Sherman, G.W., & Ammon, B.D. (1993). *Rip-roaring reads for reluctant teen readers.* Englewood, CO: Libraries, Unlimited.

Spencer, P. (1994). *What do young adults read next? A reader's guide to fiction for young adults.* Detroit, MI: Gale Research.

Taylor, D. (1994). *The juvenile novels of World War II: An annotated bibliography.* Westport, CT: Greenwood Press.

Tiedt, I.M. (2000). *Teaching with picture books in the middle school.* Newark, DE: International Reading Association.

Yaakov, J. (1999). *Children's catalog* (18th ed.). New York: H.W. Wilson.

fathers or any adult men reading anything at all. This situation is most prevalent among adolescents of minority groups. In their investigation of the causes for high unemployment and underemployment among black males, Chung, Baskin, and Case (1999) found that black males tend to have lower educational attainment and terminate formal schooling earlier than white males. The principal reason for this pattern is the absence of role modeling by fathers for many black boys (Weber, 1993). Unfortunately, absent fathers are all too common in the black community, according to the Bureau of the Census (1997); in 1995, 58% of all black households with children under 18 were headed by a single female. In large urban areas, as many as 40% of African American boys do not graduate from high school, whereas 40% of African American men have problems with literacy (Wright, 1991/1992). These disheartening facts clearly point to the importance of male role models in the academic and social development of male adolescents, particularly black teen and preteen boys.

This is why we brought adult men who were dedicated readers into the classroom as part of our Real Men unit at West Oso Junior High School (described in more detail in Chapter 5). These men read aloud from their favorite books and talked about the importance of active literacy. One splendid role model who had a powerful impact on the seventh graders was my former colleague Dr. Malcolm Booker. Here was a black man with an exceptional knowledge of science education, who from the most humble beginnings achieved academic acclaim as a university professor and researcher. What Malcolm took the most pride in, however, was his personal and professional habit of daily, regular reading. He exuded enthusiasm for reading books and magazine articles, and provided a real-life example of the benefits of literacy. He was able to establish a special rapport with the African American and Hispanic American students because of his background of poverty, his unemployed and absent father, and his high school and college athletic prowess, which the boys found irresistible because of their dreams of basketball and football stardom.

Although Dr. Booker was raised primarily by his mother and had few male role models, research proves that any adult male role model can have a major effect on black men's academic achievements and career aspirations (Chung et al., 1999). Teachers, then, need to arrange for as many classroom visits as possible by adult men who embody active literacy and honorable masculinity. These men should come from all walks of life—both blue- and white-collar workers, people from the local college or university, members of the clergy, workers from retirement centers, and so on.

Another male role model who I was particularly proud to have as a speaker was Al Townsend, a garage mechanic. I discovered that Al, who had become a friend of mine as a result of the numerous service calls I made about my aging car, had an insatiable appetite for books on virtually any topic. When my wife dropped me off at his garage one day, I was stunned to find Al lounging in his grease-smeared, although commodious, old office chair reading David Guterson's *Snow Falling on Cedars* (1995). We immediately fell into a long conversation about our mutual love of reading, finding we share many interests in authors and genres. As we talked, I began to notice, among auto parts, tools, and engines in various stages of repair, numerous paperback and hardbound books. His loft above the shop was a veritable archive of literature he "simply couldn't part with." In class, Al read from one of his favorite science fiction novels, *Lathe of Heaven* by Ursula LeGuin (1997), and said that his modest means as an auto mechanic did not prevent him from taking joyous flights of imagination through books. He said, "Reading, for me, turns my hot, greasy shop into a cool, fresh garden." Enough said!

Boy Talk

Nick, 16, Meets Nick Adams, a Hemingway Persona

Mr. Burns knew I wasn't into the Hemingway story in our literature book. It was called "The Short Happy Life of Francis Macomber" (1995). I just couldn't relate to it. I like to hunt, and the African safari thing would be cool, but the plot seemed kind of silly. It was like a 1930s thing with these rich Americans who don't have much of a marriage and the husband trying to prove he's a big man by killing a lion.

Mr. Burns and I can talk about most things. He likes to hunt too. In fact, we hunted deer last fall during deer season. He told me he was kind of a hippie when he was in college. Not really a hippie, more like a wanderer. He hitchhiked all across the country, living out of a sleeping bag and meeting up with all kinds of interesting people. He said what had inspired him to do this was reading *The Nick Adams Stories* (Hemingway, 1981). He gave me his copy of the book and told me to give these stories a try. He thought I would like them a lot more than the Francis Macomber story.

First off, my name is Nick, and when I started reading about Nick Adams it was almost like meeting someone I knew. He reminded me of Mr. Burns but also a little of myself. The story I really got into was "The Fighter." Nick sneaks onto a train and gets thrown off in the middle of nowhere in Northern Michigan. But he can handle it. He has his bedroll, and he knows how to take care of himself in the woods. He's young like me, though, and when he comes upon a small fire and a couple of older guys, you don't know what might happen to him. One guy is a former boxer and talks to Nick about some of his experiences. But his mind's gone and that makes the scene a bit threatening. They give Nick something to eat, but soon Nick moves on down the tracks to get away from the crazy old fighter.

The story seems simple enough, but I got this feeling that it was important for Nick to have the experience he had—almost like when I shot my first deer. You can't wait to do it, but when it finally happens, you feel a little sick and weird inside. The sound of the rifle shot seems to ring in your head for a long time, and you wonder if it was worth it. But you've got to get over this if you're ever going to hunt again. Mr. Burns says hunting is excusable if you don't abuse it and use as much of the deer as possible for meat.

It's amazing how much more I liked these stories than I did the one in our literature book. There's really no comparison. *The Nick Adams Stories* are about someone my age who likes being in the woods and tramping around. Nick is free, young, and not afraid to do things by himself. That's how he's sort of like me. I have one good friend called Jared. Nick has one good friend, too, named Bill Wemmish. I only wish these kind of stories were in our literature book. I think many more guys like me would enjoy reading them instead of the Hemingway story that's in there now.

Final Thoughts

It has been said that creativity cannot be taught. I'm not sure I agree. I do know that some teachers using unconventional methods find a way to engender a will to learn in their students.

The strategies described in this chapter reflect, if not purely original thinking, an attitude of openness about instructional possibilities for enticing boys to engage in active literacy. No one told Kenny about the Guys' Rack; this is an idea that leapt into his mind as a result of serious thinking about the needs of his male students. Patty's companion introduction is something she picked up at an inservice several years ago, although she was able to give it special expression when used with both the students from the Real Men unit and my undergraduates. The point is this: Teachers who think seriously about their craft find ways to reach students. All teachers who work with teen and preteen boys should be prepared to become nonconformists if necessary and to advocate their male students' rights and needs as readers.

Chapter 5 presents a detailed description of the Real Men unit. Using abundant anecdotal evidence in the form of actual classroom vignettes and stories of behind-the-scenes planning, I present a complete account of how the teachers and I designed the unit, selected appropriate literature, implemented the instructional strategies, and documented and evaluated the students' responses. In so doing, I demonstrate how the seventh-grade males were invited to participate in an authentic unit intended to help them look critically at popular notions of masculinity, develop positive male values, and become more engaged readers and learners.

Achieving a Language Curriculum With Literature for Boys: The Real Men Unit

> One of the most important ways in which our society introduces its young to acceptable social behavior and to important social practices is through language—particularly printed language—and the school's role in this introduction is obviously crucial. (Gilbert, 1989, p. 3)

A toy gun lay in the middle of the desktop. Patty Walter and Teri Placker stood on opposite sides of the desk staring intently and angrily at one another. Fourteen seventh-grade boys and two seventh-grade girls looked curiously at this scene as I read aloud from *Scorpions* (Myers, 1990). The scene was of 12-year-old Jamal, the main character, trying to decide whether to take a handgun, given to him by a gang member, to school. Jamal's classmate Dwayne, who is taller and stronger, has been goading Jamal to fight him. Jamal knows the odds of getting beaten up are high unless he uses his newfound source of confidence—the handgun. I read just to the point before Jamal makes his decision, and Patty began reaching slowly for the handgun. Then I abruptly closed the book. The students were disappointed; they asked me to read on, but I refused. Patty and Teri reminded their combined classes that this was the kind of excitement they would experience over the next several weeks as we read *Scorpions* together.

The three of us were introducing a new unit that became affectionately known as Real Men. I had just finished a brainstorming activity with the students, resulting in a web of popular images and stereotypes of men, which I had written on the board. We followed that activity with a book talk on *Scorpions*, Walter Dean Myers's gripping, pathos-filled tale of young boys and gangs in New York City. It was the beginning to an exciting critical study of men and boys in today's society.

The unit developed and taught by Patty, Teri, and me was devoted to exploring what it means to be man. We built activities around the book's events and characters, striving to make the seventh graders more aware of the prevalence of male violence and selfishness. These activities were also intended to help students reflect on their everyday experiences with other boys and men who accept violence and selfishness as necessary features of masculinity. We ultimately hoped that the students would become engaged readers and be more critical of their own attitudes about stereotypical masculinity.

We discovered that careful instruction and interaction with an exciting young adult novel that speaks to traditional male interests helped the boys as well as the two girls in class to become more engaged readers and learners (Brozo & Schmelzer, 1997).

The Students

The four students I highlight in my discussion of the Real Men unit are Ricardo, DeWayne, James, and Shantala. I included a female in this profile to make sure that teachers recognize the value of this unit (and others similar to it) for helping to clarify and transform girls' attitudes toward boys and men. Girls, especially those whose lives are filled with negative male images, are also in desperate need of positive male images. The following students who participated in the unit exemplify the worthwhile nature of our work.

Ricardo is a small-framed Hispanic American boy who lives with his mother, grandmother, and two younger sisters. His father moved back to Matamoros, Mexico, and rarely visits the family. Ricardo and his family live in a cramped two-bedroom apartment in Section 8 housing (federally subsidized). The apartment complex is notorious for high rates of teenage pregnancy, delinquency, and gang-related crime. Despite this atmosphere, Ricardo has managed to keep himself out of serious trouble, although other boys have begun pressuring him to join their gang. He has a desire to take on the roles of protector and supporter for the females in his life but is still too young and without the resources to really make this kind of contribution. In response to the dream of a better life by Jamal, Ricardo wrote in his journal:

> For my future I want to live in a reg. hous [sic] and I don't know where
> I want to work. And my dream is to travel around the world.

DeWayne is a tall, lanky African American boy with alert eyes and a wide smile. DeWayne told us at the beginning of the unit that he lived with his mother, father, brothers and sisters. Within a few weeks, however, we discovered that DeWayne had actually been living for some time with a grandfather who was trying to care for all the kids. The grandfather characterized DeWayne's father as a "crack head," although he was eager to figure out a way to move DeWayne and his siblings out of his household. DeWayne's journal response reflects his desire for a carefree lifestyle with no restrictions:

> I want to have a nice car. I would put the top back and wear my shades and cruise for miles and miles. Maybe even right out of Texas.

James is a handsome, streetwise African American. He was the only student in the class whose father, although not his mother, lived with him; however, James's father, a hairdresser, is often not around during critical after-school and early evening hours to supervise his son. James told us about coming home from school one afternoon and mindlessly punching the television's remote control only to discover that the television, the stereo, and other household appliances had been stolen by his drug-addicted aunt, who had broken in through a window earlier that day. James's journal entry concerning his future reflects his dreams to become a high roller, surrounded by wealth and glitter:

> My dream is to become a business owner and have lots of money and a lot of sports cars. I would like to live in a manshion [sic] in Las Vegas. The kind of job I would want will be a casino owner.

Shantala is a tall, athletic African American girl. She is 13 years old, and her mother lives in Houston, Texas, USA. As a little girl, Shantala was given to a woman who is not a family member. There is no father in the home, and Shantala does not know her real dad. She wrote the following about her dreams in her journal:

> What kind of future do I want? To be in the WNBA. In a big house. A good job, a job that pays a lot of money.

These four adolescents well represent the attitudes, desires, and life worlds of the seventh-grade classes. They are not unique in the sense that their home lives are not any better or worse than their 12 other classmates. Virtually all experience the daily challenges that come with inadequate housing, not having two parents in the home, and limited financial resources. These factors, as I have advanced in previous chapters, clearly place Ricardo, DeWayne, James, and Shantala at risk of failing to live out their dreams. We found, however, that by introducing them to activities and experiences designed to question masculine stereotypes spread by popular culture, these students showed remarkable depth of sensitivity and understanding. They also demonstrated a heightened degree of enthusiasm for reading, about males both good and bad, as well as crafting written and oral responses to what they were learning.

The Genesis for the Unit

My relationship with Patty dates back to graduate reading classes she had taken with me some 10 years ago. We discovered a mutual interest in creating learning environments for secondary students that broke the mold. Patty's keen and critical mind, her sensitivity to adolescents' desires and needs, and her vast reserve of active language strategies (rooted in her background in theater) made her an ideal collaborator. Her school had coincidentally been the site of other research I had conducted.

Teri had been an undergraduate student of mine, and I had not seen her for a few years until she was reintroduced to me during a teacher inservice workshop I had given at the same school. She had recently become a member of Patty's seventh-grade language arts team. When she showed up in one of my required reading classes for master's students, I immediately recognized in Teri another kindred spirit whose goals were to make learning for adolescents critical, stimulating, and personally meaningful.

By November, Patty, Teri, and I had agreed to teach a language unit for their seventh graders. Both Patty and Teri were well acquainted with my keen interest in boys' literacy development. They thought this should be the unit's focus because we shared concerns about masculinity and reading. By a twist of good fortune, they were teaching the same reading course in adjacent classrooms during fifth period. The class was for seventh graders who had difficulty reading, and not surprising, mostly boys made up these classes. By combining the sections, we were able to expose a larger group of males to our readings and activities while coordinating instruction as a team.

Planning the Unit

We focused on the goals of the project at our initial meetings. After considerable discussion we derived the following main thrusts for the Real Men unit:

- Use literature as a catalyst for critical explorations of masculinity.
- Critically explore images of violent and selfish masculinity in popular culture and media.
- Foster engaged reading and learning.

With these guidelines, we got down to the business of fleshing out a curriculum. We decided to devote the last 8 weeks of the school year, 2 days per week, to the Real Men unit, and that it would be taught by the three of us. We also agreed that, in addition to the use of magazine articles, essays, and stories dealing with masculinity, a young adult novel would be used as the students' core literature source.

Finding an adolescent novel that would be just right for these unique seventh graders would take some time. We wanted to be certain that whatever we used as the primary reading source would engage the students' imaginations throughout the 8 weeks. We were fortunate to be living in a city with a wonderful bookstore specializing exclusively in children's and young adult books. The bookseller, a former elementary school teacher, has been a good friend and invaluable resource to me and many teachers in the area. With her help, we selected Walter Dean Myers's *Scorpions* to anchor the unit. This book was chosen primarily because, similar to our students, the two main characters in the story are in seventh grade and are both African American and Hispanic American; furthermore, the events in the story take place in a Harlem neighborhood, where events are similar to the daily events that take place on the streets and alleys of Molina, Texas. We recognized the book's potential for providing our students with an excellent focus for critical exploration of masculinity, as it is perceived by adolescents of minority groups living in poverty and without fathers or other positive male role models. Here was a book that could speak intimately to our Molina youth, offering a counterpoint to the negative images they see—honorable forms of masculinity that they could explore concurrently through other readings and activities. Using a small research grant, I was able to purchase copies of *Scorpions* for each student participating in the Real Men unit.

Gradually, Patty, Teri and I began detailing the strategies we would use in the unit. We built our activities around events and characters from different chapters, striving to reveal how mass media, commercialism, and everyday experiences with other boys and men who are poor role models can distort aspects of masculinity.

The next phase of planning involved making decisions about and developing documentation methods to assess the degree to which we achieved our goals for the Real Men unit. We agreed that numerous data sources would provide vital information on our unit goals. These data sources are detailed in the following sections.

Responses to the "To Be a Man" Survey

We created the "To Be a Man" survey to have students reflect on statements based on issues and events from *Scorpions*. The students had to respond either *yes, no,* or *unsure* to the assertions about masculinity, particularly violent masculinity, inherent in each statement, then supply a reason for their choice. The survey, given to students before the readings began, served as a baseline for their attitudes on stereotypical masculinity and violence. (The results of Ricardo's, DeWayne's, James's, and Shantala's preunit surveys are highlighted in Figure 9.)

Teacher Anecdotal Logs

I have been involved in classroom-based research for many years, so I know that it is important for teachers to keep their own record of observations and feelings about their work. This documentation serves as a reflection on teaching, offering crucial feedback on teacher instruction and student learning. Throughout the unit, Patty, Teri, and I used our own written records of classroom events and our responses to them as a focus for weekly discussions. The process of testing our perceptions against the students' perceptions ultimately led to a deeper understanding of individual student behavior, as well as greater sensitivity to classroom dynamics as a whole.

Student Work and Unit Projects

Student projects revealed a great deal about their level of involvement in the strategies and activities that prompted these projects, as well as their evolving sense of masculine identity. Some examples of unit projects included movie posters, scene reenactments, clay figurines with descriptions, life-size posters of characters with descriptions, and a three-dimensional model of a setting in the story.

Compare-Contrast Essay

Students wrote a compare-contrast essay when they finished reading *Scorpions*. It was intended to elicit their ideas about how Jamal is similar to and different from a "real man." As an end-of-unit activity, we wanted to discover whether students could analyze the behavior of a boy who chooses a form of destructive masculinity by comparing it to the expected behavior of a male who expresses his masculinity in honorable ways.

Week One: Introductions and Predictions

Patty, Teri, and I concluded our book talk on *Scorpions* and handed out copies of the book while telling the class that the tragedy of handgun violence is only one aspect they can expect to read about in this novel. After the students had received their copies, they began thumbing through the pages to locate the

FIGURE 9
Sample Preunit Responses From "To Be a Man" Survey

1. When a man is being hassled by another man, he needs to fight to get the man to back off.
   Ricardo's response—"Yes."
   Ricardo's reason—"Because the guy will keep messing with him."
2. Men who walk away from fights are sissies.
   DeWayne's response—"Yes."
   DeWayne's reason—"When you got to fight, you got to fight."
3. Men need weapons like knives and guns to show how strong they are.
   James's response—"Unsure."
   James's reason—"Men should be able to have guns and knives."
4. You can't really be a man unless you are in a gang.
   Shantala's response—"Unsure."
   Shantala's reason—"You got to be really tough to be in a gang."
5. Men like to fight because that's just who they are.
   Ricardo's response—"Yes."
   Ricardo's reason—"We're stronger than girls, so we have to do the fighting."
6. Men who go to prison are real men.
   DeWayne's response—"Yes."
   DeWayne's reason—"My uncle knows this guy who was in prison because he killed someone, and he thinks he's cool."
7. If a man killed someone, other men would think he was really cool.
   James's response—"Yes."
   James's reason—"Where I live, you got to fight because people always messing with you."
8. Real men protect their families by fighting.
   Shantala's response—"Unsure."
   Shantala's reason—"If you don't want to get killed there you better be a man."
9. As soon as a boy turns 13, he needs a gun.
   Ricardo's response—"Yes."
   Ricardo's reason—"People know you're serious with a gun."
10. Sometimes being violent is the only way for a man to make others understand he means business.
    DeWayne's response—"Yes."
    DeWayne's reason—"I've seen it."

scene we had just simulated in our book talk, as well as to gain a sense of the book's length. Prior to our book talk, we had administered the "To Be a Man" survey, asking both male and female students to complete it honestly. I present examples of postunit survey responses later in the chapter.

Following the book talk, the three of us explained the goals of the unit. I said we would be exploring the consequences of good and bad decisions through the novel, listening and conversing with guest speakers, writing, sharing, and reflecting. The ultimate intent of the unit, we stressed, was to help the class better understand and appreciate positive aspects of masculinity, so as to guide them in their own decision making about who they wanted to be. I told the class when the unit was completed I wanted them to be able to recognize what a real man was. To this statement, James replied, just loud enough for me to hear, "I am a real man." The boys around him chuckled. I did not challenge him.

I led the students in a group brainstorm to discuss their attitudes, perceptions, and experiences related to masculinity. I used the "Television Man" and "Real Man" as the central images for two large webs, which I displayed on poster board. By using television's portrayals of men, I knew it would be easier to draw out the numerous stereotypes of masculine behavior from television-culture children. First, I asked students to turn to their neighbor, discuss what men on television are usually like, and jot down brief notes on these conversations. The class quickly fell into animated chatter about television personalities from sitcoms, commercials, sports teams, and music videos. When I opened the discussion to the entire class, nearly everyone was eager to provide input. Figure 10 illustrates the web brainstorm of some characteristics and images of the television man. James was quick to point out that they "have a lot of money...they gotta be rich." Elton said a television man "always has a good car and a good job." "They're good looking and dress in suits," intoned Maria (to the hissing of several boys). James, in his supercilious and blasé manner, offered, "TV guys are tough; they use weapons like guns and do expensive drugs." Lalo, who often spoke with a sense of higher moral conscience, said flatly, "TV men are disrespectful of women and the law." Shantala's characterization of a television man was, "They immature, they always fighting and drinking, and they players, you know, they mess around on they women." Her last statement brought a great burst of laughter from the guys, although they did not deny that Shantala's perceptions were accurate.

Overall, I was impressed with the class's ability to think critically about stereotypical portrayals of males on television. To contrast these negative images, I asked the class to help me create another brainstormed web (see Figure

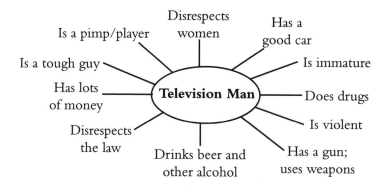

FIGURE 10
Web of Class Brainstorm of a Television Man

Is a pimp/player

Disrespects women

Has a good car

Is a tough guy

Is immature

Has lots of money

Television Man

Does drugs

Disrespects the law

Is violent

Drinks beer and other alcohol

Has a gun; uses weapons

11) based on real men. Students were once again asked to talk it over first with a partner before we shared our ideas with the class.

Ricardo began with, "A real man is loyal and honest...someone you can count on, you know, you can trust." These words have special importance because Ricardo's father had broken his promise to buy Ricardo a hunting rifle after Ricardo raised his grades. This is a dad who does not live in the same household with his son and has never been the kind of adult male Ricardo could ever "count on." John, a strapping, brooding 13-year-old who also lives without a father, added "He's gotta keep his word." Willis and DeWayne agreed that a good man should "have an education." Shantala rejoined, "A good man dresses nice and is polite. He opens a door for a woman, you know, shows respect." "He needs to have a steady relationship," stated James, whose father's womanizing had been a regular source of annoyance for the cool seventh grader. He recounted on several occasions how for each new "squeeze" his dad would bring home, James was expected to act as though she might become his next "mom." Adding a last characteristic of a good man to our web, Tony suggested, "He should be able to find a pretty good job and keep it, so he can take care of his family and have a car." Tony's absent father had totaled his mother's car, which she depended on to go to the store, doctor's office, and the social service office. His father had neither insurance nor resources for acquiring another vehicle.

It became clear to Patty, Teri, and me that the seventh graders' perceptions of the qualities of real men reflected their own negative experiences with

FIGURE 11
Web of Class Brainstorm of a Real Man

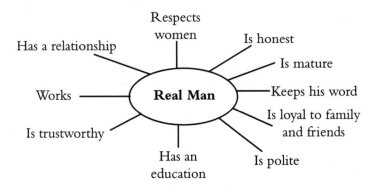

estranged fathers and other adult males. Fathers, and even mothers, behaving poorly was all too common in the students' daily lives.

Following the brainstorming activities, I shared a My Bag to give the students a fuller personal introduction. I included items that reflected both my traditional interests and hobbies, as well as my devotion to personal and social literacy and my commitment to my family. Students were very inquisitive about each item; while passing around photographs of my daughter and wife, students wanted to know their names, ages, favorite things to do, schools attended, as well as how long I'd been married, if I had any other children, why I had only one, and so forth. The class showed particular interest in the various books I pulled out of my bag. The greatest response came when I passed around a textbook that I had authored. DeWayne was amazed that I had written "such a thick book!" We told students they would have the opportunity to put together and share their own My Bags over the next couple of class sessions, which clearly pleased most class members.

Before the period ended, we invited questions about the day's activities. Students were eager to know more about the novel, barraging us with questions about the characters and the plot. We did our best to respond with answers that revealed little yet continued to pique their interest in *Scorpions*.

At the beginning of the next session, I was greeted by the students with smiles, nods, a "little skin," and letters of introduction that they had written. That night I lay in bed reading about their lives and felt hollow inside. The comfort of my new four-bedroom suburban home, although a mere 5 miles from Molina, must seem as far away and unattainable to them as Park Avenue appears to the characters of Jamal and Tito from their Harlem tenement. The crush of poverty, absent dads, and the dangers and discomforts that come with these conditions emerged from the still awkward hands of our young students' letters. Although heartrending, their stories reinforced the legitimacy of my work with them. Consider how James described the way things are on the streets where he lives:

> One thing I do not like about my neighborhood is everybody is trying to kill everyone. What I mean by this is you can be walking down the road and a car is coming...they will get in front of you and they won't move until you get close to them, and then they will move. Or they would carry guns or knifes [sic] around and threaten you, and the only thing you can do is run.

In her letter, Shantala included what had happened the afternoon and night before:

> I came home and my sister went in my room and pulled everything out of my dresser and my closet and messed up my bed, and I told my mom and she said don't worry about it and they will clean it up and they never did so I had to do it. And after I finisted [sic] I went in the kichen [sic] and their [sic] were no food left for me, and my dad made it worstest [sic] because he came over and it never got better.

Among the items in DeWayne's letter was this small but revealing anecdote from the day before:

> I was riding my bike and ran into a car. That was backing up and I hit it and I flew over the back end of the car. I hit the grown [sic] hard. Everybody was laughing at me, and they didn't help me up or nothing....

Finally, Ricardo's letter made me realize that the fiction we had created in our book talk is perhaps too real for some students. His words made my skin tingle:

> I could relate to this book talk because it happened to my friend. He got shot sitting on the swings in the park. He was sitting on the swing

with a gun in his pocket with the clip hanging out, and a gang drove by and saw it...he got shoot [*sic*] with a 357 magnam [*sic*].

The students' letters reminded me that countless boys enter school classrooms each day wearing the psychic and for some, physical scars of their harsh worlds. That is why we allowed the students in this unit the safety and freedom to interrogate their own and others' conceptions of masculinity, look critically at pop culture images of maleness, and consider other possibilities of masculinity characterized by positive archetypal male traits, such as honor, commitment, and intellectual prowess.

We spent most of this day getting through the first couple of chapters in *Scorpions*. Instead of round-robin oral reading, we employed a simplified Readers Theatre, assigning the roles of narrator, Jamal, Tito, Mama, Sassy, and Mack. We had created simple stage flats (recall Patty's theater background) of a cityscape on large sheets of poster board and attached them to one of the classroom walls. Here students took positions for reading their parts and used simple gesturing. We rotated the male roles, so every boy in class had a chance to participate. Shantala and Maria, our only girls, traded off taking on the persona of either Mama or Sassy.

I was surprised to find students enthusiastically embracing their roles. I attributed this to the style of teaching the seventh graders had become used to with teachers like Patty and Teri, who exploited the theatricality of different novels and stories by having students participate in reenactments, impromptu dramatic interpretations, and Readers Theatre.

At the end of the period, students had to summarize what they had learned and make predictions in their journals about the action in subsequent chapters. Ricardo predicted the following in his journal:

> Tommorow Jamal will probably join a gang. The gang he will get in is called the Scorpions. After he is in the gang he will sell drugs to buy a VCR and get his brother out of jail.

James speculated in his entry:

> What I think will happen is that Jamal is going to pressure Dwayne to join a gang, and Dwayne will. When he gets in the gang, he will start selling drugs. Dwayne will be making all the money, and he won't give it to Jamal. Jamal will kill him and brag about it.

DeWayne guessed that

> The problem will be about selling drugs. I think that Jamal will have pressure to join a gang. I think Jamal will join the gang and take a gun everywhere he goes. Jamal will probably kill someone and then go bragging to other people. He'll end up in prison like his brother.

The students' predictions reflect an uncomfortable level of familiarity with situations involving drugs, violence, gangs, and the criminal justice system. The students projected scenarios for the characters in *Scorpions* that approximated the lives of people who might live next door, down the street, or around the corner. These personal connections with the book's action and themes were what Patty, Teri, and I had hoped to achieve by using this novel. Another reason we chose the book was to have it serve as a reference for dishonorable forms of masculinity; that is, the central characters, seventh graders themselves, behave in ways we wanted our students to evaluate and ultimately disavow.

Week Two: Story Impression Writing and Skits

A strategy I found to work extremely well with our seventh graders as a prereading motivator for the next chapter in *Scorpions* was story impression writing. Before students gathered their copies of the book, which were kept in a bookcase in the room, I wrote several words on the board. These words came directly from the pages we were about to read, and I asked students to use them in a short paragraph describing what was about to happen in the book. These story impression words helped the students form an impression of the action in the story, and their writing about that action served as a prediction of what they thought would happen next. As students read, they compared the actual events with their predictions. The aim of this strategy, then, is to hold students' interest for the duration of the reading and encourage careful reading.

The story impression words I gave the class in the order in which they appear in the chapter were *Jamal, bet, running, principal's office, Tito and Jamal, boat basin,* and *yacht.* Then, I helped students find a partner and directed them to write journal entries using each of these words. Students got to work quickly and fell into animated discussion with their coauthors as they crafted their entries. When they finished, I asked the students to share what they had written with the class. This gives all students a chance to ruminate on plot possibilities before learning what actually happens. Here is Ricardo and John's story impression:

Jamal and another student make a *bet* for money or something. Someone sees it and goes *running* to the *principal's office* to tell. *Tito and Jamal* get kicked out of school and go down to the *boat basin*. They sneak onto a *yacht*.

DeWayne and James's story impression was by far the most elaborate and interesting; however, it revealed a knowledge about petty gambling and thievery that made me and the teachers uncomfortable.

One day while *Jamal* was *running* to school he saw some kids in the back of the school rolling dice. They *bet* Jamal $5 that he couldn't roll a seven. Jamal said yes because he wanted to make some money to help his mama pay for Randy's new trial. As soon as Jamal picked up the dice, the principal came. All the other kids ran and Jamal was stuck with the dice. The principal told him to come to the office after first period, Jamal said alright. When Jamal went to the *principal's office*, the principal said you should be suspended for betting and bringing dice to school. Jamal denied it and said the dice weren't his. The principal didn't know Jamal was telling the truth so he suspended him and made him leave. Jamal met up with Tito after school and walked down to the *boat basin*. Jamal asked Tito to look out while he snuck into a *yacht* to try to find something to hock so they could get some money for Randy's new trial.

My goal with this strategy was to create a heightened sense of eagerness in the students to read. As we read, I asked students to indicate whether they found corroboration for their story impressions.

When we concluded reading the chapter, I directed the class's attention to one of Jamal's statements from the chapter. In this chapter, the reader learns something important about Jamal that Patty, Teri, and I decided would serve as a critical source of reflection on how males should behave in the face of taunting. In the story, Dwayne, a tall seventh grader, is egging Jamal on and seems to have it in for him. About Dwayne's persistent harassment, Jamal thinks, "The only way to deal with somebody stupid like Dwayne...was to punch him out" (Myers, 1990, p. 60). We formed groups of three students, presented the students with this quote, and directed them to create short skits showing how interpersonal conflict can be resolved without fighting. Felipé, James, and Maria's skit was typical of the performances by the class. Felipé introduced the scene as follows:

Felipé: I'm asking a girl [Maria smiles coyly] to go to the movies with me, and this guy [James nods his head] says I'm messin' around with his girlfriend. So....

Felipé:	Hey, Maria, you want to go to the movies with me?
Maria:	What's playin'?
Felipé:	It's a cool movie called *The Road to El Dorado*.
Maria:	Okay.

[James walks up, pulls Maria to the side, and confronts Felipé.]

James:	[with hostility] You messin' with my girl?
Felipé:	I wasn't tryin' to...
James:	Where you two goin'?
Felipé and Maria:	We're goin' to the movies. You wanna come?
James:	Okay.

When the skit concluded, the class discussed how the three students were able to diffuse a potentially volatile situation by simply including James in their plans. James was angry and suspicious at first but was immediately calmed by Felipé and Maria's invitation to join them. In this way, James could see that Felipé and Maria were not attempting to conceal anything from him.

Another skit, however, was difficult for the class to accept as "something they would do." In the scene, John and Noe meet up after a football game; John challenges Noe to a fight. Noe walks away. John goads him by calling him a "sissy" and threatens to tell everyone that he "chickened out." In spite of these taunts, Noe keeps walking away until John eventually gives up. The male students could not believe the honorable way was to let John get away with his name-calling and threats. Noe best summed up this sentiment when he said, "He don't bother me in here, but if we were on the street, I'd jump him." With that, the two boys engaged in a mock fistfight.

Week Three: Anticipation Guide and Compare-Contrast Activity

I began the third week by taking the class through an anticipation guide for the chapter we were about to read. This strategy involves presenting students with statements related to the text they will read that day and asking them to guess whether the statements are true or false. This strategy increases students' interest and their desire to read the text closely to find support for prereading guesswork. Usually as students read the text, they refer to their anticipation guide statements for possible connections. This time, however, students could amend their initial hunches if they found that they were incorrect, although they had to be prepared to defend their pre- and postreading indications. Figure 12 shows the anticipation guide I presented the seventh graders. By taking a position on each of these statements about possible plot twists, the students were much more focused as we read Chapter 6, periodically checking their anticipation guides for accuracy.

After rechecking students' anticipation guide responses in a class discussion, I pulled another line from the chapter to use in a compare-contrast activity of males who make good decisions and males who do not. In the book, Jamal, reflecting on his situation, reveals his sense of despair over the inevitability of a future marked by crime. He thinks, "If you were part of the life they were living, then after a while you did something and the police came and got you" (Myers, 1990, p. 117).

I asked students to first discuss these lines with their neighbors and think about whether people have control over their behavior and whether people (male and female, young and old) have the choice to make good decisions or bad decisions. After a few minutes, Patty, Teri, and I led the class in a mini-debate. I was stunned to discover how many boys held sentiments similar to Jamal's. For instance, James commented that police stop people in cars just because they are black. Armando recounted a harrowing night when police with guns barged through his apartment's front door, believing the apartment was a crack house. They were all watching television, he said, and he was so scared he could hardly breathe.

We followed up the discussion by asking students to work in pairs to find pictures in magazines of males behaving in both admirable and reprehensible ways. Students made two columns on a piece of poster board and placed their pictures in the appropriate column labeled either "Positive" or

---

FIGURE 12
Anticipation Guide for Chapter 6 of *Scorpions*

Prereading			Postreading	
T	F	1. Jamal and Tito throw the gun into the river.	T	F
T	F	2. Tito shoots the gun in the park.	T	F
T	F	3. Jamal lies to Mama about getting in a fight.	T	F
T	F	4. Dwayne tells the principal about the gun.	T	F
T	F	5. The police arrest Jamal at his apartment.	T	F
T	F	6. Dwayne fights Jamal again.	T	F

"Negative." Not surprisingly, many students included a picture of a man and woman together, happy and in love, as positive. For example, Ricardo and John found a photo of smiling newlyweds and wrote beneath it, "This is a good man because he loves his wife." Lester and DeWayne also placed a picture of a bride and groom in their Positive column with the caption, "Is marrieing [sic] a woman he loves."

Other themes of honorable male behavior that the students chose included scenes of family life where the father is present. The caption of James and Felipé's picture of a father throwing a baseball around with his three sons read, "Good decision because the dad is spending time with his kids." Shantala and Maria also had a picture of a man holding his baby. They wrote beside it, "He is spending time with his child." Lester and DeWayne chose to portray positive male behavior through men who had jobs, particularly those with skilled professions. They glued a photo of a group of astronauts to their poster and wrote simply, "They have a good job." James and Felipé showed a man standing in the foreground with a proprietary look on his face, and a long cotton field and harvester behind him. They wrote underneath the picture, "Has a job and is a farmer."

Negative portrayals of men invariably involved guns and knives. There were several pictures of men and boys buying, holding, and shooting handguns and rifles. One ominous photo on Noe and John's poster was of a big man with his face in shadow; he was holding a pistol and his unbuttoned shirt revealed a long red scar running the length of his torso. They had written beside it, "He been cut so he have a gun." There were also pictures of men in prison garb. Shantala and Maria had a series of faces of infamous men, such as John Wayne Gacey ("He killed over 30 boys"), O.J. Simpson ("He killed his wife"), and even President Clinton ("He slept with another woman").

This activity and the minidebate showed Patty, Teri, and me that the students could distinguish between the media's portrayal of positive and negative male images. Even though they had been exposed to many negative male role models in their own lives, similarly to Jamal, they had definite notions about what constituted positive and negative behavior of boys and men.

Week Four: University Field Trip

This was a special week for all of us. The seventh graders were given a field trip to the university to explore the campus, and most importantly, to spend time with my secondary content area reading undergraduates. The hour and a half was chock-full of activities, readings, and strategy demonstrations that kept everyone excited and involved.

Although only half a dozen miles from the junior high, this was the first time any of these adolescents had been on the campus of Texas A&M University in Corpus Christi. I watched with delight as the seventh graders gazed in awe at the large buildings and manicured grounds. The campus is actually quite small and, because of hurricane codes, none of the buildings are over three stories. This field trip, nevertheless, was nothing short of an adventure for kids whose experiences are so circumscribed by their families' limited resources.

First, the students were to be guests in my undergraduate class. My undergraduate students had been prepared for their arrival, and as soon as the seventh graders entered the classroom, the university students introduced themselves to a seventh grader. These students paired off and found a place to sit and visit. When everyone was settled, I introduced Patty and Teri. Patty reviewed what her students planned to do and gave directions to begin the first activity.

We began the class with companion introductions as a method of getting to know one another (see Chapter 4). Each junior high-graduate student pair went to the front of the room and introduced each other using the companion introduction strategy.

The next strategy began with the seventh graders assembling chairs in the middle of the room, where each took a seat. James suddenly stood up and said, "Jamal gets the job at Mr. Gonzalez's grocery store." Popping up right after him was Maria, who added, "He works after school and on weekends." She is followed by Noe, who contributed, "Jamal got paid after his first week and was real proud." John jumped up next and said, "Then Indian and Angel from the Scorpions came into the store, and Jamal got fired."

The students were demonstrating for my undergraduates a strategy known as *popcorn review*. Any student can begin the review by "popping" up to state a detail from the story. This detail begins a sequence of events, which entails the next person who pops up to correctly supply the following event and so on. Like popping corn, it is the random order in which students stand up to provide a brief description of the story's next event that gives the strategy its name. My undergraduate students were impressed, and we briefly discussed how they could use this strategy when teaching in science, history, English, and virtually any other content area. The seventh graders invited the undergraduates to take their places and demonstrate a popcorn review of their new learning. My undergraduates who were kinesiology majors decided to give it a try and showed the rest of us how they could use the strategy to review bone and muscle connections. For instance, the first student stood up and said "radius," the next student said "ulna," the next "tarsal," and so on.

The following activity was the most enjoyable because it combined humor with review. Imagine a group of four students standing in a row in the front of the classroom. Each is wearing a long, white lab coat and a Groucho Marx mask with the fake plastic glasses, big nose, and mustache. Here is the context for the strategy known as Professor Know-It-All. The sight of these students in their ridiculous costumes was enough to ensure that all of us were paying attention. A seventh grader sitting among us asked the Know-It-Alls, "Where did Jamal hide the gun?" With this, the "professors" huddled in consultation, then turned to the class. They provided an answer in a complete sentence with each student saying one word of the sentence, and the last student saying the appropriate end punctuation. To the preceding question, the student-professors replied,

DeWayne:	Jamal
Ricardo:	hid
John:	the
Shantala:	gun
DeWayne:	under
Ricardo:	the
John:	cushions
Shantala:	in
DeWayne:	the
Ricardo:	couch
John:	period.

This group of Professor Know-It-Alls fielded several more questions before a new team was asked to take over. This form of review and the popcorn review takes a process that is usually boring and gives it a fresh, humorous twist. By reviewing story content or other subject matter in these ways, students prompt and monitor each other instead of passively waiting for the teacher to ask questions and call on someone for an answer. Giving students the responsibility for review creates conditions in which they can become more invested in the learning process; it also increases their level of engagement with the strategies.

When class concluded, several of my students and I accompanied Patty and Teri's seventh graders to the university student center for drinks and snacks. This extra time gave the adolescents a chance to fraternize with college students and talk about campus life.

Based on residual conversation with the undergraduates and the seventh graders, that afternoon was a rousing success. One never knows the full impact of these kinds of encounters on either solidifying in a 20-year-old preservice teacher's mind that he or she chose a well-suited profession or exciting a 13-year-old's imagination to eventually realize a dream of attending college. Comments made to me by my university class, however, suggested a new resolve about teaching. One of my students remarked, "I really enjoyed those West Oso kids. I know that's a tough place to teach, but it would be really rewarding to work with students like that." The seventh graders also used words like *cool* and *neat* to characterize their field trip to the university campus. Felipé asked me, "You think I could get a scholarship to go there?," and I overheard James tell Noe, "I could be doin' that in 6 years."

Week Five: Columbine Tragedy Strikes at Our Core

> Dear Jamal,
>
> I know your [*sic*] having some hard times but just solve it not by violence, comprimise [*sic*]. You don't need a gun to protect yourself; just have God in your heart. So just throw the gun away, okay.
>
> Your friend,
> Tito

The preceding letter was actually written by Ricardo after we prompted students with the following question (which we asked them to respond to in their journals): If you were Tito, what would you say in a letter to Jamal about what he should do with the gun? From the time Jamal receives the handgun from Mack, *Scorpions* deals with Jamal's dilemma about whether to use the gun in a way he thinks his older brother Randy would respect or get rid of it. Javier responded,

> Dear Jamal,
>
> I'm sorry I'm convicing [*sic*] you to throw away the gun, but I dont want you to get heart [*sic*], but now I think you should keep the gun for pretaction [*sic*].
>
> Tito

With the issue over the handgun coming to a critical point in which Jamal either gives the gun back to Mack and disavows membership in the

Scorpions or continues to hold on to it until real tragedy befalls him, we decided the opportunity was ripe for an extensive and critical exploration of gun violence among young people. Just as we were initiating discussion and activities to help the class better understand the seriousness of this topic, Ms. Guerra, principal of West Oso, announced over the intercom, "Teachers and students, I have terrible news to report to you. In Littleton, Colorado, in a high school called Columbine High, two teenagers have just shot and killed several of their classmates and they have killed themselves. I would like all of you to join me in a moment of silence for the victims. Thank you."

The news stunned all of us. It was one thing to use a fake handgun as a prop for our book talk, to talk about gun violence in our streets, homes, and schools, but it was something entirely different to have that reality thrust upon us in such a horrifying way that day. Patty immediately turned on the television. We spent the rest of the period watching the ongoing news coverage of the chilling events in Columbine.

Patty, Teri, and I lingered in a stupor after the bell rang, and the students shuffled out of the room. We could hardly bring ourselves to talk. At that moment, our lessons seemed so trivial beside this palpable tragedy of horrific proportions. For me, it brought on an uncomfortable, almost eerie feeling of déjà vu. Five years earlier, I was in this same school doing a lesson with a group of eighth graders when Ms. Guerra interrupted class activities to announce the shooting death of Selena, who was perhaps the brightest and most promising Tejano music star ever, and whose parents still lived in Molina, which made her death especially devastating to West Oso students.

Late that night, I called Patty to commiserate and seek fortification. I wondered if we should not close down shop, if our efforts were too insignificant to matter, if mere words like the Reagan-era mantra "just say no" could ever be enough? Could this really make a difference in the lives of disturbed youth or youth living in grinding poverty with out-of-control adults who could not provide any moral or behavioral compass for their children? Patty finally brought me out of my despicable state of self-pity by reminding me that our seventh graders were precisely the group in greatest need of our message of honorable masculinity. Incidents of gun violence, although increasing among white suburban youth, occur overwhelmingly in nonwhite, economically depressed communities like those where our students and families reside. She also reminded me that gun violence was hardly foreign to our students. Many of our students, like James who revealed the random shooting death of his best friend at the hands of local gang members, were already well acquainted with gun violence, crack houses, gang wars, and deadbeat dads. The Columbine incident would not change that. What might change that, she added, was our work in sensitizing boys to positive male images; thus, even if we gird one young man with the confidence to stay clear of gangs and drugs, we might consider our work to have been a success.

With a new resolve, I began the next class session with a debate activity. The debate forced the students to focus on critical issues related to gun violence. I divided the class into two large groups, giving each instructions to adopt the perspective we were giving them and build an argument in defense of that perspective. The different perspectives were as follows:

Perspective 1—You are a group of owners of gun stores. You have always followed the law, making sure the guns you sell go to people with proper identification and permits. A group of citizens wants to close your store because it feels your stores make it easy for criminals to get and use guns in crimes and homicides. Be prepared to defend your right to operate a gun store.

Perspective 2—You are a group of citizens who wants to close local gun stores. You believe that because these stores make guns too easy to buy, guns get into the hands of criminals. All of you have had loved ones killed by criminals with handguns. Be prepared to argue why the gun store owners should close their shops or leave town.

We reminded students that the handgun in Jamal's possession could have begun its journey at a gun store, then to a law-abiding citizen, then to a criminal in a robbery, then to a pawn shop dealer, then to a gang member like Mack, and finally to Jamal.

Students were directed to first brainstorm ideas in support of their perspectives by working in pairs. This way, all students were likely to have something to contribute when we opened the discussion to the larger group. We prodded Perspective 2 students to think about what they knew of guns from personal experiences. We challenged students working with Perspective 1 to consider a person's legal right to sell and buy guns, and whether that meant they should be held responsible for someone else's reckless use of a gun. As the groups consolidated their arguments, we asked that each select a spokesperson. Afterward, all students were told to be ready to join in the discussion.

The debate began slowly as each side stated its position. As spokesperson for the gun shop owners, DeWayne said, "No one could put them out of business just because they didn't like guns." He went on to say, "We don't like that people use guns to kill other people, but it's not our fault." As spokesperson for the antigun citizens, James countered, "We don't want to have to put you out of business either, but it's your guns that killed my son, so we don't have no choice." Members of each group angrily joined in after hearing this statement. The students argued over whether guns or people shooting the guns were responsible for murder when guns were used. James even used the incident at Columbine to further his argument for the citizens.

After nearly everyone made at least one contribution to the debate, the dialogue wound down. We then asked group members to spend a few minutes talking among themselves about ways to reduce gun violence, assuming gun manufacturers and shops are not eliminated. Patty wrote students' ideas on the board as they shouted them out. The list of ideas included insightful recommendations:

- Parents should watch their kids, so they do not mess with guns.
- Parents should not leave guns lying around the house.
- Adults should help kids stay away from gangs because gang members always have guns.
- People who sell guns should be helped to make money some other way.
- Kids who bring guns to school should be kicked out for good.
- If kids kill someone with their parents' gun, the parents should have to go to jail too.

I reflected on our students' suggestions for reducing gun violence and wondered if any of them would fall victim to a criminal's bullets. Every day in the United States, children and young adults are killed by guns in homicides and in either purposeful or accidental self-infliction (Garbarino, 1999). These statistics rise precipitously in streets and alleys, tenements, and abandoned buildings of our inner cities, where poverty is high, education levels are low, and positive adult role models are scarce—situations similar to the lives of our seventh graders. Further increasing the chances that these boys will become victims of gun violence are the statistics cited in the Introduction, which indicate that 95% of all murders are committed by males, and males make up 70% of all homicide victims (Garbarino, 1999). Would James, for instance, one day find himself mistaken for a gang member and be gunned down while walking to the park? Would DeWayne awake one morning to find desperate crack heads pilfering his apartment and be forever silenced by a handgun? These are unthinkable notions, but always on my mind as I slap hands with the guys exiting the classroom after another engaging lesson.

Week Six: Preparing for the Unit Projects

As we approached the conclusion of *Scorpions*, Patty and Teri began preparing the students for their unit projects. The students' options included movie posters, scene reenactments, clay figurines with descriptions, life-size posters of characters with descriptions, and a three-dimensional model of a setting in the story. Patty and Teri also invited students to propose their own projects, and at least a few students followed up on the offer. For instance, DeWayne asked if he could do an interview with a gang member or crack dealer (people from his neigborhood that he knew) and compare their lives with the life of either Randy or Mack from *Scorpions*. Teri was concerned about the liability for DeWayne's safety if something went wrong, especially if it were discovered that DeWayne was fulfilling a school assignment. I suggested that he might be able to get the information about a gang member through a secondhand source, perhaps a former gang member. DeWayne told us he could ask his uncle who had always said he used to be in a gang. James, meanwhile, wondered if he could match words from popular rap songs to the novel's main characters. Patty thought this was an excellent way to demonstrate appreciation of character and gave immediate consent. Noe, the student in our unit with the most advanced knowledge about computers, proposed a PowerPoint presentation with photos and graphics that covered the main story line. Although not an uncritical devotee of computer technology, Patty did encourage her students to use this medium for creating interesting language-based projects, so Noe's idea was also given approval.

Once Patty, Teri, and I received commitments from every student to do a particular project, we stocked the classroom with necessary resources, such as poster board and paper, markers, variously colored clay bars, shoe boxes, and other material to help students complete the assignment. Part of each class session was reserved for work on the unit projects.

One of the activities the teachers and I used during this time involved revisiting the pop culture images of boys and men. I brought in a dozen or so copies of *Men's Health*, *Esquire*, and *GQ* magazines, Patty collected an assortment of teen music magazines and local newspapers, and Teri gathered photograph books of movies and films. We distributed these sources to students and had them pair up to review them. Each pair of students was given a wide piece of poster board and instructed to divide it into four columns. In the left column (labeled "Male Images"), we asked students to keep a running list of how these magazines and books portray males (for instance, what the males are doing and what they look like). In the second column (labeled "Interpretations"), students were to write what these male images suggested to them (for example, physical strength, control, money, power, violence, authority with weapons, lady's man, and so on). In the third column (labeled "*Scorpions*'s Males"), students were to briefly describe similarities between boys from *Scorpions* and the male images in the first column. In the fourth and last column (labeled "My

Behavior"), we asked the students to indicate their own behaviors or actions that coincided with male images in the first column. Before the period ended, the pairs shared their work with the rest of the class.

Exploring media portrayals of boys and men would appear to be an effective approach to take to help young men think critically about how gender stereotypes are promulgated by commercial advertisers. Su Langker (1995), a teacher of media studies in Sydney, Australia, reports on her success with junior high students as they deconstruct advertisers' images to reveal manipulations of young men. The students discovered that ads were replete with ethnic and gender stereotypes, portrayals of males as sexual objects, and messages that reinforce popular notions of the expendable man (such as, fighting machine, soldier of fortune, and so on).

Felipé and Ricardo were the first to share their work with the class. Felipé held up one end of the poster board as Ricardo held the other, and they explained what they had written in each of the columns. The first image of a man in their Male Images column was Clint Eastwood as Dirty Harry, which was taken from one of the movie books. In the photograph, Harry is holding his trademark long-barrel magnum with a caption that read, "Go ahead, make my day." Ricardo said,

> This is a man who thinks he's tough because he's got a gun. Mack and Jamal think they're tough too because they scare people with guns. Jamal scared Dwayne when he pointed it at him when they were fighting. I shot a rifle when I went hunting with my grandfather. I never pointed it at anyone.

Felipé and Ricardo both said they never shot a pistol, although they had both handled one.

DeWayne and John shared their poster and described an entry across all four columns. DeWayne explained,

> Here's a picture of Charles Barkley, and it say next to him, "You gotta have protection." He so big he don't need no protection, so if you ain't big like him, you gotta get protection somewhere. In *Scorpions*, Mack says the same thing to Jamal when he give him the gun.

At this point, John broke in to say something about the last column. "My little brother, Carlos, was gettin' picked on by these older boys, so I had to walk him to school and tell them that if they messed with Carlos I would get 'em. They didn't touch him after that."

Shantala and Maria, who often worked together as they were the only females in class, had a different take on the assignment. Their poster identified several images of men either driving fast, expensive sports cars or in the company of adoring women. Describing one of the male images on their poster, Maria said,

> There's this man sitting at the table with a real pretty girl and some fancy food there. It say underneath "impress her with do-it-yourself gourmet." We thought this guy is only a player [slang for someone who acts slick around women]...he not cookin' to be nice but to get this girl 'cause she ain't got no ring on or nothin'. He just a phony. We couldn't think of nothin' from *Scorpions* like this, but my mom told me my dad used to do stuff like that, you know, then he left us anyway.

James and Noe found a picture of a man in a red convertible. The man was wearing sunglasses and had a very attractive woman sitting next to him. James explained,

> He was going real fast because the road is all fuzzy and everything, so we thought guys like him have cool cars they can get pretty girls with. In the book no one has any money, but everyone tryin' to act cool anyway. There ain't no girls in there except Mama and Sassy. On my street, guys in low riders act real cool and always have girls hangin' around 'em.

The next opportunity Patty, Teri, and I had to reflect on that day's activities, we agreed that the students seemed to have a fairly critical understanding of the spurious nature of mass media's images of males. Talking about false men is one thing; however, avoiding the everyday traps that entice men to behave in false ways is something entirely different. This is also true for the two females in our class. It might be easy for Maria and Shantala to say to their teachers and fellow students that men who do things to impress women may have dishonorable motives. Will they, however, be able to resist the wiles of an insincere man? Young girls in Maria's and Shantala's neighborhoods are getting pregnant at alarming rates, with little expectation or hope of the fathers sticking around to offer financial and emotional support. What does this say about Maria's and Shantala's futures?

We concluded our reflective session by ironing out the details on the end-of-unit activity—a school party to celebrate positive masculinity. It was only 2 weeks away. I had made arrangements with numerous male friends and colleagues to attend the party and share their personal feelings about being both men and readers. Patty and Teri were attempting to invite the students' fathers but held little hope that they would show up; after all, only James lived with his dad, and his father worked during the day. Teri would make arrangements for refreshments. Our agenda included teacher introductions, brief presentations by the male guests, one-on-one visits between students and guests, and student presentations of their projects, each of which would be displayed. Patty, Teri, and I also agreed to re-administer the "To Be a Man" survey after the party instead of at the book's conclusion.

Week Seven: End-of-Book Journal Entry

Students worked busily on their unit projects as they finished the last couple of chapters of *Scorpions*. Right after we read aloud the last word of the story, Patty asked students to open their journals and write a letter to Walter Dean Myers, telling him what they had learned as a result of reading his book. Ricardo wrote,

> Dear Walter Dean Myers,
>
> By reading your book named "Scorpions" I learned that life has many osticels [*sic*] like gangs, drugs, and other things. In the story Jamal is asked if he wants to be in a gang that his brother Randy was in. A friend of Randy's was named Mack and gave Jamal a gun. Just like in this story, I may or may not be asked to join a gang. But I am going to be on track and won't pick the same decission [*sic*] that Jamal had picked.
>
> Your reader, Ricardo

DeWayne reveals a very different reaction in his letter. His words left us all with the sinking feeling that despite what we had done in the unit, despite the message of honorable masculinity that pervaded the unit, despite the school's intolerance of fights and other violence, the logic of "street justice" may prevail for some of these kids.

> Dear Mr. Myers,
>
> I liked your book. I'm glad you had Jamal keep the gun. Dwayne could have messed with him again. The next time Dwayne might have a gun and try to scare Jamal and then Jamal could just pull out his gun and shoot Dwayne. Jamal needed the gun so the next time he go [*sic*] to the Scorpions hideout and a man tries to mess with him, he can either shoot the man or shoot at the man's ear.
>
> Your reader, DeWayne

The seventh graders pressed the issue of the surprise ending. Everyone sensed that Jamal's decision not to give the gun back to Mack or throw it in the river would lead to nothing but trouble. Jamal agrees to meet with the Scorpions in a remote area of the park late one night in what seems to be a bold statement, rejecting any thoughts that Jamal will be walking in his brother Randy's footsteps. Despite Tito's entreaties, he refuses to take the gun with him. This leads readers to conclude that if anyone gets shot, Jamal will not be the perpetrator. Two shots do pierce the air that night in the middle of a violent confrontation between Jamal and two members of the Scorpions. The students eagerly finished the last pages to find out which character had been holding the gun that fired those shots.

Week Eight: Real Men Finale

Although it all seemed to be over far too quickly, the unit's finale had arrived. The teachers and I had set up for the party in the back of the cafeteria. Student posters adorned the walls, and clay figurines and three-dimensional models covered a long table. Another table held several copies of *Scorpions* and a variety of student work created during the unit. Punch, cake, and cookies covered a third big table.

When I arrived, Patty pulled me aside and told me softly that Ricardo would not be joining us today because he was suspended from school. She handed me a folder and said, "Read this." I tucked it into my briefcase. Later that morning, I opened the folder Patty had handed me, which held two pages of her project notes. I began reading and found that Ricardo apparently had been a lookout for a friend of his who had been caught stealing money from a teacher's desk. Soon after, Ricardo was in trouble again for hitting a boy in the jaw. His home life was not good either. Both his father and sister were in jail, and his grandmother, with whom he lives, recently became ill. Patty spoke with Ricardo about this incident and discovered that Ricardo thought he had been right to hit that boy.

Patty tried to reason with Ricardo by speaking about Jamal's actions in *Scorpions* and connecting Ricardo's actions to Jamal's. She asked Ricardo whether Jamal had been right to pull a gun and if Jamal could go to jail for his actions. Ricardo responded just as Patty thought he would, because Ricardo knew Jamal's actions were wrong and knew the consequences Jamal could face because of these actions. She ended their conversation by asking Ricardo,

Patty: So do you really think hitting that boy was the right thing to do?

Ricardo: [After a long pause] No, I guess not....

Patty: What could you have done?

Ricardo: Told you or another teacher, or just ignored him....

Ricardo's behavior represents the difficulties of helping young men adopt new expressions of masculinity, which is a challenge everyone faces when going against the grain of popular images of masculinity. Envisioning new images of masculinity was particularly challenging with the children of Molina because of their familiarity with the violent masculinity that dominates their community and lives.

Patty did, however, seem to get through at some level with Ricardo. One of the more challenging boys in the seventh grade and growing up in circumstances that will require every bit of his willpower to surmount, he was brought to notice parallels between his troubles and those of Jamal. Ricardo seemed to understand that punching a classmate was a poor decision. This realization also acknowledges the emptiness of his own macho bravado toward the incident. His duplicity in stealing money is obviously very serious and demonstrates the fine line that Ricardo and many other seventh-grade boys walk daily between self-discipline and delinquency. I will always remember Ricardo for his ability to evaluate his actions and those of his partner critically—much the same way he learned to critically evaluate Jamal's behavior throughout the novel.

Patty's notes brought me a joy that reinforced the satisfaction I felt over the celebration of the unit's finale, which had just ended. The party in the cafeteria began with Patty speaking about the unit's goals, what we had done along the way, and what we hoped to accomplish within the next hour. With her cue, students approached our male guests to form teams for personal introductions. We allowed these groups to converse for a few minutes, then had the group share what they learned with the whole class. We chuckled as our adult guests stretched their short-term memories to introduce the seventh graders within their groups.

After these introductions, the students presented their unit projects. DeWayne held up his three-dimensional model of Jamal's apartment and described the scene in which the preacher prays with Mama, Jamal, and Sassy for the older brother Randy, who was injured in a prison fight. James made clay figurines of the main characters. He displayed these figurines while supplying character sketches of each, then answered questions about the characters. Ricardo's life-size poster advertising *Scorpions* was on the wall. Because of his suspension that day, Teri pointed it out to the group and explained what Ricardo had intended with his picture of a scorpion above the words *Scorpions are back!* Shantala and Noe reenacted the scene from the novel when Sassy discovers the hidden gun in the sofa cushions. They rewrote the book's dialogue and memorized their lines. They also used simple props, such as a toy gun and a pillow on a folding chair.

When the students completed their presentations, Patty invited them to partake of the refreshments. Afterward, she asked our male guests to share some of their thoughts about being male and being a reader. Dr. Chuck Dugan, a kinesiology professor and former all-American gymnast, began by reading an excerpt from the poem "I Celebrate Myself," which is from one of his favorite books, *Leaves of Grass* by Walt Whitman (1993). He read the following lines:

> I celebrate myself, and sing myself,
>
> And what I assume you shall assume,
>
> For every atom belonging to me as good belongs to you.
>
> I loafe and invite my soul,
>
> I lean and loafe at my ease observing a spear of summer grass.
>
> My tongue, every atom of my blood, form'd from this soil,
>
> this air,
>
> Born here of parents born here from parents the same, and
>
> their parents the same.
>
> I, now thirty-seven years old in perfect health begin,
>
> Hoping to cease not till death.

Chuck went on to explain his philosophy about health: In order to be totally healthy, people must be both physically and intellectually active. He warned that the biggest mistake is to become imbalanced, forgetting to stimulate either the body or the mind. "Reading," continued Chuck, "is the best way to guarantee that our minds stay in great shape. That's why I read every day...it's a kind of mental exercise."

Another marvelous male guest was Dr. Malcolm Booker, whom I have mentioned in Chapter 4. Malcolm candidly described his humble beginnings in rural Louisiana, his basketball scholarship to a state college, and, the pinnacle of his academic efforts, the completion of his doctoral degree in education at the University of Florida. He emphasized that life's circumstances give people plenty of reasons to avoid the difficult steps, to seek to "feel good" only for the moment, and to find excuses for bad behavior and decisions, which are truly within their own control. Despite the many questions students had about his exciting college basketball career, Malcolm adroitly refocused his answers on the importance of disciplining oneself, setting goals, and becoming as highly literate as possible. For example, after Felipé queried him about whether he ever played basketball with Michael Jordan, Malcolm laughed and responded, "I had dreams of playing big-time roundball, but when I broke my ankle in junior year, and it never healed properly, my playing days were over." He went on to say:

> I knew many guys who were convinced that nothing would stop them from becoming pros...but when they got injured or flunked out, they had no backup plan, no Plan B. My best advice to all of you, especially if you like sports and think you're really good: Keep playing hard, work on your game to become as good as you can, but work just as hard on your school lessons, so if one plan doesn't work out, you'll have another ready to go. The one sure way to be ready is to be a reader.

Malcolm concluded his presentation by reading passages from Martin Luther King Jr.'s "Letter from Birmingham Jail" from *Why We Can't Wait* (1963). Looking out on the diverse group of young adults, he intoned,

> Moreover, I am cognizant of the interrelatedness of all communities and states. I cannot sit idly by in Atlanta and not be concerned about what happens in Birmingham. Injustice anywhere is a threat to justice everywhere. We are caught in an inescapable network of mutuality, tied in a single garment of destiny. Whatever affects one directly, affects all indirectly. Never again can we afford to live with the narrow, provincial "outside agitator" idea. Anyone who lives inside the United States can never be considered an outsider anywhere within its bounds. (p. 34)

After brief presentations from our last guests, the final day of our Real Men unit drew to a close. Rene Zamora a successful investment banker revealed his love of books from the thriller genre. Doug Horner a local actor read dialogue from *A New Way to Pay Old Debts* (Massinger, 1910), an Elizabethan play that was being staged in town. Doug said, "It has everything to do with choices young men make to be deceitful and unkind or decent and honorable." The lines he read that stuck out in my mind were those from Lady Allworth to her son:

> You are yet
> Like virgin parchment, capable of any
> Inscription, vicious or honourable. (p. 869)

The point, of course, Doug observed, is that even though boys are vulnerable to external influences, they must strive to reject the vicious and emulate the honorable.

All the guests were perfect. Each uniquely embodied the characteristics of honorable masculinity and clearly stressed the importance of active literacy in shaping their personal and professional lives. When the final bell rang, the finality of the moment hit me. I hoped that these young people might take the memory of this unit with them and make good decisions as they enter adulthood.

Revisiting the "To Be a Man" Survey

Although the unit officially ended, Patty, Teri, and I still had a great deal of work to finish. It was time to re-administer the "To Be a Man" survey to the students and compare the results from 2 month earlier to determine any self-reported changes in attitude toward stereotypical male behavior.

Demonstrating this change in attitude using self-report measures is similar to research conducted by Albert Farrell and Aleta Meyer (1997). In their study, they examined the impact of a school-based curriculum designed to reduce violence for sixth-grade students from inner-city Richmond, Virginia, USA. At the beginning of the school year, students completed a survey reporting the number of incidences of assaultive violence they had engaged in. Farrell and Meyer re-administered the survey after an 18-session violence-prevention program. Results showed highly significant reduction in the frequency of violence and several other related problem behaviors for boys. Most of these differences were maintained through the end of the school year.

We were heartened after reading our students' responses to the postunit survey. (The results of Ricardo's, DeWayne's, James's, and Shantala's surveys are highlighted in Figure 13.) Students' responses suggested that the unit was a success; however, it is impossible to know whether their responses reflected a genuine change in attitude or a desire to tell us what we wanted to hear.

Boy Talk

Adrian, 17, Discovers His Father's History in Elizabeth Becker's *America's Vietnam War: A Narrative History*

At one of my dad's veterans' rallies, I found out something really interesting (at least to me). You know how most people think vets are all messed up on drugs, live on welfare, and are screwed up in the head and everything? Actually, that's not true. Most vets are very successful. Most of them have good jobs and families and have gotten over their war experiences without committing suicide or turning into monsters like the movies always show.

My dad's a good example. He went to college when he got out of Vietnam. He started working for a Xerox company, and now he owns

FIGURE 13
Sample Postunit Responses From "To Be a Man" Survey

1. When a man is being hassled by another man, he needs to fight to get the man to back off.
   Ricardo's response—"No."
   Ricardo's reason—"Because they can talk it out."
2. Men who walk away from fights are sissies.
   DeWayne's response—"No."
   DeWayne's reason—"Even if you're stronger, what's the use of fighting."
3. Men need weapons like knives and guns to show how strong they are.
   James's response—"No."
   James's reason—"If they're going hunting or something, that's okay, but they don't have to use them [guns and knives] to fight."
4. You can't really be a man unless you are in a gang.
   Shantala's response—"No."
   Shantala's reason—"You're a man, staying out of gang."
5. Men like to fight because that's just who they are.
   Ricardo's response—"No."
   Ricardo's reason—"We have control of what we do."
6. Men who go to prison are real men.
   DeWayne's response—"No."
   DeWayne's reason—"That don't sound cool to me."
7. If a man killed someone, other men would think he was really cool.
   James's response—"No."
   James's reason—"You protect them better by having a good job and a good house."
8. Real men protect their families by fighting.
   Shantala's response—"No."
   Shantala's reason—"Prison ain't no place to prove you're a man."
9. As soon as a boy turns 13, he needs a gun.
   Ricardo's response—"No."
   Ricardo's reason—"A boy only needs a gun for hunting."
10. Sometimes being violent is the only way for a man to make others understand he means business.
    DeWayne's response—"No."
    DeWayne's reason—"There are other ways, like what you say that let's people know you ain't messing."

Kinkos, the copy place out near the mall. It's because of him I've always been interested in history, especially war history. When I read *America's Vietnam War: A Narrative History* (Becker, 1992), I felt like I was getting the true story of how the war started and why we fought it in the first place. As I was reading it, I talked with my dad about the stuff I was learning. He gave me his understanding of the facts, from how he felt when he was first drafted and later when he studied the history of the war.

Chapter 6 about the Tet offensive is right at the time my dad was in Viet Nam [*sic*]. He was near Khe Sanh when the North Vietnamese attacked. Every week the news would show the number of dead American soldiers and Vietnamese [people], but it could never tell the real story about guys getting blown up and tortured or families getting burned. The real massacres happened in Hue. Becker talks about how many people were slaughtered after the city was taken over by the North Vietnamese and Viet Cong. They killed 1,000 innocent civilians and 3,000 other people. Many of them were Americans. When the Americans finally recaptured the city, they found mass graves where the thousands of people were buried.

Dad said he had orders to go to Hue. Many of his buddies had gone and been killed there. But when the North Vietnamese were pushed back, he didn't have to go. What a lucky thing, too, because at least 10,000 soldiers died there. He could have been one of them.

My dad doesn't think of himself as some kind of macho man for fighting in the war. And he doesn't totally agree with why we fought the war in the first place. But he agrees with Elizabeth Becker when she says Vietnam veterans have unfairly become "the symbol of lost American innocence twisted into madness" (p. 3). Dad says all wars are a form of madness, but the men fighting them don't have to come out crazy.

Final Thoughts

What I cannot adequately recount in my description and analysis of the Real Men unit are the small, everyday exchanges that took place with these young men—the facial expressions, the body language, the sighs and guffaws, the sarcasm, and most importantly, the occasional and fleeting glimpses into their souls. On the other hand, to tell all would somehow be cheating, like revealing a secret. Only those of us who lived this unit can ever know the full impact of the experience; furthermore, it is impossible to know whether the unit will have a lasting effect on the students. Experienced teachers accept the fact that their protégés will rarely, if ever, visit them in the future to show them who they have become and to tell teachers how much they meant to them, personally and professionally.

Someday Patty, Teri, or I may hear from one of our students from the Real Men unit. That student may have good news about his life, the honorable choices he has made, how he has kept out of trouble, how he stayed the course in school, and how he has come back to acknowledge the contribution that our instruction has made to his life. Far more likely, however, we will go on with our hopes for these young men, knowing that we humbly tried to make a difference by shifting their thinking about males and themselves in less stereotypical directions.

Community Partners
in Boys' Literacy Growth

I have no idea how my parents or someone else could get me to read because I don't like reading. No one ever read to me before I fell asleep.
No one ever bought me a book or some reading material they knew I
might be into. And no one ever said, "You can do it, man," or something like that.

—Esteban, ninth grader

For someone who says he does not have a suggestion for how adults can
encourage their sons to read, Esteban certainly gets to the heart of the
matter, doesn't he? Parents and other adults can take advantage of
Esteban's "advice," however, by giving boys everything that Esteban was de-
prived of and by helping to condition boys to love reading.

Every concerned adult can inspire teen and preteen boys to read. At
school, this includes teachers, aides, counselors, administrators, older students,
and other staff members. Evelyn Dandy (1998) of Armstrong Atlantic State
University in Savannah, Georgia, USA, developed Armstrong's Pathways to
Teaching program. This program is designed to take noncertified school district employees and offer them tuition and other support to enable them to
take college courses and become fully licensed teachers. Dandy's program
identifies workers, such as janitors and lunchroom staff, in minority schools
who seem to have genuine promise in helping children develop and retain
positive attitudes toward their education. More specifically, the male personnel often become magnets for young boys who are attracted to anyone offering them a positive model of what it means to be a man. The idea for the
program came to Dandy as she observed how support staff at schools often
acted as nonsanctioned counselors, mentors, supporters, and disciplinarians—
roles sorely needed for many inner-city minority youth.

The following vignettes are testimony to the fact that almost anyone at home or in neighborhoods and communities can help boys stay the course in reading and learning. In each of the following cases, teachers of these teen and preteen boys played a supportive role for the people who were interested in making a difference in boys' literacy futures.

Buddy Reading: Being Cool, Being a Reader

Think about how atypical the following scene is. Mando, a 15-year-old Hispanic American in a taut, white sleeveless undershirt that exposes his muscular shoulders and arms, and Rickey, a 6-year-old Latino child, sit on the front stoop of Rickey's house...reading a book together. Mando has a crew cut, and his left forearm bears the name of his current or former sweetheart Delia. It is a muggy, hot summer morning in Corpus Christi, Texas, but these boys are being real "cool" sharing Rickey's favorite story, *Where the Wild Things Are* (Sendak, 1988). As Mando reads, with Rickey leaning in closely, he points to each word and invites Rickey to read along or say the words on his own. They soon finish the story for the second time, and Mando heads down the street to join his buddies, who are on their way to the park with a basketball. Rickey puts down the book and reaches for the large metal dump truck beside him, zooming it across the porch.

This is Molina, the same neighborhood I have referred to often in this book. Gangs are down the street, crack houses are around the corner, pit bulls pace menacingly behind chicken-wire fences, and some men sleep off drug or alcohol binges or congregate on street corners, throwing dice and drinking from paper bags. What makes Mando so special? He was in a *buddy reading* program the previous year. His English teacher, Maria, paired Mando with Rickey to help him learn to read; she also knew that they lived on the same block. Twice a week, Mando practiced his reading skills and thought more seriously about what it takes to be a good reader, while Rickey had the opportunity to see a "big, tough boy" reading, read along with him, and talk about stories together. Mando, who also has three younger sisters, took a shine to this young *vato* (loose translation for *buddy*).

Because Rickey lived so close, Mando continued reading with him a couple of days a week during the summer. Mando knew Rickey's mother and realized she was trying to raise five children on her own while working as a waitress 6 days a week at Rinconcitos, a Mexican restaurant.

Every concerned adult can exploit boys' inner Patriarch by creating situations in which young men can provide reading and learning guidance for boys. Practical knowledge and research evidence lend credence to this learning-by-teaching model. Through years of scientific investigation, for example, Merlin Wittrock (1990) has proven that when students *generate* their own learning, it is more permanent and meaningful. In other words, when students become teachers, as in Mando's case, they generate learning for themselves and others.

In homes where the father is absent, older boys often take on the role of surrogate dad. Evidently, mothers who do not have husbands often groom their older sons for parent-like responsibilities in order to share the chores of raising other children (Silverstein & Rashbaum, 1995). Although child psychologists have voiced caution about mothers who expect their sons to be husband substitutes, one extremely helpful role an adolescent boy can play in a single-parent household is that of a model and encourager of reading and learning.

Stewart, a superintendent and dear friend of mine, died tragically a couple of years ago. His passing was made all the more heartrending because of the two young daughters and adolescent son he left behind. Stewart's widow Traci, who is a local elementary school principal, has strived to avoid pressuring her son, Roger, into the role of surrogate fatherhood. She has, however, continued to hold her family together by preserving a family ritual of nightly reading. Roger's participation in reading to and with his sisters has become more prominent since his father's absence, perhaps because Traci has given him wide latitude with respect to the kinds of things the family reads. According to Traci, Roger usually suggests books and stories for the family to read. For instance, after the four of them saw the movie *Sleepy Hollow* (Burton, 1999), Roger tracked down a copy of Washington Irving's *The Legend of Sleepy Hollow* (1990) and read it to his sisters. Afterward, they talked about the similarities and differences between the film and the story.

Teachers can work with concerned individuals outside of the family to help boys find buddies for shared reading opportunities. Taking advantage of the inner Patriarch, coaches, pastors, and recreation counselors can bring older and younger boys together through reading. This is precisely what Daniel, a youth center volunteer, was able to do after talking with a local junior high school teacher who made the suggestion. When the boys who showed up to use the basketball courts were forced indoors because of rain, wind, or chill, Daniel urged the older boys to read with the younger ones. The center has a television, shelves full of board games, and several portable tables. Daniel made certain that there were plenty of paperback books on hand as well. Although there is only one rickety bookcase, usually crammed with books, Daniel stores others in cardboard boxes and milk crates. Daniel explained how he kept such a steady supply of books for a relatively small cost:

I lose 10 or so books a month, but I consider that to be a good problem.... It usually means kids are taking the books home and reading them. I buy them for almost nothing at garage sales and Goodwill stores. The library has donated discarded books...so most of them are giveaways anyway. Some of the guys will ask me if they can have a book, and I always say it's okay.

Daniel proceeded to describe how he encourages, but never forces, the children to read. He hopes to connect boys who are trying to make good choices with others, both young and old, doing the same. Daniel has watched many such relationships form. For example, 15-year-old Antoine is often seen playing with and mentoring 8-year-old Thomas. Both boys are growing up without their fathers. Their relationship started when they began reading *Trino's Choice* (Gonzalez-Bertrand, 1999) together.

While monitoring the center, Daniel spends as much time as feasible reading. As he terms it, he is a "born-again" reader, and he wants the kids to see him enjoying books. He loved *Trino's Choice* because it takes place in San Antonio, the city of his birth. He was brought to remember many of the same troubles that Trino experiences, such as growing up without an adult male's guidance, living in poverty, being constantly threatened by gangs, and just squeaking by in school. As Daniel said,

> It was easy for me to sell this book because I lived the life, and it was hard getting out. These boys around here, especially the teenagers, all have problems at home and at school. Most don't have dads living with them. They can barely pay their bills. They live in Section 8 housing [federally subsidized] that's crowded, noisy, and not the best place for a young man to feel good about himself.

Antoine and Thomas were hooked by the first chapter and returned to the center nearly every day for a while to read it. Antoine asked Daniel to keep the book with him, so it would be there when they came back. The book eventually disappeared from the center's collection altogether, but no one is complaining—except the other boys who have heard about it and now want to read it. Daniel plans to replace the missing copy because,

> What's special about the story is it's realistic and it shows how a kid...can decide to stay out of trouble and make something of himself. I tell these kids that even if they feel they were born with bad luck, they can give themselves a chance for something better...but it's up to them. Being a good reader is the way I finally made it out, so I know it can really help.

Because he stands up against criminality and turns courageously toward positive influences, Trino offers readers an image of the Warrior archetype.

From Hobbies to Books: Using Toy Soldiers to Engender Reading

As a preteen, Theo still seemed to be interested in little more than playing with his toy soldiers. His parents, Jack and Peggy, had busy careers that subjected them to long days and weekends at work. When Theo's reading scores edged near the minimally acceptable cutoff on the district's standardized test, Peggy and Jack found themselves at school one afternoon, meeting with his teacher Karlene. She recommended some tutoring and agreed to provide it herself a couple of days after school.

Theo came to the reading clinic in September of the new school year. He was 11 years old and in the sixth grade. Karlene was surprised by Theo's lackluster reading performance. She had come to discover that despite material privilege, a nuclear family, and educated parents, Theo exhibited the signs of a classic nonreader. What further surprised her was his unenthusiastic reaction to her questions about his interests. He reported no hobbies, no involvement with sports, and few regular or predictable activities that he looked forward to after school or on weekends.

Her follow-up chat with Jack and Peggy focused on helping them see the connection between having an interest in something and being motivated to read about that interest. Boys often need help discovering their interests; yet, in households where parents are extremely busy, boys are usually left to their own devices to discover what turns them on. Unfortunately, all too often, default leisure-time activities will be chosen, such as watching television and playing computer games. Karlene, therefore, urged Theo's parents to get more involved in how Theo spent his free time. This would help them find ways of engaging Theo in reading. She advised that the best way to accomplish this might be to capitalize on anything that Theo had already found enjoyable.

Theo's parents cleared their schedules for the next few weekends and dedicated themselves to spending time with Theo both outdoors and indoors. For instance, they went to the zoo for the first time in 2 or 3 years, an evening baseball game played by a local minor league squad, and the beach. Some indoor activities included putting puzzles together, playing board games, watching movies, and upon Theo's urging, setting up his arsenal of plastic soldiers and weapons on a mock battlefield. Theo was proud of his replicas of U.S., German, and Japanese soldiers.

Theo's response to these activities convinced Jack and Peggy that they should begin with his only genuine interest—his toy soldiers. While looking at various sets of army men in a hobby shop, Jack and Theo became inspired to build a diorama of a World War II battle. As a boy, Jack was an avid modeler, building everything from airplanes to ships to cars. His boyhood hobby was all but forgotten until he and Theo brainstormed about the diorama project. Their work would require research of World War II, as well as techniques for creating miniature though lifelike displays. Jack found Theo to be as enthusiastic about this family project as anything he had ever done and reasoned it was because they were working as a unit, father and son—a rarity of late.

They began their project by making trips to the local library and various bookstores for appropriate reference material. They checked out *The Attack on Pearl Harbor: Battles of World War II* (Rice, 1997) and *Battles of World War II* (Taylor & Taylor, 1998). These books are junior high level histories of various battles, such as the Nazi invasion of Poland, the D-Day invasion, the Battle of the Bulge in Europe, and battles in Pearl Harbor, Guam, and the Philippines. The books include plenty of black-and-white and color photos of actual battle scenes. For information on creating dioramas and miniature displays, Theo and Jack found two excellent resources at a couple of bookstores: Jerry Scutts's (2000) *World War II Dioramas* and Francois Verlinden's (2000) *Building Military Dioramas*. These books displayed a variety of war dioramas showing burnt buildings, weathered machines and men, and field hospitals, and included detailed descriptions of the techniques for recreating them.

Theo and Jack set aside time each evening to look through and read the books they had gathered in preparation for creating their own diorama. Theo toiled cheerfully on every detail as the two of them spent the next 2 months bonding in a way that they had never done before. The project became so all-encompassing that Jack began taking less and less work home; he also limited his weekend work to a couple of hours on Sunday evenings. Activity on the diorama became a kind of curative for the workaholic funk Jack had found himself in. It also gave him and Theo time to renew the critical father-son bond, which had become frayed.

On a large piece of plywood, Jack and Theo crafted a remarkable replica of the Ardennes (forest), which was the last-gasp offensive of another German invasion into France, as well as a turning point in the Battle of the Bulge. U.S. and German soldiers were arrayed in opposition among hedgerows, trees, and burnt-out buildings, and they were also in foxholes and behind tanks. Borrowing techniques from the diorama books to create further realism, Theo and Jack had rigged a device that would emit smoke onto the mock battlefield. In addition to this achievement of visual authenticity, Theo could recount each detail of the battle, demonstrating the power of personal interest as a motivator for learning.

As for the payoff on the "literacy ledger," Jack was able to reintroduce Theo to the pleasure of reading by finding out what his interests were, then engaging him with the appropriate literature. Similar to Theo, many boys who have adequate literacy skills will often stop reading when (a) reading at home is not being modeled and (b) school reading has more to do with skill, lessons, and tests than with personal enjoyment and growth. As a result of the diorama project, Theo continued to seek and read books about World War II. Peggy even found a slim but exciting book titled *Pearl Harbor Is Burning! A Story of World War II* (Kudlinski, 1993) that Theo quickly finished. All of these books now leave him asking for more. According to Karlene, Theo's renewed interest in reading surely contributed to the improvement he demonstrated on the district's standardized reading test the following year.

Even Cowboys Get the Blues: Reading as Adolescent Therapy

South Texas ranchers are a rugged breed. The endless hot, sunny, dry, and windy days leave the boys and men who spend their time working outside as weathered and tough as the land, which is strewn with mesquite, yucca, and prickly pear cacti.

Sonny's 16-year-old son Kip had devoted his young life to ranching. He was the heir apparent to his dad's 700-acre spread and 500 head of mixed Santa Gertrudis, Red Brangus, and Texas Longhorn; that is, until the bottom dropped out for Sonny and hundreds of other small to midsize ranchers in the mid-1990s. The area was hit by a severe drought, coming on the heels of nearly 10 years of drier-than-average weather. Land for grazing withered, feed and hay prices soared, and water holes evaporated. Sonny could not afford to maintain his herd and pay the mortgage on a new barn. By the end of the summer, with no drought relief in sight, Sonny was forced to sell his entire herd at ridiculously low prices.

Kip was devastated. What hurt most was the realization that it could take years for his father to rebuild a herd that was large enough to make the ranch profitable. Meanwhile, predictions of continuing drought conditions seemed to come daily from meteorologists and agronomists. Kip had no backup plan. He had been squeaking by in school like the other rancher boys who fully expected to continue in the footsteps of their fathers and grandfathers who had been ranchers.

This tale came to me by way of Kip's English teacher, Marc. Kip's father was a lanky man in his mid-50s, who with a Stetson in his grooved hands, called on Marc, who was grading papers in his classroom. Sonny was a sincere and intelligent man who knew Kip was going to need help building his reading and learning skills in order to complete high school and learn a new trade. He confided in Marc that he did not want Kip to become a rancher because it had become too risky, offering an unpredictable living.

Sonny told Marc he could not remember ever seeing his son reading a book simply for the fun of it, and that he did not spend much time reading his schoolbooks, either. First, Marc told Sonny to do whatever he could in a positive way to induce Kip to read. Marc suggested he begin by finding books about ranching, cattle, and the Wild West and make them available to Kip. Sonny revealed that he himself had become a nonreader given the arduous, time-consuming demands of maintaining a ranch. Because he was now entering a form of semiretirement, however, he would have much more time to read. Marc emphasized how important it was for Sonny to take advantage of his role model status by demonstrating the pleasure of reading. Kip and Sonny would also have more leisure time as ranching chores wound down. Last, Marc reinforced the fact that Kip would not become a competent reader unless he read often. "Reading itself will help build his reading skills," Marc stressed. Their conversation ended with Marc giving Sonny directions to the big discount bookstore, so he could make a stop before heading back to the ranch.

The next morning, Marc found a voice-mail message from Sonny, thanking him for his time and help. He also let Marc know that he had purchased a handful of "really good books" about ranching and cowboys that he was sure would interest Kip. He promised to read them as well.

Sonny was true to his word on all counts. Marc became aware of the full measure of Sonny's commitment to get Kip enthused about reading as he watched Kip evolve into a young man who read and enjoyed books. Kip told Marc about such books as *Bob Sharp's Cattle Country: Rawhide Ranching on Both Sides of the Border* (Sharp, 1985), which is Sharp's memoirs of rawhide ranching in northern Mexico during the 1920s and 1930s. Sharp, the son of a dentist, dropped out of college in 1922 to work with cattle on the Mexico-Arizona border, eventually becoming the top hand in the ranching empire of Colonel William Green. Kip loved this book and the others that his dad brought home. Sonny was equally engrossed by these books, which described through pictures and text a life similar to the one Sonny and his father had cut out for themselves.

Another favorite book that Kip shared with Marc and talked about unceasingly if given the chance was Dick Hyson's (1998) *The Calling*. As the book's title suggests, the desire to become a rancher is not unlike other occupations of destiny. Frank Dalton is the main character, who is half Comanche, half white. He teaches the young tenderfoot R.C. Roth what the cowboy world is all about. Kip said Hyson's storytelling is straightforward and true to life, based on his own ranch family experiences. Other books with a distinctly Texan flavor include Kathleen Jo Ryan's (1999) *Deep in the Heart of Texas: Texas Ranchers in Their Own Words* and Louise O'Connor's (1991) *Cryin' for Daylight: A Ranching Culture in the Texas Coastal Bend*. Ryan's book was especially poignant because actual ranchers disclose, in a one-on-one interview format, glimpses into the lives of people involved in cattle ranching. Kip said that he and his father talked a great deal about a couple of ranchers' stories concerning the challenges of passing the ranch on to the younger generation. One rancher, like Sonny, tells of dissuading his son from taking on the unpredictable lifestyle of cattle ranching even though the son feels it is in his blood.

In the end, Kip seemed to profit handsomely from his new habit of independent reading. The last I heard, Marc told me Kip had graduated from high school and joined the Reserve Officers' Training Corps (ROTC) at a local community college. "He wants to work on radar, or so he says," Marc continued, "and he asked me if there were any interesting books on that topic, too."

Driving Ms. Ritchie: Running Errands to the Bookstore

I am told by parents that next to paying for braces, the most trauma-inducing event in a parent's life is when a teenager receives his or her driver's license. One positive aspect of this is that these teens can now take themselves to and from school, work, the movies, sporting events, and dates; however, this is balanced by the downside of gas and repair expenses, higher insurance rates, and a nonstop fear of some unthinkable calamity involving teens and the family car.

When single mom Karen (also known as Ms. Ritchie) watched her son Ben open his official letter from the Texas Department of Transportation and hold his first operator's license, she said she could only stare in disbelief at this 11th grader who towered over her by nearly 6 inches. She felt totally unprepared for the move from bicycles to go-carts, and now this. Ben immediately requested to "go for a spin" in her car, which was the only one in the family. She relented and was struck by a brainstorm while cruising the neighborhood.

Ben, like most guys his age, was becoming increasingly involved in extracurricular activities, such as work, homework, and track practice, leaving little room for leisure reading. Karen, an elementary school teacher, was particularly sensitive to Ben's growing disaffection with reading. When Ben was in seventh grade, she began noticing what seemed like a complete reversal of his earlier fascination with reading. This coincided with a prodigious growth spurt, Karen's divorce from Ben's father, and a spot on the junior varsity track team as a distance runner. Karen has always been a compulsive reader, finding solace and escape from work and parenting in books, especially murder mysteries. Her estranged ex-husband read the weekend paper—period.

As Ben entered adolescence, Karen found herself and Ben in constant power struggles over how he should spend his free time. She demanded that he read, and she thrust books upon him with the vague hope that they would rekindle his passion for literature. Ben refused to read any of them. Karen said that for at least 2 years, the only material she ever saw him read was his monthly magazine on running, and then for just the first few days of its arrival. She felt as if she had hit a dead end.

As Ben drove and talked about the kind of car he wanted to buy, Karen hatched a new plot to engage Ben in reading. "Ben, I've got a couple of library books in the backseat that are due. Do you know how to get to the Greenwood Branch?" Karen asked. It was brilliant—Ben could drive her car, but she would send him on frequent errands to the bookstore and library where he would have to pick up, look for, and buy books.

This first time, Ben sat in the car while Karen returned her books and checked out some new ones. On the next trip, she coaxed him inside; he sat thumbing through magazines as she perused the shelves of the mystery-thriller area. The big payoff came when she started asking Ben for rides to the bookstore. The large Barnes & Noble bookstore held some tantalizing incentives, such as the coffee shop, which sold baked goods that Ben found irresistible. The drive was longer, as well, and required negotiating several heavy-traffic avenues, meaning that their trips to the bookstore would often last an hour or longer. In time, Ben fell into a routine that is familiar to many patrons of these new, larger bookstore chains: With a cup of coffee and biscotti, he would lounge in one of the commodious chairs or sofas and read while Karen browsed. When Ben met Myra, a senior, during one of their trips to the discount bookstore, it quickly became his regular haunt. Myra's devotion to books began to rub off on him, especially because one of his reasons for reading was to be able to talk with Myra. Ben continued to read even after their relationship faded because, even though he had not noticed, reading had become his new habit. As Karen put it,

I knew if I could just get him around books again, he'd eventually start taking advantage. When you're in a library or bookstore, there isn't much else you can do with yourself except read...and that's what Ben started to do.

What began as errands to the library and bookstore connected to a young man's driving privileges turned into a young man's rediscovery of reading for fun.

Baseball Saved Us:
Learning to Soft-Pedal Reading

Books are a tough sell for boys. That's all there is to it. Reading, as I have mentioned, becomes uncool for males when they are in their preteens and seems to get worse as they move through adolescence (Jensen, 1999). Why is this pattern so predictable? One compelling explanation is that U.S. culture portrays reading as a *female* activity. This is reinforced for boys nearly every day in either school, where primarily women teach them to read, or at home, where the person who reads to them is almost certainly a woman. Once adolescent boys lose interest in books, these tough sells are even less likely to be successful. Buddy's parents, Charlotte and Louis, found this out the hard way.

Buddy was a precocious boy. Small for his age and possessing a squeaky voice, he was reading well by the time he entered kindergarten at age 5. Charlotte, a bank manager, and Louis, a successful attorney, often had Buddy read in front of friends and guests. To everyone's amazement, Buddy gave near perfect oral renditions of text within popular news magazines. Teachers also showcased his exceptional decoding skills, glowing with undeserved pride—*undeserved* because Buddy's remarkable reading ability was for him, as it is for most precocious readers, a special gift that transcends instruction and easy explanation.

His reading progress continued until Buddy, quite suddenly, stopped reading at age 9. Buddy had discovered baseball and took to it with fanatical zeal. I know how a young boy's attraction to this game can be so strong that it consumes nearly every minute of his day, because I was also a baseball fanatic during my childhood. Buddy's parents watched helplessly as he eschewed reading for collecting baseball cards, playing catch with others, or just playing with the ball by himself (throwing a ball against the steps or garage, or throwing it in the air), well into the evening. He wore an Astros cap, shirt, and trousers; when he could get away with it, he even slept with his cap on.

Buddy received his lowest reading test scores ever in fifth grade, and his parents felt they could no longer ignore his disaffection with books. They enrolled him in a special summer camp for boys who were "motivationally challenged" about school, reasoning that his obsession with baseball might be knocked out of him by the rigors of scholastic boot camp. Buddy survived 2 weeks in the Texas Hill Country. After being away from the game he loved so desperately, however, he seemed to become even more obsessive about baseball and responded with greater aversion to any mention of books, school, or plans for his academic future.

At the beginning of Buddy's sixth-grade year, Charlotte responded to one of my advertisements for clinical reading services, which I had distributed throughout the community. Charlotte was disconsolate. I was, unfortunately, all too familiar with her story, which was like the countless others I have heard from parents who had taken extreme measures to get their sons to read. I was unable to be encouraging to Charlotte because our clinic's roster was full for the semester. I told her not to despair, but to be patient and, above all, not to do anything that would make the situation more intractable than it already appeared. "Motivating boys to read requires a delicate touch," I told her. "Thrusting books upon Buddy will, in all likelihood, force him to dig in his heels even more."

Within a month, I was on the telephone with Louis. His voice was edged with impatience as he cataloged the ways he had tried to "deal with" Buddy's antipathy toward reading. Louis recalled how, when growing up poor in Puerto Rico, his own father had demanded nothing short of a total commitment to his studies from him. "It paid off for me in the long run because my good grades made it possible for me to get into Baylor Law School. Buddy doesn't stand a chance at college if he keeps up this baseball nonsense." He wanted to know, because I was the "reading expert," what they should do.

Beyond my professional identity, I am also the father of a preteen, so I have plenty of empathy for parents who cannot understand why their adolescent progeny are not as serious minded about learning and reading as they themselves are. It is as though parents expect their children to be perfect academic soldiers marching in step down the path of scholastic accomplishment that the parents have devised. When children reach the middle grades and begin asserting their selfhood, it is felt most grievously by those so naive as to think conformity is somehow programmed into them. Louis, and Charlotte to a lesser extent, could not understand how Buddy, growing up in a household of privilege and being raised by university graduates and successful professionals, could be anything but a young scholar. Even more harmful, however, was Louis's savaging of Buddy's self-esteem and burgeoning masculine identity. Louis did more harm than good by devaluing Buddy's love of baseball, which is a traditional and healthy diversion for males, and giving him no alternative but to read and study.

Buddy was only behaving like a boy. The insistence that he suspend his devotion to baseball and return to a time when he read often and with uncanny ability was pure folly. This demand is similar to asking a teenager to stop growing, be in bed by 8:00 p.m., and always like what mom and dad like. The way to improve Buddy's situation was to prevent any further deterioration of his relationship with his parents and create a supportive home environment that lovingly and patiently guided him back to reading. The key to this change was in Charlotte and Louis's midst all along, but it would take a few more months of misery before they lifted the blinders and recognized the reparative—baseball.

By the beginning of the second grading period that year, Buddy had developed psychosomatic stomach ailments, such as cramps, gas, sourness, and tightness. These ailments, which had started once or twice a week, became daily complaints. Doctors found nothing and suggested therapists and antianxiety drugs. There was finally a breakthrough just before Christmas.

Louis's brother John, also Buddy's favorite uncle, was an executive in an auto parts manufacturing plant based in San Juan, Puerto Rico. He invited Buddy to spend a week with him during the upcoming school holiday. That week, the two of them indulged themselves with baseball. The Puerto Rican, Cuban, and Dominican clubs boast some of the best athletes the major leagues have ever signed, such as Roberto Clemente and Tony Perez from years past, and current stars Sammy Sosa and Pedro Martinez. Buddy and his uncle were at the ballpark every day, enjoying the outstanding play of these clubs. It was just the antidote for a young man beleaguered by demanding parents and psychosomatic distress.

Something else happened on that holiday, however, which initiated Buddy's journey back to reading. John's Christmas present to his nephew was the following books: *Cal Ripken, Jr., Quiet Hero* (Nicholson, 1993), *Slugger Season: McGwire and Sosa* (Driscoll, 1998), and *What Hearts* (Brooks, 1992). Brooks's book tells a serious story about Asa, who is a boy about Buddy's age. Throughout his parents' divorce, seven moves in 3 years, and a new life with a gruff "fake" dad, Asa finds solace and courage in the one thing he knows well—baseball. In this way, *What Hearts* evokes the Warrior archetype. The other books that John gave Buddy also provide links to positive male archetypes. The two biographies recount the lives and athletic prowess of Cal Ripken, Mark McGwire, and Sammy Sosa, and remind young readers that honorable sports figures are still around. These men have conducted themselves with humility and gratitude both in and out of the ballpark, and each man is a generous contributor to programs for youngsters. McGwire even convinced his team, the St. Louis Cardinals, to use his son as a batboy so he could spend more time with him.

Uncle John's gifts were refreshingly absent of demands or threats. They were offered openly, freely, and without parental or authoritative strings. Buddy thanked his uncle and set the books aside. He did not look at them again until his flight home, when he opened the Cal Ripken book and read the inscription: "From one baseball nut to another. Enjoy! Love, Uncle John."

A philosophy professor who graciously mentored me during my stormy sophomore year at college once told me that, sometimes, when people stop trying so hard to get what they want, things will come to them. This insight often needs repeating. Charlotte and Louis had to learn it or they might have created an insuperable emotional rift between themselves and their son. After talking with John and doing some serious self-examination the week that Buddy was away (when the emotional waters were calm), Louis took his first step toward reparation. For Christmas, he bought Buddy a first-baseman's glove.

As he ruminated over his past failures to mold his son into a faithful student and cheerful reader, Louis realized that he had plenty of latent feelings about baseball. He had also loved the game as a youngster. He was a talented baseball player and was ready to play wherever and whenever, but the exigencies of a poverty-stricken life on the outskirts of San Juan had forced him to give up his love for the game. His father worked tirelessly to support Louis, John, and their three sisters, and they were all successful. Buddy's obsession with baseball reminded Louis of a life of dissipation he was destined to live had he not a strong need to survive and the incentive of a better life, so Louis had worked hard, was studious, and above all, had given up that "silly pastime." Louis began to realize, however, that he still enjoyed baseball and decided to reconnect with his son by allowing himself to share his own love of baseball with Buddy.

I am pleased to report that this tale has a happy ending. Buddy started reading again that spring. It began with the sports page from the newspaper. Both he and Louis read stories together about the Astros: their spring training; which players were traded, acquired, and injured; batting averages; pitching records; and so on. The two of them made it to baseball's opening day game. (Louis allowed Buddy to miss school so they could be together on such a memorable occasion.) Buddy soon found himself reading books about baseball. He finally returned to the three books from his uncle and read them with a ferocity that reminded Charlotte and Louis of the "old" Buddy. The next fall, Buddy was allowed to join Little League as long he kept up his grades. The last report I had gotten on him was that he had qualified for the district's special middle school for children who qualify as gifted and talented students, and he was doing fine.

Charlotte called to tell me one last thing as well. She said that Buddy had bought his father a special birthday present—a picture book titled *Baseball Saved Us* (Mochizuki, 1993). This is a splendid book for boys both young and old. It takes place during a time of national embarrassment in the United States, when Japanese Americans were interned in camps during World War II. The main character and narrator is a boy of around 10 or 11, who describes how the inmates band together to create a life of dignity and diversion from the barbed wire, spartan accommodations, and incessant watch of guards wearing dark glasses and carrying automatic rifles. The story culminates in a baseball game played by the adolescent Japanese American boys within the prison grounds. The narrator has the deciding hit and wins the game for his team. As the boy rounds the bases, he notices that the guard who looks the most menacing allows a subtle grin to spread over his face, acknowledging the boy's feat. Buddy wrote on the inside cover, "The title of this book reminded me of us. I hope you like this story as much as I did. Love, Buddy."

Family Book Club: Bargaining With Chores

In my small family of three, it is crucial that we all pitch in. So, theoretically, every third day is my turn to clean up after dinner, and, theoretically, every other third day is my daughter Hannah's turn. As a preteen, she is given to a natural inclination toward shirking anything that smacks of parental-imposed responsibility and constantly tries to negotiate an alternative chore. Despite her complaints, this system works fairly well but depends on each of us holding our end of the bargain.

Bargaining with after-dinner chores was worth it to single mom Roberta, whose three adolescent sons hated doing dishes more than any other household chore. Ever since they were old enough to help, Roberta has had them clearing the table; wrapping leftovers; and washing, drying, and putting the dishes away. It was becoming more of a struggle every evening, though. The boys fought her and each other over details and technicalities, made excuses, feigned illnesses, and procrastinated—all in an effort to either lessen the chore or get out of doing it entirely. Roberta was no pushover, however, and managed to get them to finish the job most evenings.

Getting the boys to read was another matter altogether. Roberta was not winning this fight. The days when her sons sat on her lap and listened excitedly to stories or fell asleep in her arms to a bedtime story were a faint memory. The boys spurned the idea of leisure-time reading as emphatically as doing dishes. When Rashad, the youngest, was placed in a remedial reading class at the start of junior high, Roberta realized it was time to find ways to get him and his older brothers more involved with reading at home.

Although of modest means, Roberta held the family together on a nurse's income and had been fortunate to have a day shift for the past 3 years that gave her time in the late afternoons and evenings to be with her sons. She confided her concern about Rashad to a colleague whose son had been in a similar class the year before and had made rapid progress. This prompted Roberta to get in touch with Rashad's reading teacher.

When Lynn, the reading teacher, met Roberta she was immediately struck by her level of commitment to her boys and her dedication to shift their attitudes about reading. During the course of their conversation, Lynn asked many questions about Rashad's out-of-school interests. It was then that she discovered Rashad's nemesis—doing dishes. After years of working with parents to find ways of linking literacy to home and community interests and activities, it did not take long to hit on the idea of offering the boys a reprieve from doing the dishes if they would agree to replace this activity with reading. Like most new ideas, it remained somewhat ill defined until Roberta could experiment with possible options to see which worked best.

On her first attempt, Roberta had the guys simply read silently from any source they wanted while she did the dishes. This seemed to work for a week or so, but before long, they were finding ways around it by doing homework (which had always been an activity for after their cleanup), complaining about not having anything good to read, or pretending to lose a favorite book, magazine, or newspaper section. Not to be taken advantage of, Roberta used a new strategy in which the boys took turns reading aloud, not unlike a teacher's old reliable, round-robin reading. This, however, could not be sustained for more than a couple of days before boredom set in, resulting in a ridicule match whenever one of them stumbled on a word.

Finally, Roberta decided she needed to be directly involved with the boys' reading and discussions in order to keep them attentive and involved. Her solution was to let the after-dinner cleanup wait for 30 minutes while she and her sons read together. It worked. The threats of reassigning after-dinner chores if they did not participate in reading dwindled and eventually disappeared as they rediscovered the pleasure of family reading. Before long, Roberta started referring to them as the "Cooper Book Club," and the name stuck.

Roberta found that the reading material that brought out the best reading and discussion was what the boys picked out themselves. Each had his turn, so no one felt left out. Roberta would occasionally introduce something for the boys to consider. Her material was often rejected, although there were significant exceptions. She managed to get articles on health, diet, and nutrition past the Cooper advisory board. The boys also agreed to read articles about God and spirituality, which were some of Roberta's favorites. In turn, Roberta read articles about sports figures, such as Deion Sanders, Kobe Bryant, and Tim Duncan, and musical stars, such as Snoop Doggy Dog, Puff Daddy, and Salt-N-Pepa. They read anything and everything that was mutually agreeable, regardless of the source. For example, a CD's liner notes were often part of the after-dinner discussions, as were sports trading cards. No one would dare judge these sources as quality literature; however, simply getting her boys back into the habit of reading for enjoyment was most important to Roberta.

Roberta noticed other benefits that came with her boys' reading habits. For example, dinner conversation was usually centered on what the family was currently reading or about to read; thus, as a result of the Cooper Book Club, there was an increase in text-related conversation between the boys and their mother. This is not an insignificant aspect of Roberta's efforts. Michael Schwarzchild (2000) says that despite the seeming banality of family mealtime,

> Quality mealtime conversation between parents and children has been shown to increase children's mental and verbal abilities...develop important skills...such as...taking turns speaking, and listening to the person talking. Meals are one of the best times for children to pick up new words. Kids whose families chat most during mealtimes have larger word inventories. (p. 95)

In addition to increasing languaging about texts, quality mealtime conversation between parents and children has been shown to reinforce family unity (Bowden & Zeisz, 1997). Another potential bonus of the dinnertime book club is the way youth begin associating a pleasurable time in their day, in this case eating, with literacy (Sawyer, 1987). In Roberta's sons' minds, the pleasing aromas, tastes, and general atmosphere of mealtime has become connected in a positive way to reading, discussing, and sharing. How different these connections are when compared to the all-too-frequent negative associations many boys have with school-based reading because of either stale instruction, unappealing texts, or fear of humiliation in a setting that places their vulnerability on the line virtually every day.

The Cooper Book Club ultimately heightened the boys' awareness of books. In the past, for example, they would walk down the aisle in a supermarket with books and magazines or an entrance to a mall bookstore and not notice either. Roberta's sons were now giving these places a second glance. In fact, the family discovered the novel *Hoops* (Myers, 1999) as a result of a mall bookstore's display of Walter Dean Myers's novel *Monster* (2000), which caught Rashad's eye.

Roberta found *Hoops* to be a perfect match for her sons, who were basketball-playing, Michael Jordan wanna-bes. Rashad and his brothers could not get enough of this story and were ready to reread as soon as they had finished it. Roberta wisely acquiesced, reasoning that, like the desire to watch a great movie again, a great book deserves to be read more than once.

When Roberta had first come to Lynn about her concerns for Rashad, Lynn, a former student of mine, told Roberta about my reading clinic. Roberta did contact me about 9 months before the clinic, but I did not have any openings for new clients. By the time I contacted her to let her know of an opening in clinic, Roberta, to my delight, graciously turned down my offer for the best of reasons. She explained that she had told Rashad if he did not improve his reading scores, he would be required to go to the university for remediation. He came through, and Roberta credited this in large part to the help he was getting from Lynn and his new reading habit. As Roberta detailed the changes she had noticed in all her sons, such as their willingness and eventual excitement to read, a sense of ease came over me. I looked out my office window at the students walking across campus and wondered if I might see Rashad among them someday, attending the university, though *not* for remediation.

Boy Talk

Marcus, 13, Better Understands His Own Quest After Reading Katherine Paterson's *Parzival: The Quest of the Grail Knight*

Ever since I can remember, I liked anything that had to do with knights and castles and King Arthur. It's always been a place I can go to in my mind to get away from being bothered by things around me. We live in a small apartment, and I have to share a room with my younger brother who's at the age when he wants to hang around with me all the time. It's noisy around my apartments. There's nowhere you can find peace and quiet. I also have two sisters, and they drive me crazy. They're older and like to call me "immature" just to make me mad.

I remember when I was a kid, I used to collect all the Christmas trees people threw out after Christmas and build a hideout with them. I would crawl inside and pretend to be Robin Hood, hiding in the middle of a forest somewhere in England from the Sheriff of Nottingham. One of my friends would play him. We made swords out of a couple pieces of wood and would go to battle for any noble cause.

I read everything I could find about knights. We only had a couple of books in our school library, but I found some really good ones at the downtown library. The best one is the one I just read called *Parzival: The Quest of the Grail Knight* (Paterson, 2000). Parzival only has his mom like me. And like me, his mom can't really teach him much about how to be a man or a knight. When he reaches my age, he's considered a man and has to act like one by being brave, doing good deeds, and staying loyal to the king. He's a special knight because he is brought to the Wild Mountain Castle to see the king who is very sick and about to die. But Parzival doesn't know the right questions to ask to make the king better, so he must go on a quest for the Holy Grail. I didn't know what a grail really was until I read this book. It's supposed to be the cup that Jesus drank from at the Last Supper.

His quest is a great story with lots of dangers and challenges that he has to overcome. This makes the story of Parzival and King Arthur something I like to read about today even though the author says it's 800 years old. All the years I used to wish I was someone like Parzival so I could have all these great adventures. But really, I always kind of knew that the story is like a Bible story in a way. These things might have happened or they might not have, but we can learn from them anyway. I think my quest is to try to stay away from drugs and gangs and get a good education, so I can help my mother and my brother. This isn't the same as defeating big, supernatural knights in a joust like Parzival does, but it might be just as hard because there are a lot of drugs and gangs in my neighborhood.

Final Thoughts

Trying to spark a reluctant boy to read can be a full-time, often frustrating enterprise for parents and other adults. Male youth often find themselves in a handicapping cycle that begins with peer pressure that urges them to avoid reading because it is not "cool." This disuse leads to a loss of reading skill, which then brings on a disdain for reading because it is associated with incompetence and vulnerability. This disdain causes boys to form a mask of indifference to reading, which leads to a further decline in reading ability. Demanding boys to read may condemn them to relive this cycle throughout adolescence and may actually help create the "hardened" nonreader.

Parents and adults can help struggling readers reverse cycles of aliteracy through a number of caring and clever strategies. Teachers of adolescents should be advocates of these positive interactions between boys, books, and adults. Teachers also should seek to enlist more men in programs and activities that allow men to be role models of active literacy and honorable masculinity. For example, teachers can encourage members of communities to start father–son reading clubs. One such club called "Books and Balls" works as follows: Sons choose a book for the club to read; then once a month, fathers and sons meet at a local indoor soccer arena to eat pizza and discuss the books before they play soccer (Maughan, 2001). Another book club, which teachers who work with African American boys should be aware of, called "Men of Books" was started by and for African American males (Houser, 2001). The goal of this club is to make the statement that black males are readers, and black male authors have something to say to black men and boys. Men of Books provides a forum for enjoying fiction and exchanging thoughts on social and political problems.

All the strategies in this chapter are unique yet share some important features: Instead of being pulled, kicking and screaming to books, boys were invited to engage in literacy with few strings attached, with literature that was personally exciting, and by adults who were readers themselves.

Conclusion

Since completing *To Be a Boy, To Be a Reader*, I am even more convinced of the importance of connecting boys with books. New evidence (Herbert, 2001) suggests that the situation for many adolescent boys is as dire as many teachers and parents believe, and that this problem demands urgent attention. Bob Herbert describes nearly 5 million people in the 16-to-24 age group who are known as "nowhere kids." These are young people who "live their troubled lives beneath the radar of most public-policy planners" (p. 15). Herbert characterizes this hard-to-reach group of people as follows:

> Most lack basic job skills as well as solid literacy...they are neither working nor looking for jobs. They are not in vocational training. They are not in manufacturing. They are not part of the information age. They are not included in the American conversation. (p. 15)

And most are male. As this book has stated, to presume that reading itself will transform conditions that plague young men such as poverty, alcohol and drug abuse, crime, and irresponsible fathering is recklessly naive; however, to ignore the potential of active literacy for ensuring that fewer adolescent males become nowhere kids is equally naive.

For this growing population of disenfranchised boys and for adolescent males from all of society, we must find books and literature that engage their unique imaginations and offer models of positive masculinity. Basic literate behaviors that struggling and reluctant male readers exhibit daily such as reading motor vehicle and computer manuals, clothing labels, and gang graffiti (Aronson, 2001; Moje, 2000) provide teachers and other adults with starting points. However, adolescent boys will develop higher levels of literacy only through sustained print encounters with increasingly challenging texts.

What the future holds for adolescent boys' literate lives depends in no small part on the recognition by teachers and parents that boys' literate health is vitally important to all of society. It is my hope that this recognition will lead to initiatives and practices that are both imaginative and practical and that will take place in classrooms, libraries, and homes. These practices should strive to bring together teachers, parents, and adolescents with good books. If you gain any new understandings from *To Be a Boy, To Be a Reader* about how to help adolescent males find entry points to active literacy, I hope they are these:

- *The material matters.* In fact, in a recent survey to determine what makes middle school students want to read, the students expressed that the most important reason was *interest* in the reading material (Ivey & Broaddus, 2001). Teachers and parents must make the commitment to determine boys' interests and provide them with reading material tied to those interests.

- *Parents and teachers should respect boys' interests.* Arthur Applebee's (1993) discovery that the core list of required books in most secondary schools in the United States has been unchanging for many years offers a clue as to why many adolescent boys become disaffected readers. Although books such as *Lord of the Flies* (Golding, 1999) and *A Separate Peace* (Knowles, 1990) may have a place in the literature curriculum of secondary schools, other books that reflect the lives and interests of teen and preteen boys should be a part of that curriculum as well. We have known for many years that a large number of adolescents prefer to read nonfiction, yet it is rare to find this genre in middle school and high school classrooms and libraries (Bean, 2000; Sullivan, 2001; Worthy, Moorman, & Turner, 1999). When boys say they like anything with sports, action, and scary stuff, they mean it. We should honor boys' interests by making literature on these topics, especially young adult literature, available to them.

- *Books with positive male archetypes are important.* Teen and preteen boys can become engaged readers by reading books that portray males in nonstereotypical ways. Quality young adult fiction and nonfiction that honestly depicts boys and men will help dispel myths about masculinity while offering positive images of masculinity for adolescent males to emulate.

- *All adults can model the pleasures and benefits of active literacy.* As illustrated in Chapter 6, teachers who are struggling to make a difference in the literate lives of adolescent males are urged to consider how they can work with parents and other community members to support initiatives and practices that engage and keep boys reading. Any effort is worthy that works against the disaffection toward reading that many young men feel.

One Final Story

I recently had a delightful surprise when I was going through my e-mail. A friend had forwarded a letter he had received from a high school English teacher (H. Parkhurst, personal communication, November 1, 2001). The teacher's message described the attitudes of most of her teen male students in a basic English class—disinterested, hostile, listless, uncooperative. She said that these attitudes changed when she found Terry Davis's *If Rock and Roll Were a Machine* (1994). Davis's book depicts 16-year-old Bert Bowden's change from a bright, confident, and popular young man to one who is riddled with self-doubt after a teacher humiliates him in class. Bert embodies the Pilgrim archetype when a couple of adult friends show a willingness to help, and he embarks on a quest to regain his confidence.

After reading this novel of adolescent angst and maturation, the attitudes of the teenage boys in the English teacher's classroom changed. Disinterest gave way to enthusiasm, hostility to curiosity, and opposition to participation. The teacher also noted that one young man who had described himself as a nonreader for life and was convinced nothing could change his mind was now the most involved student in her class.

Stories like this epitomize the importance of matching boys' needs and interests with good books. I have been heartened to learn of others who have begun to champion boys' literacy needs. Efforts such as "GUYS READ," a literacy initiative launched by children's book author Jon Scieszka, should help raise both teachers' and parents' consciousness about the significance of helping all boys become active readers. Scieszka's campaign, which is also supported by Penguin Putnam and the Association of Booksellers for Children, focuses on the special reading needs of boys (Maughan, 2001). The goal is first to get boys excited about reading, then to get boys to move on to reading more sophisticated books. The campaign includes a website that lists specific books that may interest boys, as well as brochures and other promotional material about GUYS READ. Undoubtedly, sensitivity to boys' needs is the crucial first step, but to make a difference in the literate lives of boys, teachers will also need resources that familiarize them with appropriate titles and successful teaching practices to assist them in their efforts to reach boys through books. It is my hope that *To Be a Boy, To Be a Reader* will become one of these useful resources.

Appendix

Literature With Positive Male Archetypes

Chapter 1 presented evidence that boys have consistent preferences for certain types of literature. These preferences develop at a very young age for both boys and girls and appear to be related to general patterns of play and social behavior. For example, researchers investigated preschoolers' choices of fairy tales that they would most like to have read to them; they found clear gender differences in children as young as 2 years old (Collins-Standley, Gan, Yu, & Zillmann, 1996). Girls ages 2 to 4 had a strong and growing preference for romantic tales, whereas boys showed a growing preference for violent and scary tales. The researchers advance the possibility that these gender-specific genre preferences are part of a "behavior-fosters-interest complex," whereby constitutional factors are likely influencing gender-specific preferences for particular fairy tales (p. 301). In other words, very early in their development, boys acquire more pleasure from stories that help consolidate their unfolding sense of self as males.

This appendix contains 300 titles of current young adult literature organized around the 10 male archetypes described in Chapter 2. These books were screened and selected by me and come principally from titles that I discovered during my research for this book. Other books were included as a result of recommendations from students, teachers, and colleagues. Still others were included because of their quality as judged by young adult literature experts (for example, Donelson & Nilsen, 1997; Herz & Gallo, 1996; Odean, 1998). The titles, grouped according to the most salient archetype, are further classified into the following three categories to aid in the selection of books for teen and preteen boys: Adolescent Novels, Informational Books, Easier Reading. It is important to note that the male characters and figures in these books almost always exhibit behaviors consistent with more than one archetype. For purposes of simplification, therefore, I have placed each book within a category based on the archetypal qualities that are dominant in the book's main character or historical figure. This means that in some cases two biographies of the same man may be placed under different archetypes. Teachers can use the guidelines articulated in previous chapters as well as their own creative imaginations for helping boys develop a positive sense of masculinity through enjoyable experiences with the following books. Although I have categorized the young adult literature in these ways, teachers who may feel a book fits better in another category should feel free to use it that way.

Pilgrim

Adolescent Novels

The Car (Gary Paulsen) New York: Bantam Doubleday Dell, 1995

The Fields and the Hills: The Journey, Once Begun (Harald Bakken) New York: Clarion Books, 1992

If Rock and Roll Were a Machine (Terry Davis) New York: Laurel-Leaf, 1994

One Fat Summer (Robert Lipsyte) New York: HarperCollins, 1991

Pacific Crossing (Gary Soto) Orlando, FL: Harcourt Brace Jovanovich, 1992

Parzival: The Quest of the Grail Knight (Katherine Paterson) New York: Puffin, 2000

Playing Without the Ball (Rich Wallace) New York: Knopf, 2000

Running Wild (Thomas Dygard) New York: Penguin, 1998

The Snake-Stone (Berlie Doherty) New York: Viking/Penguin, 1998

Whirligig (Paul Fleishman) New York: Henry Holt and Company, 1998

The Wreckers (Iain Lawrence) New York: Bantam Doubleday Dell, 1999

If Rock and Roll Were a Machine (Terry Davis) New York: Laurel-Leaf, 1994

Informational Books

Across America on an Emigrant Train (Jim Murphy) New York: Clarion Books, 1993

Black Pioneers: An Untold Story (William Loren Katz) New York: Atheneum, 1999

Children of the Dust Bowl: The True Story of the School at Weedpatch Camp (Jerry Stanley) New York: Crown Publishers, 1992

The Circuit: Stories From the Life of a Migrant Child (Francisco Jimenez) Albuquerque, NM: University of New Mexico Press, 1997

Columbus and the World Around Him (Milton Meltzer) Danbury, CT: Franklin Watts, 1990

Flying to the Moon: An Astronaut's Story (Michael Collins) Somerville, MA: Sunburst, 1994.

Grass Sandals: The Travels of Basho (Dawine Spivak) New York: Atheneum, 1997

A Hope in the Unseen: An American Odyssey From the Inner City to the Ivy League (Ron Suskind) Louisville, KY: Broadway Books, 1999

Out of Darkness: The Story of Louis Braille (Russell Freedman) New York: Clarion Books, 1997

Tea That Burns: A Family Memoir of Chinatown (Bruce Edward Hall) New York: Free Press, 1998

Easier Reading

3 NBs of Julian Drew (James Deem) New York: Avon, 2000

Bearskin (Howard Pyle) New York: Books of Wonder, 1997

Beyond the Sea of Ice: The Voyages of Henry Hudson (Joan Elizabeth Goodman) New York: Mikaya Press, 1999

Children of Bach (Ellis Dillon) New York: Scribner, 1992

China Boy (Gus Lee) East Rutherford, NJ: Plume, 1994

Countdown (Ben Mikaelsen) New York: Disney Press, 1997

Crow and Weasel (Tom Pohrt) Somerville, MA: Sunburst, 1998

Dance of the Sacred Circle (Kristina Rodanas) Boston: Little, Brown, 1994

Secret of the Dolphins (Edward Packard) New York: Bantam, 1993

Stranded at Plimoth Plantation 1626 (Gary Bowen) New York: HarperCollins, 1994

Taking Sides (Gary Soto) San Diego, CA: Harcourt Brace, 1992

The True Adventures of Daniel Hall (Diane Stanley) New York: Penguin, 1995

The Watsons Go to Birmingham—1963 (Christopher Paul Curtis) New York: Bantam Doubleday Dell, 1995

Patriarch

Adolescent Novels

California Blue (David Klass) Topeka, KS: Econo-Clad Books, 1999

Canyon Winter (Walter Morey) New York: Puffin, 1994

The Fool's War (Lee Kisling) New York: HarperCollins, 1992

Gypsy Davey (Chris Lynch) New York: HarperCollins, 1994

Hoops (Walter Dean Myers) Minneapolis, MN: Econo-Clad Books, 1999

The Maze (Will Hobbs) New York: Avon, 1999

Shadow Boxer (Chris Lynch) New York: Harper Trophy, 1995

True Friends (Bill Wallace) New York: Holiday House, 1994

Informational Books

Andrew Carnegie: Steel King and Friend to Libraries (Zachary Kent) Springfield, NJ: Enslow, 1999

The Meaning of It All: Thoughts of a Citizen Scientist (Richard Feynman) Cambridge, MA: Perseus, 1999

Michael Jordan: Basketball Great (Sean Dolan) Topeka, KS: Econo-Clad Books, 1999

Patriarch: George Washington and the New American Nation (Richard Norton Smith) Boston: Houghton Mifflin, 1997

Steve Young: Complete Quarterback (Terri Morgan & Samuel Thaler) Minneapolis, MN: Lerner, 1995

William Bradford: Rock of Plymouth (Kieran Doherty) New York: 21st Century/Millbrook, 1999

Easier Reading

The Backyard Tribe (Neil Shulman) New York: St. Martin's, 1994

Frederick Douglass: The Last Day of Slavery (William Miller) New York: Lee & Low Books, 1995

The Harmony Arms (Ron Koertge) New York: Avon, 1994

Martin Luther King (Rosemary Bray) New York: Greenwillow, 1995

Running Loose (Chris Crutcher) New York: Bantam Doubleday Dell, 1986

Thomas Jefferson: A Picture Book Biography (James Giblin) New York: Scholastic, 1994

Too Long a Stranger (Janette Oke) Minneapolis, MN: Bethany House, 1999

Warrior

Adolescent Novels

Against the Storm (Gaye Hicyilmaz) Boston: Little, Brown, 1992

The Contender (Robert Lipsyte) New York: HarperCollins, 1991

Dust Devils (Robert Laxalt) Reno, NV: University of Nevada Press, 1997

Ghost Soldier (Elaine Alphin) New York: Henry Holt and Company, 2001

Ironman (Chris Crutcher) New York: Greenwillow, 1995

Jesse (Gary Soto) New York: Scholastic, 1996

The Last Mission (Harry Mazer) New York: Dell, 1981

No Man's Land: A Young Soldier's Story (Susan Bartoletti) New York: Scholastic, 1999

The Proving Ground (Elaine Alphin) New York: Henry Holt and Company, 1993

Ran Van: The Defender (Diana Wieler) Toronto, ON: Groundwood Books, 1998

Reef of Death (Paul Zindel) New York: Disney Press, 1999

Scorpions (Walter Dean Myers) New York: Harper Trophy, 1990

Trino's Choice (Diane Gonzales-Bertrand) Houston, TX: Arte Publico, 1999

The Walls of Pedro Garcia (Kevin McColley) New York: Delacorte, 1993

When the Mountain Sings (John MacLean) Boston: Houghton Mifflin, 1992

Wrestling Sturbridge (Rich Wallace) New York: Knopf, 1997

Informational Books

A Boy Becomes a Man at Wounded Knee (Ted Wood with Wanbli Numpa Afraid of Hawk) New York: Walker and Company, 1995

Colin Powell: A Man of War and Peace (Carl Senna) New York: Walker and Company, 1992

Fire in Their Eyes: Wildfires and the People Who Fight Them (Karen Magnuson Beil) San Diego, CA: Harcourt Brace, 1999

I Was a Teenage Professional Wrestler (Ted Lewin) New York: Hyperion, 1994

Jesse Owens (Tom Streissguth) New York: Lerner, 1999

Jim Thorpe: Twentieth-Century Jock (Robert Lipsyte) New York: HarperCollins, 1993

The Life and Death of Crazy Horse (Russell Freedman) New York: Holiday House, 1996

The Long Road to Gettysburg (Jim Murphy) Boston: Houghton Mifflin, 2000

Nelson Mandela: Voice of Freedom (Libby Hughes) Lincoln, NE: iUniverse.com, 2000

Still Me (Christopher Reeve) New York: Ballantine, 1999

Troy Aikman: Super Quarterback (Bill Gutman) Brookfield, CT: Millbrook Press, 1997

A Young Patriot: The American Revolution as Experienced by One Boy (Jim Murphy) Boston: Houghton Mifflin, 1996

Easier Reading

Backfield Package (Thomas Dygard) New York: Morrow, 1992

The Brave (Robert Lipsyte) New York: Harper Trophy, 1993

The Heartbeat of Halftime (Stephen Wunderli) New York: Avon, 1996

Mandela: From the Life of the South African Statesman (Floyd Cooper) New York: Philomel, 1996

On My Honor (Marion Bauer) New York: Dell Yearling, 1987

The Printer's Apprentice (Stephen Krensky) New York: Bantam Doubleday Dell, 1995

Roughnecks (Thomas Cochran) San Diego, CA: Gulliver Books, 1999

Toussaint L'Ouverture: The Fight for Haiti's Freedom (Walter Dean Myers) New York: Simon & Schuster, 1996

What Hearts (Bruce Brooks) New York: HarperCollins, 1992

Magician

Adolescent Novels

At All Costs (John Gilstrap) New York: Warner Books, 1999

Cyclops (Clive Cussler) New York: Pocket Books, 1995

Dither Farm (Sid Hite) Topeka, KS: Econo-Clad Books, 1999

Dragonwings (Laurence Yep) New York: Harper Trophy, 1989

Escape From Exile (Robert Levy) Boston: Houghton Mifflin, 1993

Golden Compass (Phillip Pullman) New York: Del Rey, 1999

Moonfall (Jack McDevitt) New York: HarperCollins, 1999

Plunking Reggie Jackson (James Bennett) New York: Simon & Schuster, 2001

Stars (Eric Walters) Topeka, KS: Econo-Clad Books, 1999

Striking Out (Will Weaver) New York: HarperCollins, 1993

The Shark Callers (Eric Campbell) San Diego, CA: Harcourt Brace, 1995

The Subtle Knife (Phillip Pullman) New York: Dell Yearling, 1999

The Transall Saga (Gary Paulsen) New York: Laurel-Leaf, 1999

Informational Books

The Abracadabra Kid: A Writer's Life (Sid Fleishman) New York: Morrow, 1998

Always Inventing: A Photobiography of Alexander Graham Bell (Tom Matthews) Washington, DC: National Geographic Society, 1999

Bard of Avon: The Story of William Shakespeare (Diane Stanley) Topeka, KS: Econo-Clad Books, 1999

Bill Peet: An Autobiography (Bill Peet) Boston: Houghton Mifflin, 1994

The Casebook of Forensic Detection (Colin Evans) Chichester, UK: John Wiley & Sons, 1998

Gutenberg (Leonard Everett Fisher) New York: Simon & Schuster, 1993

Harry Houdini (Adam Woog) San Diego, CA: Lucent Books, 1995

Matthew Brady: His Life and Photographs (George Sullivan) New York: Cobblehill Books, 1994

Outward Dreams: Black Inventors and Their Inventions (James Haskins) New York: Starfire, 1992

Rocket Boys: A Memoir (Homer Hickam Jr.) New York: Delacorte, 2000

Rocket Man: The Story of Robert Goddard (Tom Streissguth) Minneapolis, MN: Carolrhoda Books, 1995

Tibaldo and the Hole in the Calendar (Abner Shimony) New York: Copernicus Books, 1997

Easier Reading

The Adventures of Ali Baba Bernstein (Johanna Hurwitz) New York: Avon, 1995

Amazing and Death Defying Diary of Eugene Dingman (Paul Zindel) New York: Starfire, 1989

The Gift-Giver (Joyce Hansen) New York: Clarion Books, 1989

Harry Potter and the Chamber of Secrets (J.K. Rowling) New York: Scholastic, 1999

Harry Potter and the Sorcerer's Stone (J.K. Rowling) New York: Scholastic, 1999

The Iron Ring (Lloyd Alexander) New York: Penguin, 1999

Knights of the Kitchen Table (Jon Scieszka) New York: Penguin, 1994

Leonardo da Vinci (Diane Stanley) New York: Morrow, 1996

The Librarian Who Measured the Earth (Kathryn Lasky) Boston: Little, Brown, 1994

Mozart Tonight (Julie Downing) New York: Bradbury Press, 1991

Mutation (Robin Cook) East Rutherford, NJ: Berkley Publishing Group, 1991

The Real McCoy: The Life of an African American Inventor (Wendy Towle) New York: Scholastic, 1993

The Tempest by William Shakespeare (Ann Keay Beneduce) New York: Philomel, 1996

The Wonderful Towers of Watts (Patricia Zelver) New York: Tambourine Books, 1994

King

Adolescent Novels

Borderlands (Peter Carter) New York: Farrar, Straus & Giroux, 1993

Last Days of Summer (Steve Kluger) New York: Morrow/Avon, 1999

Walker of Time (Helen Hughes Vick) Sacramento, CA: Roberts Rinehart, 1993

When Heroes Die (Penny Durant) Topeka, KS: Econo-Clad Books, 1999

Informational Books

Arthur Ashe: Breaking the Color Barrier (David Wright) Springfield, NJ: Enslow, 1996

Cesar Chavez (Ruth Franchere & Earl Thollander) New York: HarperCollins, 1970

Franklin D. Roosevelt (Karen Bornemann Spies) Springfield, NJ: Enslow, 1999

The Greatest: Muhammad Ali (Walter Dean Myers) New York: Scholastic, 2001

King of the World: Muhammad Ali and the Rise of an American Hero (David Remnick) Elk Grove, CA: Vintage Books, 1999

Lincoln: A Photobiography (Russell Freedman) New York: Clarion Books, 1989

The Sea King: Sir Francis Drake and His Times (Albert Marrin) New York: Atheneum, 1995

Ship of Gold in the Deep Blue Sea (Gary Kinder) Elk Grove, CA: Vintage Books, 1999

The Tall Mexican: The Life of Hank Aguirre All-Star Pitcher, Businessman, Humanitarian (Robert Copley) Houston, TX: Arte Publico, 2000

Winston Churchill: Soldier, Statesman, Artist (John Severance) New York: Clarion Books, 1996

Easier Reading

The Book of Three (Lloyd Alexander) New York: Dell Yearling, 1999

The Fire Pony (W.R. Philbrick) Topeka, KS: Econo-Clad Books, 1999

Ghost Canoe (Will Hobbs) New York: Avon/Camelot, 1998

Honest Abe (Edith Kunhardt) New York: Greenwillow, 1993

Invitation to the Game (Monica Hughes) New York: Aladdin, 1993

A Little Bit Dead (Chap Reaver) Topeka, KS: Econo-Clad Books, 1999

A Picture Book of Sitting Bull (David Adler) New York: Holiday House, 1993

Wildman

Adolescent Novels

Angels of the Swamp (Dorothy Whittaker) New York: Walker and Company, 1992

Brian's Return (Gary Paulsen) New York: Random House, 1999

Brian's Winter (Gary Paulsen) New York: Scholastic, 1996

Crash (Jerry Spinelli) New York: Knopf, 1996

Danny Ain't (Joe Cottonwood) New York: Scholastic, 1992

Far North (Will Hobbs) New York: Avon, 1996

Jason's Gold (Will Hobbs) New York: Morrow, 1999

Lockie Leonard, Human Torpedo (Tim Winton) Boston: Little, Brown, 1991

The Last Safe Place on Earth (Richard Peck) New York: Laurel-Leaf, 1996

The Loop (Nicholas Evans) New York: Dell, 1999

Never Cry Wolf (Farley Mowat) New York: Bantam, 1983

The River (Gary Paulsen) New York: Dell Yearling, 1993

Slam! (Walter Dean Myers) New York: Scholastic, 1998

We Are All Guilty (Kingsley Amis) New York: Viking, 1991

Wilderness Peril (Thomas Dygard) New York: Puffin, 1991

Informational Books

Born Naked (Farley Mowat) Boston: Houghton Mifflin, 1995

The Climb: Tragic Ambitions on Everest (Anatoli Boukreev & G. Weston DeWalt) New York: St. Martin's, 1998

Gone A-Whaling: The Lure of the Sea and the Hunt for the Great Whale (Jim Murphy) New York: Clarion Books, 1998

The Hemingway Cookbook (Craig Boreth) Chicago: Chicago Review Press, 1998

Ice Story: Shackleton's Lost Expedition (Elizabeth Cody Kimmel) New York: Clarion Books, 1999

Into Thin Air: A Personal Account of the Mt. Everest Disaster (Jon Krakauer) Waxhaw, NC: Anchor Books, 1999

Jack London: A Biography (Daniel Dyer) New York: Scholastic, 1997

The Man Who Was Poe (Avi) New York: Avon, 1997

Pirates (David Spence) South Bend, IN: Consortium Books, 2001

The Saga of Lewis and Clark Into the Uncharted West (Thomas Schmidt & Jeremy Schmidt) New York: Doris Kindersley, 1999

To the Top of the World: Adventures With Arctic Wolves (Jim Brandenberg) New York: Scholastic, 1997

Within Reach (Mark Pfetzer) New York: Puffin, 2000

Easier Reading

Angel Falls: A South American Journey (Martin Jordan & Tanis Jordan) New York: Kingfisher, 1995

Antar and the Eagles (William Mayne) Garden City, NY: Doubleday, 1990

Captain Hawaii (Anthony Dana Arkin) New York: HarperCollins, 1994

Capturing Nature: The Writings and Art of John James Audubon (Peter Roops & Connie Roops) New York: Walker and Company, 1993

Climb or Die (Edward Myers) New York: Hyperion, 1996

Cowboy Charlie (Jeanette Winter) San Diego, CA: Harcourt Brace, 1995

Hatchet (Gary Paulsen) New York: Scholastic, 1999

Hugh Glass, Mountain Man: Left for Dead (Robert McClung) New York: Beech Tree Books, 1993

Into the Deep Forest With Henry David Thoreau (Jim Murphy) New York: Clarion Books, 1995

Lewis and Clark: Explorers of the American West (Steven Kroll) New York: Holiday House, 1994

A Picture Book of Davy Crockett (David Adler) New York: Holiday House, 1996

Prince Henry the Navigator (Leonard Everett Fisher) New York: Macmillan, 1990

Walden (Robert Sabuda) New York: Philomel, 1990

Healer

Adolescent Novels

Blue Skin of the Sea (Graham Salisbury) New York: Laurel-Leaf, 1994

Bud, Not Buddy (Christopher Paul Curtis) New York: Random House, 1999

Chinese Handcuffs (Chris Crutcher) New York: Dell, 1996

Holes (Louis Sacher) New York: Random House, 1999

Just Like Martin (Ossie Davis) New York: Puffin, 1995

Midget (Tim Bowler) New York: Aladdin, 2000

The Moves Make the Man (Bruce Brooks) New York: Harper Trophy, 1996

Night of Fear (Peg Kehret) Topeka, KS: Econo-Clad Books, 1999

Twelve Days in August (Liza Ketchum Murrow) New York: Holiday House, 1993

Twelve Shots: Outstanding Short Stories About Guns (Harry Mazer) New York: Laurel-Leaf, 1998

Informational Books

Gandhi: Great Soul (John Severance) Boston: Houghton Mifflin, 1997

John Muir: Wilderness Protector (Ginger Wadsworth) Minneapolis, MN: Lerner, 1992

Life in Prison (Stanley Williams) New York: SeaStar Books, 2001

Stella (Peter Wyden) Waxhaw, NC: Anchor Books, 1993

The Wreck of the Henrietta Marie (Michael Cottman) New York: Harmony Books, 1999

Easier Reading

Alexander Graham Bell (Leonard Everett Fisher) New York: Atheneum, 1999

The Chemo Kid (Robert Lipsyte) New York: HarperCollins, 1992

Dear Benjamin Banneker (Andrea Pinkney) San Diego, CA: Harcourt Brace, 1994

Flander's Field: The Story of the Poem by John McCrae (Linda Granfield) Garden City, NY: Doubleday, 1995

Keeper of the Universe (Louis Lawrence) Boston: Houghton Mifflin, 1993

Mariposa Blues (Ron Koertge) Madison, WI: Demco Media, 1993

Raptor Rescue: An Eagle Flies Free (Sylvia Johnson) New York: Dutton, 1995

Rescue Josh McGuire (Ben Mikaelsen) New York: Hyperion, 1993

Sticks (Joan Bauer) New York: Bantam, 1997

A Sunburned Prayer (Marc Talbert) New York: Aladdin, 1997

Prophet

Adolescent Novels

An Eye for Color (Norman Silver) New York: Dutton, 1993

A Fisherman of the Island Sea (Ursula LeGuin) San Diego, CA: Harcourt Brace, 2001

Maniac Magee (Jerry Spinelli) New York: Harper Trophy, 1990

The Postman (David Brin) New York: Bantam, 1990

S'gana the Black Whale (Sue Stauffacher) Anchorage, AK: Alaska Northwest Books, 1992

Seventh Son (Orson Scott Card) New York: Tor Books, 1993

Slave Day (Rob Thomas) New York: Simon & Schuster, 1997

Informational Books

Art Attack: A Short Cultural History of the Avant-Garde (Marc Aronson) New York: Clarion Books, 1998

Einstein: Visionary Scientist (John Severance) New York: Clarion Books, 1999

Flash! The Associated Press Covers the World (Vincent Alabisco) New York: Abrams, 2000

I Have a Dream: The Life and Words of Martin Luther King, Jr. (Jim Haskins) Brookfield, CT: Millbrook Press, 1992

Jacques Cousteau: Champion of the Sea (Catherine Reef) Breckenridge, CO: Twenty-First Century Books, 1992

Malcolm X: By Any Means Necessary (Walter Dean Myers) New York: Scholastic, 1995

Martin Luther King: The Peaceful Warrior (Edward Clayton & David Hodges) Huntington Beach, CA: Archway, 1996

Men of Color: Fashion, History, Fundamentals (Lloyd Boston) Wedmore, UK: Artisan, 2000

Now Is Your Time! The African-American Struggle for Freedom (Walter Dean Myers) New York: HarperCollins, 1992

Easier Reading

Coming Home: From the Life of Langston Hughes (Floyd Cooper) New York: Philomel, 1994

Gandhi (Leonard Everett Fisher) New York: Simon & Schuster, 1995

Gulf (Robert Westall) New York: Scholastic, 1996

Leagues Apart: The Men and Times of the Negro Baseball League (Lawrence Ritter) New York: Morrow, 1995

The Moon Is a Harsh Mistress (Robert Heinlein) New York: Tor Books, 1996

Rudy (James Ellison) New York: Bantam, 1993

Starry Messenger (Peter Sis) New York: Farrar, Straus & Giroux, 1996

Trickster

Adolescent Novels

In a Dark Wood (Michael Cadnum) New York: Penguin, 1999

Inca Gold (Clive Cussler) Topeka, KS: Econo-Clad Books, 1999

Juggler (John Morressey) Minneapolis, MN: Econo-Clad Books, 1999

Oddballs (William Sleator) New York: Puffin, 1995

Rama: A Legend (Jamake Highwater) Bridgewater, NJ: Replica Books, 2001

Slot Machine (Chris Lynch) New York: Harper Trophy, 1986

Someone Was Watching (David Patneaude) Topeka, KS: Econo-Clad Books, 1999

Stone Cold (Pete Hautman) New York: Aladdin, 2000

The Good Liar (Gregory Maguire) New York: Clarion Books, 1999

There's No Surf in Cleveland (Stephanie Buehler) New York: Clarion Books, 1993

A Wizard of Earthsea (Ursula LeGuin) New York: Bantam, 1984

Informational Books

Boy: Tales of Childhood (Roald Dahl) New York: Viking, 1988

Mark Twain: America's Humorist, Dreamer, Prophet (Clinton Cox) New York: Apple Publishing, 1999

Prince of Humbugs: A Life of P.T. Barnum (Catherine Andronik) New York: Atheneum, 1994

Easier Reading

The Adventures of Reddy Fox (Thornton Burgess) New York: Dover, 1992

Anything Can Happen in High School (and It Usually Does) (William McCants) Topeka, KS: Econo-Clad Books, 1999

Attaboy, Sam! (Lois Lowry) New York: Dell Yearling, 1993

Charles Dickens: The Man Who Had Great Expectations (Diane Stanley) New York: Morrow, 1993

Creepers (Keith Gray) New York: Putnam, 1997

Darnell Rock Reporting (Walter Dean Myers) New York: Dell Yearling, 1996

The Fat Man (Maurice Gee) New York: Aladdin, 1999

Jumper (Steven Gould) New York: Tom Dougherty Associates, 1993

Pish Posh, Said Hieronymous Bosch (Nancy Willard) San Diego, CA: Harcourt Brace, 1991

Robin Hood (Margaret Early) New York: Abrams, 1996

The Shakespeare Stealer (Gary Blackwood) New York: Puffin, 2000

Skellig (David Almond) New York: Dell Yearling, 2000

Lover

Adolescent Novels

Heart of a Champion (Carl Deuker) New York: Avon, 1994

A Life for a Life (Ernest Hill) New York: Simon & Schuster, 1998

My Brother Stealing Second (Jim Naughton) New York: HarperCollins, 1989

Nowhere to Call Home (Cynthia DeFelice) New York: Farrar, Straus & Giroux, 1999

The One Who Came Back (Joann Mazzio) Boston: Houghton Mifflin, 1992

Phoenix Rising (Karen Hesse) New York: Puffin, 1995

Rats Saw God (Rob Thomas) New York: Aladdin, 1996

A Solitary Blue (Cynthia Voight) New York: Scholastic, 1993

Staying Fat for Sarah Byrnes (Chris Crutcher) New York: Laurel-Leaf, 1995

Tiger, Tiger, Burning Bright: A Novel (Ron Koertge) New York: Orchard, 1994

Under the Blood Red Sun (Graham Salisbury) New York: Dell Yearling, 1995

Informational Books

Carl Sandburg: A Biography (Milton Meltzer) New York: 21st Century/Millbrook, 1999

Face Forward: Young African American Men in a Critical Age (Julian Okwu) San Francisco, CA: Chronicle Books, 1997

In a Sacred Manner I Live (Neil Philip) Boston: Houghton Mifflin, 1997

Jack and Rochelle: A Holocaust Story of Love and Resistance (Lawrence Sutin, Rochelle Sutin, & Jack Sutin) St. Paul, MN: Graywolf Press, 1996

Learning About Dignity From the Life of Martin Luther King, Jr. (Jeanne Strazzabosco) New York: PowerKids Press, 1997

Modoc: The True Story of the Greatest Elephant That Ever Lived (Ralph Helfer) New York: HarperPerennial, 1998

Ralph Bunch: Winner of the Nobel Peace Prize (Anne Schraff) Springfield, NJ: Enslow, 1999

Talking Peace: A Vision for the Next Generation (Jimmy Carter) New York: Penguin, 1993

Easier Reading

The Barn (Avi) New York: Avon, 1996

The Cay (Theodore Taylor) New York: Avon, 1991

A Couple of Kooks and Other Stories About Love (Cynthia Rylant) New York: Orchard, 1990

Fast Sam, Cool Clyde, and Stuff (Walter Dean Myers) New York: Viking, 1988

Freak the Mighty (Rodman Philbrick) New York: Scholastic, 2001

Harris and Me (Gary Paulsen) New York: Dell Yearling, 1995

Lives and Legends of the Saints (Carole Armstrong) New York: Simon & Schuster, 1995

The Pool Party (Gary Soto) New York: Dell Yearling, 1995

Saint Valentine (Robert Sabuda) New York: Atheneum, 1992

Shadow Like a Leopard (Myron Levoy) Lincoln, NE: iUniverse.com, 2000

Shiloh (Phyllis Reynolds Naylor) New York: Aladdin, 2000

Soldier's Heart (Gary Paulsen) New York: Laurel-Leaf, 2000

Teammates (Peter Golenbock) San Diego, CA: Harcourt Brace, 1990

Walt Whitman (Nancy Loewen) Mankato, MN: Creative Editions, 1993

References

Alexander, P., Kulikowich, J., & Hetton, T. (1994). The role of subject matter knowledge and interest in the processing of linear and nonlinear texts. *Review of Educational Research, 64,* 210–253.

Alloway, N., & Gilbert, P. (1997). Boys and literacy: Lessons from Australia. *Gender and Education, 9,* 49–58.

American Psychiatric Association. (1994). *Diagnostic and statistical manual of mental disorders* (4th ed.). Washington, DC: Author.

Anderson, R., Wilson, P., & Fielding, L. (1988). Growth in reading and how children spend their time outside of school. *Reading Research Quarterly, 23,* 285–303.

Anderson, W. (1990). *Green man: The archetype of our oneness with the Earth.* New York: Harper & Row.

Applebee, A. (1993). *Literature in the secondary school: Studies of curriculum and instruction in the United States.* Urbana, IL: National Council of Teachers of English.

Arnold, P. (1995). *Wildmen, warriors, and kings: Masculine spirituality and the Bible.* New York: Crossroad Publishing.

Aronson, M. (2001). *Exploding the myths: The truth about teenagers and reading.* Lanham, MD: Scarecrow Press.

Atwell, N. (1987). *In the middle: Writing, reading and learning with adolescents.* Portsmouth, NH: Heinemann.

Ayers, W. (1999). Juvenile criminals should not be treated as adults. In L. Egendorf & J. Hurley (Eds.), *Teens at risk: Opposing viewpoints* (pp. 70–74). San Diego, CA: Greenhaven Press.

Baines, L. (1994). Cool books for tough guys: 50 books out of the mainstream of adolescent literature that will appeal to males who do not enjoy reading. *The ALAN Review, 22,* 43–46.

Baker, L., & Wigfield, A. (2000). Dimensions of children's motivation for reading and their relations to reading activity and reading achievement. *Reading Research Quarterly, 34,* 452–477.

Barrs, M., & Pidgeon, S. (1994). *Reading the difference: Gender and reading in elementary classrooms.* York, ME: Stenhouse.

Bean, T. (2000). Reading in the content areas: Social constructivist dimensions. In M. Kamil, P. Mosenthal, P.D. Pearson, & R. Barr (Eds.), *Handbook of reading research* (Vol. III, pp. 629–644). Mahwah, NJ: Erlbaum.

Benton, P. (1995). "Recipe fictions...literacy fast food?" Reading interests in year 8. *Oxford Review of Education, 21,* 99–111.

Birkerts, S. (1994). *The Gutenberg elegies: The fate of reading in an electronic age.* New York: Fawcett.

Blankenhorn, D. (1995). *Fatherless America: Confronting our most urgent social problem.* New York: Basic Books.

Bowden, B., & Zeisz, J. (1997). *Supper's on: Adolescent adjustment and frequency of family mealtimes.* Paper presented at the 105th Annual Convention of the American Psychological Association, Chicago.

Bromley, K. (1993). *Journaling: Engagement in reading, writing, and thinking.* New York: Scholastic.

Bromley, K., & Powell, P. (1999). Interest journals motivate student writers. *The Reading Teacher, 53,* 111–112.

Browne, R., & Fletcher, R. (1995). *Boys in schools: Addressing the real issues—behaviour, values and relationships.* Sydney: Finch Publishing.

Brozo, W.G., & Schmelzer, R.V. (1997). Wildmen, warriors, and lovers: Reaching boys through archetypal literature. *Journal of Adolescent & Adult Literacy, 41,* 4–11.

Brozo, W.G., & Simpson, M.L. (1999). *Readers, teachers, learners: Expanding literacy across the content areas.* Columbus, OH: Merrill/Prentice Hall.

Bugel, K., & Buunk, B. (1995). Sex differences in foreign language text comprehension: The role of interests and prior knowledge. *The Modern Language Journal, 80,* 15–31.

Bureau of the Census. (1997). *Statistical abstract of the United States.* Washington, DC: U.S. Government Printing Office.

Bureau of Justice Statistics. (1991). *Survey of state prison inmates.* Washington, DC: Bureau of Justice.

Bureau of Labor Statistics. (1999). *Unemployment and the newest high school dropouts.* Washington, DC: U.S. Department of Labor.

Canada, G. (1998). *Reaching up for manhood: Transforming the lives of boys in America.* Boston: Beacon Press.

Chung, Y.B., Baskin, M.L., & Case, A. (1999). Career development of black males: Case studies. *Journal of Career Development, 25,* 161–171.

Clary, L. (1991). Getting adolescents to read. *Journal of Reading, 34,* 340–345.

Collins-Standley, T., Gan, S.-L., Yu, H.-J., & Zillmann, D. (1996). Choice of romantic, violent, and scary fairy-tale books by preschool girls and boys. *Child Study Journal, 26,* 279–302.

Connell, R.W. (1989). Cool guys, swots and wimps: The interplay of masculinity and education. *Oxford Review of Education, 15,* 291–303.

Cooper-Mullin, A., & Coye, J.M. (1998). *Once upon a heroine: 400 books for girls to love.* Chicago: NTC/Contemporary Publishing Group.

Cowden, T., Viders, S., & Lafever, C. (2000). *The complete writer's guide to heroes and heroines: Sixteen master archetypes.* Los Angeles: Lone Eagle.

Cutler, M. (2000). Philomela speaks: Alice Walker's revisioning of rape archetypes in *The Color Purple. Melus, 25,* 161–182.

Daly, P., Salters, J., & Burns, C. (1998). Gender and task interaction: Instant and delayed recall of three story types. *Educational Review, 50,* 269–275.

Dandy, E. (1998). Increasing the number of minority teachers: Tapping the para-professional pool. *Education and Urban Society, 31,* 89–103.

Darling, S. (1997). *Opening session speech.* Paper presented at the Sixth Annual Conference on Family Literacy, Louisville, KY.

Davis, T., Byrd, R., Arnold, C., Auinger, P., & Bocchini, J. (1999). Low literacy and violence among adolescents in a summer sports program. *Journal of Adolescent Health, 24,* 403–411.

Deci, E., Vallerand, R., Pelletier, L., & Ryan, R. (1991). Motivation and education: The self-determination perspective. *Educational Psychologist, 26,* 325–346.

DeLaszlo, V.S. (1959). *The basic writings of C. G. Jung.* New York: Modern Library.

Department of Education and Science Welsh Office. (1989). *English for ages 5 to 16.* London: HMSO.

Diaz-Rubin, C. (1996). Reading interests of high school students. *Reading Improvement, 33,* 169–175.

Donahue, P., Voelkl, K., Campbell, J., & Mazzeo, J. (1999). *NAEP reading report card for the nation and states.* Washington, DC: National Center for Education Statistics.

Donelson, K., & Nilsen, A.P. (Eds.). (1997). *Literature for today's young adults* (5th ed.). New York: Longman.

Farrell, A.D., & Meyer, A.L. (1997). The effectiveness of a school-based curriculum for reducing violence among urban sixth-grade students. *The American Journal of Public Health, 87,* 979–984.

Filozof, E., Albertin, H., Jones, C., Steme, S., Myers, L., & McDermott, R. (1998). Relationship of adolescent self-esteem to selected academic variables. *Journal of School Health, 68,* 68–77.

Finders, M. (1996). *Just girls: Hidden literacies and life in junior high.* New York: Teachers College Press.

Fink, R. (1995/1996). Successful dyslexics: A constructivist study of passionate interest reading. *Journal of Adolescent & Adult Literacy, 39*, 268–280.

Gambell, T.J., & Hunter, D.M. (1999). Rethinking gender differences in literacy. *Canadian Journal of Education, 24*, 1–16.

Gambrell, L., & Codling, R.M. (1997). Fostering reading motivation: Insights from theory and research. In K. Camperell, B. Hayes, & R. Telfer (Eds.), *Yearbook of the American Reading Forum* (pp. 3–8). Logan, UT: American Reading Forum.

Garbarino, J. (1999). *Lost boys: Why our sons turn violent and how we can save them.* New York: Free Press.

Gilbert, P. (1989). *Gender, literacy and the classroom.* Melbourne, Australia: Australian Reading Association.

Gilmore, D. (1990). *Manhood in the making: Cultural concepts of masculinity.* New Haven, CT: Yale University Press.

Glasgow, J.N. (1996). Motivating the tech prep reader through learning styles and adolescent literature. *Journal of Adolescent & Adult Literacy, 39*, 358–367.

Goodman, J. (1992). *Elementary schooling for critical democracy.* Albany, NY: State University of New York Press.

Greenspan, S., & Lewis, N.B. (2000). *Building healthy minds: The six experiences that create intelligence and emotional growth in babies and young children.* Cambridge, MA: Perseus.

Grim, J.A. (1984). *The shaman: Patterns of Siberian and Ojibway healing.* Norman, OK: University of Oklahoma Press.

Gurian, M. (1997). *The wonder of boys: What parents, mentors and educators can do to shape boys into exceptional men.* Los Angeles: JP Tarcher.

Guthrie, J., Alao, S., & Rinehart, J. (1997). Engagement in reading for young adolescents. *Journal of Adolescent & Adult Literacy, 40*, 438–446.

Hedges, L., & Nowell, A. (1995, July 7). Sex differences in mental test scores, variability, and numbers of high-scoring individuals. *Science, 269*, 41–45.

Herbert, B. (2001, September 3). In America; On the way to nowhere. *The New York Times*, p. A15.

Herz, S., & Gallo, D. (1996). *From Hinton to Hamlet: Building bridges between young adult literature and the classics.* Westport, CT: Greenwood Press.

Hewlett, S.A., & West, C. (1998). *The war against parents: What we can do for America's beleaguered moms and dads.* Boston: Houghton Mifflin.

Hoffman, L. (1999, September). What boys like. *Lingua Franca, 9*, 11–13.

Hofstetter, C.R., Sticht, T., & Hofstetter, C.H. (1999). Knowledge, literacy and power. *Communication Research, 26*, 58–80.

Houser, P. (2001). Let's hear it for the boys. *Black Issues Book Review, 3*, 72–73.

Ivey, G. (1998). Discovering readers in the middle level school: A few helpful clues. *NASSP Bulletin, 82,* 48–56.

Ivey, G., & Broaddus, K. (2001). "Just plain reading": A survey of what makes students want to read in middle school classrooms. *Reading Research Quarterly, 36,* 350–377.

Jensen, P. (1999, August 15). Reading's lost boys. *The Baltimore Sun,* pp. 1L, 4L.

Johnson, R. (1989). *He: Understanding masculine psychology.* New York: Warner Books.

Johnson, D.M., & Peer, G.G. (1984). Protagonist preferences among juvenile and adolescent readers. *Journal of Educational Research, 77,* 147–150.

Jordan, E. (1995). Fighting boys and fantasy play: The construction of masculinity in the early years of school. *Gender and Education, 7,* 69–86.

Jung, C.G. (1955). *Modern man in search of a soul.* London: Harvest Books.

Jung, C.G. (1968). *Man and his symbols.* New York: Dell.

Kindlon, D., & Thompson, M. (2000). *Raising Cane: Protecting the emotional life of boys.* New York: Ballantine.

Kipnis, A. (1994). Men, movies, and monsters: Heroic masculinity as a crucible of male violence. *Psychological Perspectives, 29,* 38–51.

Klein, R. (1997, September 12). Oh boy! Why is reading such a bore? *Times Educational Supplement,* pp. 2–4.

Kleinfeld, J. (1999, Winter). Student performance: Males versus females. *The Public Interest, 134,* 3–20.

Kragler, S., & Nolley, C. (1996). Student choices: Book selection strategies of fourth graders. *Reading Horizons, 36,* 354–365.

Langerman, D. (1990). Books & boys: Gender preferences and book selection. *School Library Journal, 36,* 132–136.

Langker, S. (1995). Boys' team also does well. In R. Browne & R. Fletcher (Eds.), *Boys in schools: Addressing the real issues—behaviour, values and relationships* (pp. 190–200). Sydney: Finch Publishing.

Libsch, M., & Breslow, M. (1996). Trends in non-assigned reading by high school seniors. *NASSP Bulletin, 80,* 111–116.

Martin, C., Martin, M., & O'Brien, D. (1984). Spawning ideas for writing in the content areas. *Reading World, 11,* 111–15.

Maughan, S. (2001, May 7). You go, guys. *Publishers Weekly, 248,* 41–42.

McGuire, M. (1997). Taking a storypath into history. *Educational Leadership, 54,* 70–74.

Mead, M. (1969). *Male and female: A study of the sexes in a changing world.* New York: Dell.

Moje, E. (2000). Reinventing adolescent literacy for new times: Perennial and millennial issues. *Journal of Adolescent & Adult Literacy, 43*, 4–11.

Moore, R., & Gillette, D. (1992). *The king within: Accessing the king in the male psyche.* New York: Morrow.

Mullis, I., Campbell, J., & Farstrup, A. (1993). *NAEP 1992: Reading report card for the nation and the states.* Washington, DC: U.S. Department of Education.

Murphy, P., & Elwood, J. (1998). Gendered experiences, choices and achievement—exploring the links. *International Journal of Inclusive Education, 2,* 95–118.

National Center for Education Statistics. (1998). *The condition of education, 1998.* Washington, DC: U.S. Department of Education.

National Center for Education Statistics. (1999). *Digest of education statistics, 1998.* Washington, DC: U.S. Department of Education.

National Center for Education Statistics. (2000). *Trends in educational equity of girls and women.* Washington, DC: U.S. Department of Education.

National Institute on Drug Abuse. (1997). *Drug abuse prevention for at-risk groups.* Washington, DC: U.S. Department of Health and Human Services.

National Law Center on Homelessness and Poverty. (1997). *Blocks to their future: A report on the barriers to preschool education for homeless children.* Washington, DC: Author.

Newberger, E. (2000). *The men they will become: The nature and nurture of male character.* Cambridge, MA: Perseus.

Nichols, S. (1980). *Jung and tarot: An archetypal journey.* York Beach, ME: Samuel Weiser.

Nicolle, R. (1989). Boys and the five-year void. *School Library Journal, 35,* 130–135.

Odean, K. (1998). *Great books for boys.* New York: Ballantine.

Oldfather, P. (1995). Commentary: What's needed to maintain and extend motivation for literacy in the middle grades. *Journal of Reading, 38,* 420–422.

Ollmann, H.E. (1993). Choosing literature wisely: Students speak out. *Journal of Reading, 36,* 648–653.

Osmont, P. (1987). Teacher inquiry in the classroom: Reading and gender set. *Language Arts, 64,* 758–761.

Parke, R., & Brott, A. (1999). *Throwaway dads: The myth and barriers that keep men from being the fathers they want to be.* Boston: Houghton Mifflin.

Pearson, C., & Seivert, S. (1995). *Magic at work: Camelot, creative leadership, and everyday miracles.* Garden City, NY: Doubleday.

Petrosky, A. (1982). From story to essay: Reading and writing. *College Composition and Communication, 33*, 19–36.

Plucker, J.A., & Omdal, S.N. (1997, June 18). Beyond boredom: Addressing complex issues with real solutions. *Education Week, 16*, 32.

Pollack, W. (2000). *Real boys' voices.* New York: Random House.

Popp, M.S. (1997). *Learning journals in the K–8 classroom: Exploring ideas and information in the content areas.* Hillsdale, NJ: Erlbaum.

Pottorff, D.D., Phelps-Zientarsky, D., & Skovera, M. (1996). Gender perceptions of elementary and middle school students about literacy at school and home. *Journal of Research and Development in Education, 29*, 203–211.

Radin, P. (1969). *The trickster: A study in American Indian mythology.* Westport, CT: Greenwood Press.

Reynolds, A.J. (1991). Note on adolescents' time-use and scientific literacy. *Psychological Reports, 68*, 63–70.

Rousseau, J.J. (1979). *Emile, or on education.* New York: Basic Books.

Samuels, B.B. (1989). Young adults' choices: Why do students "really like" particular books. *Journal of Reading, 32*, 714–719.

Sanderson, G. (1995). Being "cool" and a reader. In R. Browne & R. Fletcher (Eds.), *Boys in schools: Addressing the real issues—behaviour, values and relationships* (pp. 152–167). Sydney: Finch Publishing.

Sawyer, W. (1987). Literature and literacy: A review of research. *Language Arts, 64*, 33–39.

Schaum, M. (2000). "Erasing angel": The Lucifer-trickster figure in Flannery O'Connor's short fiction. *The Southern Literary Journal, 33*, 1–26.

Schwarzchild, M. (2000). Alienated youth: Help from families and schools. *Professional Psychology: Research and Practice, 31*, 95–96.

Silverstein, O., & Rashbaum, B. (1995). *The courage to raise good men.* New York: Penguin.

Simon, R. (1987). Empowerment as a pedagogy of possibility. *Language Arts, 64*, 370–382.

Simpson, A. (1996). Fictions and facts: An investigation of the reading practices of girls and boys. *English Education, 28*, 268–279.

Sloan, G.D. (1991). *The child as critic: Teaching literature in the elementary school.* New York: Teachers College Press.

Sommers, C.H. (2000). *The war against boys: How misguided feminism is harming our young men.* New York: Simon & Schuster.

Spaulding, C.L. (1995). Motivation or empowerment: What's the difference? *Language Arts, 72*, 489–494.

Sullivan, E. (2001). Some teens prefer the real thing: The case for young adult nonfiction. *English Journal, 90*, 43–47.

Taylor, B.M., Frye, B.J., & Maruyama, G.M. (1990). Time spent reading and reading growth. *American Educational Research Journal, 27*, 351–362.

Turner, J. (1995). The influence of classroom contexts on young children's motivation for literacy. *Reading Research Quarterly, 30*, 410–441.

Turner, J., & Paris, S. (1995). How literacy tasks influence children's motivation for literacy. *The Reading Teacher, 48*, 662–673.

Weber, M.J. (1993). Immersed in an educational crisis: Alternative programs for African-American males. *Stanford Law Review, 45*, 1099–1131.

Weeks, L. (2001, May 14). Aliteracy: Read all about it, or maybe not: Millions of Americans who can read choose not to: Can we do without the written word? *The Washington Post*, p. C1.

Weston, J. (1997). *From ritual to romance*. New York: Dover.

White, B., & Johnson, T.S. (2001). We really do mean it: Implementing language arts standard #3 with opinionnaires. *The Clearing House, 74*, 119–123.

Wicks, J. (1995). Patterns of reading among teenage boys: The reading habits and book preferences of 13–15-year-old boys. *New Library World, 96*, 10–16.

Willeford, W. (1969). *The fool and his scepter: A study in clowns and jesters and their audience*. Evanston, IL: Northwestern University Press.

Wittrock, M.C. (1990). Generative processes of comprehension. *Educational Psychologist, 24*, 345–376.

Worthy, J., Moorman, M., & Turner, M. (1999). What Johnny likes to read is hard to find in school. *Reading Research Quarterly, 34*, 12–27.

Wright, W.J. (1991/1992). The endangered black male child. *Educational Leadership, 14*, 14.

Young, J.P., & Brozo, W.G. (2001). Boys will be boys, or will they? Literacy and masculinities. *Reading Research Quarterly, 36*, 316–325.

Literature Cited

Adler, D.A. (1994). *A picture book of Jackie Robinson*. Ill. R. Casilla. New York: Holiday House.

Adler, D.A. (1997). *Lou Gehrig: The luckiest man*. Ill. T. Widener. San Diego, CA: Gulliver Books.

Anaya, R. (1999). *My land sings: Stories from the Rio Grande*. Ill. A. Cordova. New York: Morrow Junior Books.

Asimov, I. (1994). *Isaac Asimov's great space mysteries*. New York: Modern Publishing.

Bakken, H. (1992). *The fields and the hills: The journey, once begun.* New York: Clarion Books.

Becker, E. (1992). *America's Vietnam War: A narrative history.* Boston: Houghton Mifflin.

Biesty, S. (1993). *Cross-sections: Man-of-war.* New York: Dorling Kindersley.

Boswell, J. (1979). *The life of Samuel Johnson.* New York: Viking.

Brooks, B. (1992). *What hearts.* New York: HarperCollins.

Brooks, B. (1996). *The moves make the man.* New York: Harper Trophy.

Burton, T. (Director). (1999). *Sleepy Hollow* [Film]. (Available from Amazon.com)

Carter, J. (1993). *Talking peace: A vision for the next generation.* New York: Penguin.

Childress, A. (1973). *A hero ain't nothin' but a sandwich.* New York: Coward, McCann, and Geoghegan.

Clayton, E., & Hodges, D. (1996). *Martin Luther King: The peaceful warrior.* Huntington Beach, CA: Archway.

Copley, R.E. (2000). *The tall Mexican: The life of Hank Aguirre all-star pitcher, businessman, humanitarian.* Houston, TX: Arte Publico.

Crutcher, C. (1995). *Ironman.* New York: Greenwillow.

Curtis, C.P. (1995). *The Watsons go to Birmingham—1963.* New York: Bantam Doubleday Dell.

Dahl, R. (1988). *Boy: Tales of childhood.* New York: Viking.

Dahl, R. (1998). *Willy Wonka and the chocolate factory.* Ill. Q. Blake. New York: Puffin.

Dahl, R. (2000). *James and the giant peach.* Ill. L. Smith. New York: Penguin.

Davis, T. (1994). *If rock and roll were a machine.* New York: Laurel-Leaf.

Doyle, A.C. (1930). *The complete Sherlock Holmes.* Garden City, NY: Doubleday.

Driscoll, L. (1998). *Slugger season: McGwire and Sosa.* Ill. K. Call. New York: Grosset & Dunlap.

Equiano, O., & Cameron, A. (2000). *The kidnapped prince: The life of Olaudah Equiano.* New York: Random House.

Franchere, R. (1970). *Cesar Chavez.* Ill. E. Thollander. New York: HarperCollins.

Frazier, C. (1997). *Cold Mountain.* New York: Atlantic Monthly Press.

Gibson, W. (1984). *The miracle worker.* New York: Bantam Skylark.

Golding, W. (1999). *Lord of the flies* (G. Hanscombe & S. Coote, Eds.). North Pomfret, VT: Trafalgar Square.

Gonzalez-Bertrand, D. (1999). *Trino's choice.* Houston, TX: Arte Publico.

Greenfield, E. (1997). *For the love of the game: Michael Jordan and me.* Ill. J.S. Gilchrist. New York: HarperCollins.

Guterson, D. (1995). *Snow falling on cedars.* Elk Grove, CA: Vintage Books.

Gutman, B. (1998). *Tiger Woods: Golf's shining young star.* Brookfield, CT: Millbrook Press.

Hemingway, E. (1981). *The Nick Adams stories.* New York: Macmillan.

Hemingway, E. (1995).The short happy life of Francis Macomber. In *The short stories: The first forty-nine stories with a brief introduction from the author* (pp. 51–76). New York: Simon & Schuster.

Hickam, H.H., Jr. (2000). *Rocket boys: A memoir.* New York: Delacorte.

Hobbs, W. (1989). *Bearstone.* New York: Avon.

Hobbs, W. (1996). *Far north.* New York: Avon.

Hughes, L. (2000). *Nelson Mandela: Voice of freedom.* Lincoln, NE: iUniverse.com.

Hunter, M. (1999). *Wrestling madness: A ringside look at wrestling superstars.* New York: Smithmark.

Hyson, D. (1998). *The calling.* Boulder, CO: University Press of Colorado.

Irving, J. (1997). *The imaginary girlfriend: A memoir.* New York: Acacia Press.

Irving, W. (1990). *The legend of Sleepy Hollow.* New York: Tor Books.

Jeffrey, L. (1997). *Simon Wiesenthal: Tracking down Nazi criminals.* Springfield, NJ: Enslow.

King, M.L., Jr. (1963). Letter from Birmingham Jail. In *Why we can't wait* (pp. 23–33). New York: Harper & Row.

Kipling, R. (1999).The man who would be king. In *The man who would be king and other stories* (pp. 1–174). New York: Oxford University Press.

Knowles, J. (1990). *A separate peace.* New York: Holt, Rinehart and Winston.

Krakauer, J. (1996). *Into the wild.* Garden City, NY: Doubleday.

Kudlinski, K.V. (1993). *Pear Harbor is burning! A story of World War II.* New York: Puffin.

Lee, H. (1960). *To kill a mockingbird.* New York: Warner Books.

LeGuin, U. (1997). *Lathe of heaven.* New York: Avon.

Lipsyte, R. (1992). *The chemo kid.* New York: HarperCollins.

Littlefield, B. (1993). *Champions: Stories of ten remarkable athletes.* Boston: Little, Brown.

Lynch, C. (1995). *Shadow boxer.* New York: Harper Trophy.

Macy, S. (1995). *A whole new ball game: The story of the all-American girls professional baseball league.* New York: Puffin.

Massinger, P. (1910).A new way to pay old debts. In C. Eliot (Ed.), *Elizabethan drama in two volumes* (pp. 859–943). New York: P.F. Collier & Son.

Matthews, R. (1999). *Explorer.* Minneapolis, MN: Econo-Clad Books.

Meader, S.W. (1934). *Lumberjack.* New York: Harcourt, Brace & World.

Meader, S.W. (1939). *Boy with a pack.* New York: Harcourt, Brace & World.

Meader, S.W. (1950). *Whaler 'round the horn*. New York: Harcourt, Brace & World.

Meader, S.W. (1963). *The muddy road to glory*. New York: Harcourt, Brace & World.

Mochizuki, K. (1993). *Baseball saved us*. New York: Lee & Low Books.

Morressy, J. (1999). *Juggler*. Minneapolis, MN: Econo-Clad Books.

Mowat, F. (1983). *Never cry wolf*. New York: Bantam.

Mowat, F. (1995). *Born naked*. Boston: Houghton Mifflin.

Myers, W.D. (1990). *Scorpions*. New York: Harper Trophy.

Myers, W.D. (1999). *Hoops*. Minneapolis, MN: Econo-Clad Books.

Myers, W.D. (2000). *Monster*. New York: HarperCollins.

Nicholson, L. (1993). *Cal Ripken, Jr.: Quiet hero*. Cambridge, MD: Tidewater.

O'Connor, L. (1991). *Cryin' for daylight: A ranching culture in the Texas Coastal Bend*. Victoria, TX: Wexford Publishing.

Paterson, K. (2000). *Parzival: The quest of the Grail knight*. New York: Puffin.

Paulsen, G. (1990). *The crossing*. New York: Laurel-Leaf.

Pound, E. (1968). *Guide to kulchur*. New York: Norton.

Rice, E., Jr. (1997). *The attack on Pearl Harbor: Battles of World War II*. San Diego, CA: Lucent Books.

Robertson, J.I. (1992). *Civil War! America becomes one nation*. New York: Knopf.

Ryan, K.J. (1999). *Deep in the heart of Texas: Texas ranchers in their own words*. Berkeley, CA: Ten Speed Press.

Schultz, R. (1992). *Looking inside the brain*. Sante Fe, NM: John Muir Publications.

Scutts, J. (2000). *World War II dioramas*. New York: Compendium.

Sendak, M. (1988). *Where the wild things are*. New York: HarperCollins.

Severance, J. (1996). *Winston Churchill: Soldier, statesman, artist*. New York: Clarion Books.

Shakespeare, W. (1969). As you like it. In A. Harbage (Ed.), *William Shakespeare: The complete works* (pp. 246–273). New York: Penguin.

Shakespeare, W. (1994). *The tempest* (B.A. Mowat & P. Werstine, Eds.). New York: Washington Square Press.

Shakespeare, W. (1998). *Twelfth night* (H. Baker, Ed.). New York: Signet.

Sharp, R. (1985). *Bob Sharp's cattle country: Rawhide ranching on both sides of the border*. Tucson, AZ: University of Arizona Press.

Soto, G. (1992). *Pacific crossing*. Orlando, FL: Harcourt Brace Jovanovich.

Spinelli, G. (1990). *Maniac Magee*. New York: Harper Trophy.

Stanley, J. (1992). *Children of the Dust Bowl: The true story of the school at Weedpatch Camp*. New York: Crown Publishers.

Stevenson, R.L. (1994). *Dr. Jekyll and Mr. Hyde*. New York: Signet.

Stewart, M. (1996). *Hakeem Olajuwon (Grolier All-Pro Biographies)*. New York: Children's Press.

Sullivan, G. (1991). *Sluggers: Twenty-seven of baseball's greatest.* New York: Atheneum.

Sutin, L., Sutin, R., & Sutin, J. (1996). *Jack and Rochelle: A Holocaust story of love and resistance.* St. Paul, MN: Graywolf Press.

Taylor, M.J.H., & Taylor, M. (1998). *Battles of World War II.* Edina, MN: ABDO Publishing.

Taylor, T. (1989). *Sniper.* New York: Avon.

Townsend, B. (1994). *Shaquille O'Neal: Center of attention.* Minneapolis, MN: Lerner.

Verlinden, F. (2000). *Building military dioramas* (Vol. I). Chicago: Verlinden Productions.

Weaver, W. (1993). *Striking out.* New York: HarperCollins.

Whitman, W. (1993). *Leaves of grass.* New York: Modern Library.

Winton, T. (1991). *Lockie Leonard, human torpedo.* Boston: Little, Brown.

Winton, T. (1999). *Lockie Leonard, scumbuster.* New York: Margaret K. McElderry.

Wood, T. (with Numpa, W.). (1995). *A boy becomes a man at Wounded Knee.* New York: Walker and Company.

Wunderli, S. (1996). *The heartbeat of halftime.* New York: Avon.

Index

Note: Page numbers followed by *f* indicate figures.

M

MACY, S., 92

MAGICIAN ARCHETYPE, 34–36; literature reflecting, 164–165; teaching of, 56–59

MALE ARCHETYPES, 14–15; cross-cultural, 25; finding/rediscovering of, 24–26; Healer, 38–40, 62–66, 168–169; King, 30–32, 52–54, 165–166; Lover, 43–45, 70–74, 171–172; Magician, 34–36, 56–59, 164–165; Patriarch, 28–30, 50–52, 137–140, 161–162; Pilgrim, 26–28, 48–50, 158, 160–161; positive, 9, 157; preferences for, 5–6; Prophet, 40–42, 66–68, 169–170; Trickster, 42–43, 68–69, 170–171; variety of, 6, 7; Warrior, 32–34, 54–56, 148, 162–164; Wildman, 36–38, 59–62, 166–168

MALE FIGHT VS. FLIGHT, 25

MALE PROTAGONISTS: preference for, 17, 19

MANDELA, NELSON, 33–34

MARUYAMA, G.M., 17

MASCULINE THEMES, 6

MASCULINITY: cultural concepts of, 25–26, 124–126; media images of, 124–126; models of, 25. *See also* male archetypes; spectrum of, 6

MASSINGER, P., 131

MATTHEWS, R., 94

MAUGHAN, S., 158

MAZZEO, J., 12, 17

McCANDLESS, Chris, 37

McDERMOTT, R., 16

McGUIRE, M., 49

MEAD, M., 28

MEADER, S.W., 13, 94

"MEN OF BOOKS," 155

MINORITY STUDENTS: reading role models for, 96–98, 130–131, 143, 155

MIXED-GENDER CLASSROOMS, 8

MOCHIZUKI, K., 150

MOCK TRIAL, 62

MOJE, E., 156

MOORE, R., 14, 25, 43, 44

MOORMAN, M., 93, 157

MORRESSY, J., 69

MOTIVATION: choice and control and, 18; fostering of, 16–18

MOWAT, F., 59–62

MULLIS, I., 92

MURPHY, P., 13

MY BAG strategy, 78–83, 110

MYERS, L., 16

MYERS, W.D., 51, 101, 105, 127, 153

N

O

P

Pilgrim archetype, 19, 26–28, 158; literature reflecting, 160–161; teaching of, 48–50

Plucker, J.A., 78

Pollack, W., 2

popcorn review, 118

Popp, M.S., 84

Pottorff, D.D., 12

Pound, E., 48

Powell, P., 84

powerlessness, 12–13. *See also* Control

Professor Know-It-All strategy, 119

Prophet archetype, 40–42; literature reflecting, 169–170; teaching of, 66–68

R

Radin, P., 69

Rashbaum, B., 138

Readers Theatre, 112

reading: buddy, 137–140; decline in, 17; family conflict over, 146–151; gender gap in, 17; incentives for, 144–146; for pleasure, 79; therapeutic, 6; as "unmasculine," 13, 16, 146

reading buddies, 83, 137–140

reading guides, 95, 96*f*

reading journal, 79–80

reading skills: academic success and, 12; level of, 3

Real Men unit, 101–135; anticipation guide in, 115–116, 116*f;* compare-contrast activity in, 115–116, 116*f;* compare-contrast essay in, 106; end-of-book journal entries in, 127–128; finale of, 128–132; genesis of, 104; goals of, 104; introductions and predictions for, 106–113; novel selection for, 104–105; personal letters in, 111–113, 120; planning of, 104–106; Professor Know-It-All strategy in, 119; Readers Theatre in, 112; skits in, 114–115; story impression writing in, 113–114; student projects in, 106; students in, 102–104; teacher anecdotal logs in, 106; "To Be a Man" survey in, 105–106, 107*f,* 108, 132, 133*f;* unit projects in, 123–127, 129–130; university field trip in, 117–120

reluctant readers: peer pressure and, 13

Reynolds, A.J., 17

Rice, E., Jr., 141

Rinehart, J., 17

Robertson, J.I., 94

role models: adult male readers as, 96–98, 130–132, 143, 155

Rousseau, J.J., 80

Russell, Mark, 69

Ryan, K.J., 144

Ryan, R., 18

S

T–U